THE POEM
MEANS

Summaries of 1000 Poems

WHAT
THE POEM
MEANS

Summaries of 1000 Poems

WHAT
THE POEM
MEANS

Summaries of 1000 Poems

HARRY BROWN
Midwestern University

JOHN MILSTEAD
Oklahoma State University

SCOTT, FORESMAN AND COMPANY

Library of Congress Catalog No. 72-104311
Copyright (c) 1970 by Scott, Foresman and Company,
Glenview, Illinois 60025.
Philippines Copyright 1970 by Scott, Foresman and Company.
All Rights Reserved. Printed in the United States of America.
Regional offices of Scott, Foresman and Company are located in
Atlanta, Dallas, Glenview, Palo Alto, Oakland, N.J., and London,
England.

FOREWORD

This is a book of summaries of the most commonly reprinted poems in English and American literature. There are approximately 1000 poems summarized, covering English and American poetry from the Renaissance to the present.

The purpose of the summaries is to take the student through the poem at the first level of meaning. They are concerned only with helping the student understand the poem. His textbook can supply biographical and historical detail, and his teacher can handle the more subtle problems of critical analysis, aesthetic appreciation, and the poet's development.

The summaries open up the poem so that the student can proceed on his own within a basic frame of reference. Each summary includes a statement of *theme* at the simplest level and a reference to important *images* and *symbols*. Where desirable, *key words* or significant *repetitions* or other *patterns* are pointed out. Often a brief statement about the overall *structure* is given, especially for the longer poems. Anything that is helpful in breaking a poem into its understandable parts is included.

Needless to say, the summaries attempt to be as objective and authoritative as possible. Subjective and dogmatic interpretations have been avoided.

The summaries are listed according to the following principles:

1) *Alphabetical listing.* Main headings are listed alphabetically by the authors' last names. Individual poems under each author are listed alphabetically, except for long poems in numbered sequences, such as Shakespeare's sonnets and Tennyson's *In Memoriam*.

2) *Selective Index.* This index at the back of the book includes the first lines or titles of individual poems from sequences and larger works.

3) *Titles of poems.* When a poem is untitled by the author or without a traditional title, the first line or first thought unit is used as the title and written conventionally.

Harry Brown
John Milstead

CONRAD AIKEN

MORNING SONG OF SENLIN

The poem presents in immediate and dramatic contrast the petty character of Senlin and the beauty and grandeur of nature.

Senlin arises in the morning, assuring himself that things are the same and that he has the same identity (lines 37-41).

As the earth revolves and the stars disappear, he stands in this void and unconcernedly ties his tie (lines 41-44).

Far off, horses neigh "And mountains flash." Senlin stands by the mirror and surprises his soul. About him is movement and beneath him are suns (lines 45-52).

Senlin proceeds "from darkness" (night, sleep) to an uncertain destination. His watch is wound and he has a key. The sky is dark. There is "a god among the stars." Senlin will think of this god and will hum a tune as he does so (lines 53-60).

The poem ends with beautiful sounds of nature: "vine leaves tap," "Dew-drops sing," and "The Robin chirps" (lines 61-64).

MUSIC I HEARD WITH YOU WAS MORE THAN MUSIC

The theme of the poem is the permanence of a loved one's impression upon the heart. The loved one is no longer present, but the speaker remembers because of the beauty of shared experiences. Ordinary bread, music, table, silver, and glass were heightened because of the beloved's touch ("in my heart you moved among them").

ANONYMOUS

WESTERN WIND, WHEN WILT THOU BLOW?

An absent lover longs to be with his loved one in his bed. He invokes the forces of nature ("Western wind," "small rain") and prays ("Christ") to be in his bed with his love in his arms.

MATTHEW ARNOLD

A FAREWELL

The speaker met his love and they greeted each other passionately. But soon he was aware that she was too restless to remain long with one love—a restlessness the speaker has observed in himself also. He, however, says that she will learn the value of love. In the light of eternity they shall one day see the real values of life in true perspective.

DOVER BEACH

The poem describes despair at the loss of faith.

The speaker opens with a description of the beautiful scene on the sea coast. He comments to his companion (his love) that the appearance of peace and beauty is deceptive, for the ocean really brings "The eternal note of sadness in." Like Sophocles, he says, we can find a thought suggested by the ocean's sound: We have lost the faith that we once had; now, we have only each other, for the world, which seemed so fair, is actually a dark and fearsome place.

IN HARMONY WITH NATURE

The poet addresses a preacher who has advocated that men should be in harmony with Nature. The poet argues that man has more good qualities than Nature has (lines 5-12). Man and Nature are not equals. If man cannot surpass Nature, he must be "her slave" (lines 13-14).

MEETING

The speaker sees the form and features of his beloved Marguerite. But he hears again the voice that prohibits him from choosing her, and he wishes that the warning were not there.

MEMORIAL VERSES

The poet reflects on the significance of three great poets, Goethe, Byron, and Wordsworth.

Byron "taught us little," but he made us feel the conflict "Of passion with eternal law." Goethe analyzed the ills of the human race, and he saw art as compensation for the terror of an age coming to an end. Wordsworth also spoke to us in a troubled time, but he brought peace and joy. Other poets may, like Goethe and Byron, show us wisdom and emotional power, but none can give us Wordsworth's "healing power," his ability to bring the emotions to life.

PARTING

As the speaker feels the "storm-winds of Autumn," he wishes that he could go with them to the mountains. As he listens to the wind, he seems to hear and see the form so precious to him. He yearns to go to the mountains, but he cannot. He asks Marguerite to forgive him, and then he reflects on her closeness to nature and her ability to soothe him.

QUIET WORK

The poet states his conviction that it is quiet sturdy work that produces great achievements. While noise and uproar accompany more sensational schemes, the "glorious tasks" are brought to fruition in silence.

REQUIESCAT

The speaker wishes peace for the woman who is now quietly buried. Her life had been one of constant movement. She was beset by the world's demand that she be gay. But her heart was tired and wanted the peace she now has.

SHAKESPEARE

Shakespeare is beyond our ability really to understand. He is as free of our questions as the lofty hill is accessible to us only at "the cloudy border of his base." Shakespeare endured all the pains of life and brought them to a victorious resolution that only he knew and expressed fully.

THE BURIED LIFE

Deep within us may exist the springs of our true being.

The speaker asks his companion to be quiet so that he may see into her soul (lines 1-11). But it is difficult even for lovers to reveal their true selves to one another. The mass of men disguise themselves and are "alien to the rest," although all have a human heart (lines 12-23). It is good if the lovers can for a moment communicate (lines 24-29). Fate, knowing man's wayward ways, decreed that "the unregarded river" of his life should flow, unobserved, deep within him so that, without his knowledge, there should be a direction to his life (lines 30-44). We often have a desire to delve deep enough to find "the mystery of this heart," but, though we strive, we hear only distant echoes that bring melancholy into our day (lines 45-76). On rare occasions, when a man is with his beloved, he "becomes aware of his life's flow" (lines 77-90). Then, with unaccustomed calm, he may know the deep direction of his life (lines 91-98).

THE FORSAKEN MERMAN

A merman who has been forsaken by Margaret, his mortal wife (or at any rate, the mother of his children), calls for her to come back to him.

The poem opens with the merman telling his children to come away, back to their home in the sea (lines 1-9). The children call once more before they go (lines 10-22), and then their father urges them to come after taking one last look "at the white-walled town" (lines 23-29). He recalls when the sound of the bells from over the bay came to them in their caverns as Margaret sat with the merman and their children, hearing the church bells calling her at Easter-time (lines 30-62). When she did not return, they followed her to the town and the merman called to her as she sat in the church, but she ignored him (lines 64-84). Yet, as Margaret sits joyfully at the spinning wheel, sorrow overcomes her and she sighs for the Mermaiden she has left. And ever after in their memory will be the thought of the faithless and cruel mortal who abandoned them (lines 85-143).

THE SCHOLAR GIPSY

The speaker relates the legend of the scholar-gypsy, who left Oxford to join a band of gypsies. The scholar learned to pursue a single aim in life instead of being distracted by divided purposes.

As the speaker rests, looking at the fields and at Oxford below, Glanvil's book makes him think of the scholar who left Oxford to join the gypsies. Later, the scholar told two former schoolmates from Oxford that he was learning the secret of controlling men's minds (lines 1-50). Henceforth, the scholar-gypsy seems to be seen in many places by many people, by shepherds, by students, by maidens, and by the speaker (lines 51-130).

Coming back to present reality, the speaker reminds himself that the scholar-gypsy has been dead long since. Yet, on second thought, the wanderer did have a secret that we lack. Whereas we are subject to the "repeated shocks" of constant change, the scholar-gypsy had "*one* aim." Because of this strength, we imagine the scholar-gypsy exempt from age, although the rest of us perish (lines 131-160). The scholar-gypsy left the world while his life was still fresh, before it had a chance to become fatigued and baffled, uncertain and half-committed. Even the best among us is dejected. Unlike us, who endure without hope, the scholar-gypsy roams "in unclouded joy." Having been born in earlier, clearer times, "Before this strange disease of modern life," the scholar-gypsy pursues his way far from us, "Still nursing the unconquerable hope." The speaker exhorts the scholar-gypsy to "fly our paths" lest he be contaminated (lines 161-231).

The poem ends quietly with a description of a grave Tyrian trader who flees at the approach of the Greek traders (lines 232-250).

THE TERRACE AT BERNE

The speaker's memory brings up visions of Berne and of Marguerite. He wonders if she has changed or if, perhaps, she is dead without his being aware of her passing. He realizes that on the sea of life people are destined to meet and part.

THYRSIS

This elegy for Arthur Hugh Clough has for its major theme the loss of spiritual insight and creative power in the modern world. Arnold refers to Clough as Thyrsis and to himself as Corydon.

The speaker opens in a nostalgic mood, noting the changes and the remembered sights in the lovely Cummer country around Oxford (lines 1-21). Only he comes here much less often than he did formerly with his friend, when they saw the elm tree, identified with the gypsy-scholar and symbol of their youthful ideal. Here they tried their pipes (that is, wrote poems), but though the speaker has lost his pipe because of worldly cares, Thyrsis "of his own will went away," leaving the peaceful country, and later was unable to bear the "storms that rage outside our happy ground" (lines 22-50).

Then comes a description in specific detail of the spring and summer. The cuckoo is introduced as a contrast to Thyrsis. The bird has flown away, but it will return next spring (lines 51-76). Thyrsis will not return. In a mythological allusion, the speaker contrasts the past with the present: the Sicilian shepherd was able to charm Proserpine so that the dead could return, but Proserpine doesn't know the Cummer land and so could not be charmed with songs related to it (lines 77-100).

Now the poet turns back to the present scene, and with the scene return the thoughts of the changes that have occurred (lines 101-130). The poet finds that he too has changed. He is less buoyant and energetic than he once was (lines 131-150).

Coming back to the present scene again, the poet flees from the approaching hunters and sees again the tree, and he calls upon Thyrsis to hear from his grave that the tree is still there (lines 151-171). Then the poet concedes that these English scenes are no longer for Thyrsis, who now hears "the immortal chants of old." The poet, however, still has hope as long as he can see the lonely tree against the western sky. Like the gypsy-scholar, he seeks "A fugitive and gracious light," as Thyrsis had done in his youth. And, though Thyrsis' flute lost "its happy, country tone," yet he still had "visions of our light" (lines 172-230). The poem concludes on the note of regret at the fact that, living in the city, the poet rarely comes to this country now, but this regret is balanced by a note of hope at the thought that the tree still endures (lines 213-240).

TO MARGUERITE--CONTINUED

Using islands as an image of men, the poet reflects on the isolation that we endure. At times it seems that we must once have been part of a single continent and so were connected, but some God ordered the severing of these islands.

WYSTAN HUGH AUDEN

AS I WALKED OUT ONE EVENING

Though it is impossible to conquer time through love, we must still try.

Stanza 1 introduces the theme of time by describing crowds ready to be harvested, as by time. In stanzas 2-5, a lover makes extravagant claims that his love will outlast time. In stanzas 6-12, the chiming clocks set straight the view of reality: time will destroy all things. The ravages of time are always imminent—"Time watches," "life leaks away," "appalling snow," "glacier knocks." In stanzas 13-14, the clocks say that despite our distress before time we must still "love." In the final stanza, both lovers and clocks are gone, while the deep river of time runs on.

DOOM IS DARK AND DEEPER THAN ANY SEA-DINGLE (SOMETHING IS BOUND TO HAPPEN)

The first line of the poem is taken from the medieval allegory *Sawle's Ward*, in which the house (the body, whose treasure is the soul) is visited by two figures—Fear, the messenger of death, and Love of Life, the messenger of mirth.

Stanza 1 shows the love of life driving a man through danger ("avalanche," "suffocating water") and loneliness ("stranger," "a bird stone-haunting"). Stanza 2 shows the drawing of the other force, comfort and security, as he dreams of home and kissing his wife. Stanza 3 is a prayer to keep him safe ("capture," "tiger's spring") and his home safe ("from thunderbolt," "gradual ruin").

IN MEMORY OF W. B. YEATS

This is an elegy to Yeats, whose inspiration we need to help us correct the ills of our times.

Part 1 describes society as unfeeling, measuring only on a thermometer the effect of Yeats' death.

Part 2 states that Yeats' poetic gift will survive the madness of his Ireland which drove him to poetry.

In Part 3, stanzas 1-4 commit Yeats to the earth, knowing time will pardon him for "writing well." Stanzas 5-9 look to Yeats for inspiration. In a world of hatred between nations, of. "intellectual disgrace," and of absence of pity, we can use Yeats' inspiration for a "healing fountain."

LOOK, STRANGER, ON THIS ISLAND NOW

The speaker invites a stranger to delight in a present experience and the memory of an experience.

The speaker asks the stranger to look at the island now revealed for his delight and to be silent so that he can hear the sea (stanza 1).

In stanza 2, he points to the sounds of the sea by the chalk wall where he hears the "knock" of the tide and the shifting shingle.

Stanza 3 draws together nature (seeds, cloud) and man's activity (ships, errands) in memory as the ships sail and the reflection of the clouds "through the water saunter."

MUSEE DES BEAUX ARTS

The poet reflects that the old master painters of the museum of fine arts (the title) were never wrong in depicting suffering.

Lines 1-13 point out that the victim suffers alone, while others are unconcerned as they eat, open a window, or walk along. While the aged are "passionately waiting/For the miraculous birth," the children are relatively indifferent. Even the most dreadful martyrdom runs its course unnoticed by even dog or horse.

Lines 14-21 give a specific instance to depict this indifference, Brueghel's painting *Icarus* (hanging in the Museum of Fine Arts in Brussels). While the boy Icarus falls into the water, the ploughman, nature (the sun), and the ship are unconcerned ("not an important failure," "sailed calmly on").

PETITION

In the form of a prayer, the poet calls for people to make a positive assertion of will.

The prayer is addressed to a Deity who will forgive everything but "negative inversion" of will. The diseases to be healed suggest the ingrown, withdrawn life — "neural itch," weaning, lying, "ingrown virginity," cowardice. The specific new "architecture" to be given those brought to life from the "house of the dead" is a "change of heart."

SEPTEMBER 1, 1939

The poet insists that the only solution to the international wrong that produced war is the assertion through love of the individual in the face of the collective mentality.

Stanzas 1-2 tell of the gloom and cause of war. Hitler launched the war September 1, 1939, a psychopathic god created by a mad culture that extended back to Luther. Stanza 3 foresees the end of "enlightenment" and the grief and pain to come from the war begun by the dictator. Stanza 4 says that opposed to the psychopathic god is the euphoric dream of collective or competitive man. In stanzas 5-7, the poet reproaches the people who "Cling to their average day," who are fearful, unhappy, victimized by windy propaganda, and all those who are imprisoned in the "conservative dark." In stanzas 8-9, the poet undoes the "romantic lie" that man can have either collective or private existence and asserts that we "must love one another or die."

THE THREE COMPANIONS ("OH, WHERE ARE YOU GOING?" SAID READER TO RIDER)

The life of venture is posed against the life of static security.

In stanzas 1-3, the defenders of security—reader, fearer, and horror—describe the terrors of the unknown and the diseased condition of those who venture. In stanza 4, the defenders of venture—rider, farer, and hearer—dismiss one by one the questions asked in stanzas 1-3, indicating that the evils feared will come to the remaining reader, not to the departing rider.

THE UNKNOWN CITIZEN

The poet uses bureaucratic jargon to satirize man's loss of identity in our bureaucratic society.

The statistics about him, his possessions, his activities, his ideas—all show the citizen to be "unknown," fully indistinguishable from the other human statistics. In ironic obverse of the saint, who is selfless through communion with a transcendent Being, the "unknown citizen" is selfless through being completely absorbed into the social order.

VILLANELLE

Time and the poet are equally powerless to reveal what is to come or to tell the reasons for what happens.

Neither time nor the poet can foretell or explain strange phenomena like weeping at clowns, winds blowing, leaves decaying, visions fading, soldiers running. Time can say only after it happened, "I told you so." The poet can only long to explain.

THOMAS LOVELL BEDDOES

SONG (OLD ADAM, THE CARRION CROW)

In a light tone, the poem shows the cycle of life and death. Adam the crow sat in the rain, with his beak full of marrow. The wind blows through a murderer's bones. Adam calls to Eve, his "carrion wife," to drink up with him. So, grisly death enables the crows to continue the life-cycle, by eating the corpse.

THE PHANTOM WOOER

A ghost that loved a lady stood by her bedside and, in words more alluring than any upon earth, called upon her to die. Put off your flesh, he says, and the tomb will be our bed.

ELIZABETH BISHOP

THE FISH

The poem moves from an unfeeling description of a hooked fish to admiration for the fish when the poet realizes the battles the fish has fought and won in earlier times.

In lines 1-21, the poet sees evidence of the fish's age and ability to overcome adverse circumstances. In lines 22-46, she gains sympathy for the fish as a being, with life-force ("terrible oxygen," "shiny entrails"). In lines 47-76, she lets the fish go after seeing the old hooks in the jaw, the hooks being evidence that the fish has battled for the right to live.

THE IMAGINARY ICEBERG

An iceberg, as seen from shipboard, is compared to the soul.

Stanza 1 asserts that we prefer the iceberg to the ship even though the iceberg were to wreck the ship. Stanza 2 describes the fascination for the iceberg as though it were a graceful dancer on the stage. Stanza 3 points out the utter self-containment of the iceberg as a jewel with its own inner light and compares the iceberg and the soul: "Both being self-made from elements least visible."

THE MAN-MOTH

The poet uses the word in the title, from a newspaper misprint for "mammoth," to refer to New York City. The man-moth suggests the fluttering spirit of man trapped in the eerie night of the metropolis. It is attracted to the danger, yet seeks to escape by climbing up and through the moon as though the moon were a hole in the night sky. But the man-moth must finally descend to its home, the death-like "subways of cement," with its only possession, a tear.

WILLIAM BLAKE

A CRADLE SONG (FROM <u>SONGS OF INNOCENCE</u>)

As the infant sleeps with sweet dreams, the mother watches tenderly through the night.

The first four stanzas tell of the sweet sleep that enfolds the "happy child." In the fifth stanza we learn that while she watches over the happy child, the mother weeps. Then the idea of divinity enters. The sleeping babe has the "Holy image" in its face. Once, also, "Thy maker lay and wept for me." Finally, still alluding to Jesus, the speaker describes the divine image that wept for all and "smiles on thee."

A POISON TREE (FROM <u>SONGS OF EXPERIENCE</u>)

The poem describes the consequences of repressing one's anger. It is executed in terms of the tree as a symbol of demonic growth within the human soul.

An open statement of anger to a friend causes the anger to end. But when the speaker concealed his anger toward an enemy, it grew in fear and deceit, and eventually it "bore an apple bright," which attracted his foe. One night the enemy entered his garden to steal the apple. In the morning the speaker is glad to see his enemy dead beneath the tree.

AH! SUN-FLOWER (FROM <u>SONGS OF EXPERIENCE</u>)

"Weary of time," the Sun-flower longs for the "golden clime," where the "journey is done." Here the sexually-thwarted youth and the repressed maiden arise from their graves and aspire as does the Sun-flower.

HOLY THURSDAY (FROM <u>SONGS OF EXPERIENCE</u>)

The poet laments that there should be so many poor, miserable children in a "rich and fruitful land." The first stanza raises the question of whether a land can be both rich and holy if its children are miserable.

HOLY THURSDAY (FROM <u>SONGS OF INNOCENCE</u>)

Stanza 1 describes a colorful procession of children as they move to St. Paul's cathedral. Stanza 2 describes the "multitudes of lambs" seated in companies. Stanza 3 tells of the singing of the children as they are guarded by the adults, "wise guardians of the poor." In the final line, the poet asks pity for poor children, for they may be angels.

INTRODUCTION (FROM <u>SONGS OF INNOCENCE</u>)

This is a symbolic narrative about inspiration. Blake begins with music ("piping") and later, under the direction of the "child" (the spirit of imagination), the piper turns to singing. With the directive to write, the child disappears and the poet sits down to write his "happy songs."

LONDON (FROM <u>SONGS OF EXPERIENCE</u>)

The poet describes the evil created by man's reason (the "mind-forg'd manacles").

As the speaker walks through London, he hears the effects of "mind-forg'd manacles" (man-made institutions and conventions). He hears them in every cry and in every prohibition. The chimney sweeper's cry reproaches the church, and the soldier's sigh "runs in blood down palace walls." Last, the speaker hears how the harlot's curse "blasts" the infant's tears and "blights . . . the marriage hearse."

NURSE'S SONG (FROM <u>SONGS OF EXPERIENCE</u>)

As she hears the voices of the children playing and the "whisperings in the dale," the nurse recalls her own youth and her "face turns green and pale." She calls the children home, and she warns them that their childhood is "wasted in play" and that their cold and dark adulthood (which is "winter and night") is wasted "in disguise," which probably means in concealing or repressing the joyful self.

NURSE'S SONG (FROM SONGS OF INNOCENCE)

The poem expresses the nurse's joy in the joy of the children. She is happy when she hears the children playing and laughing. As evening comes, she tells the children that they must go home now. But, when they protest that "it is yet day," she lets them play a while longer, and all the joy continues. The spirit of nature triumphs over adult restraint, here represented by the nurse, who finds peace in their joy.

THE CHIMNEY SWEEPER (FROM SONGS OF EXPERIENCE)

A little chimney sweeper complains that his mother and father, seeing him happy, "clothed me in the clothes of death." Now, because he can still be happy, they think they have done the child no harm. So they have gone to the church "to praise God and His Priest and King," whose Heaven is made up of "our misery."

The child senses intuitively that his parents restricted him because of his happiness (stanza 2) and that their complacent sanctimoniousness prevents them from seeing the evil that they have done (stanza 3). He can communicate neither his joy nor his bitterness to his parents.

THE CHIMNEY SWEEPER (FROM SONGS OF INNOCENCE)

A young chimney sweep describes the reality of his life and Tom's vision while sleeping.

First we learn that the speaker was sold as a chimney sweep by his father. Then he tells the story of Tom Dacre, who, after having his head shaved, had a vision. An Angel set free "thousands of sweepers" who had been put in coffins. And the Angel told Tom that if he would be a good boy, he would have God for his father. The conclusion is that "if all do their duty they need not fear harm."

THE CLOD AND THE PEBBLE (FROM SONGS OF EXPERIENCE)

Without comment, the poet describes two kinds of love.

Stanza 1 describes a selfless, even self-sacrificing love. Stanza 2 describes a completely selfish love.

THE DIVINE IMAGE (FROM <u>SONGS OF INNOCENCE</u>)

The poem identifies God and Man as one spirit. It begins by listing the virtues ("Mercy, Pity, Peace, and Love"). In lines 5 and 6 these virtues are identified as God, and in lines 7-8, these qualities are identified as Man. In the last three stanzas Blake says that God exists in the form of man, for these virtues are present in the "human form divine."

THE GARDEN OF LOVE (FROM <u>SONGS OF EXPERIENCE</u>)

The main theme is that religion places restrictions on Man's "joys and desires." The chapel and the priest have turned the Garden of Love, which had once borne flowers, into a graveyard.

THE LAMB (FROM <u>SONGS OF INNOCENCE</u>)

The poem is set up as question and answer. Stanza 1 asks the question, Who made the Lamb? and in the process describes the Lamb. Stanza 2 answers the question: Christ (or perhaps God in Christ) made the Lamb. Blake identifies the lamb and the child with Christ ("We are called by his name").

THE LITTLE BLACK BOY (FROM <u>SONGS OF INNOCENCE</u>)

Blake enters into the mind of a black child to produce both psychological and religious insight. The mother, seeing her child troubled by the difference between himself and a white child, tells him a little story. His dark color is "like a shady grove" to help him bear the rays of the sun (where God lives). The child then interprets his black skin as a special blessing, for with it (that is, his closer contact with the Sun) he can offer protection to the white child until they are both alike.

THE TIGER (FROM <u>SONGS OF EXPERIENCE</u>)

The tiger causes the speaker to ask certain questions about the power that created it.

First, he asks what "immortal hand or eye" could create the "fearful symmetry." He wonders where the fire in the eyes came from, and he is awed by the power that dared "seize the fire." He wonders "what dread grasp" would dare to handle these "deadly terrors." Then he wonders if, when peace and pity came to heaven, did this power "smile his work to see?" Did the same power that made the lamb also make the tiger? The poem ends with the question still unanswered.

TO SEE A WORLD IN A GRAIN OF SAND
(FROM AUGURIES OF INNOCENCE)

These four lines exemplify Blake's conception of "spiritual sensation." The man of vision sees the same object as ordinary people, but he sees it in its totality, that is, in its spiritual essence. Each line states a test of one's ability to see the spiritual essence.

LOUISE BOGAN

THE DREAM

A woman, through a dream, comes to a reconciliation with her suppressed sexual fears.

In stanza 1, the woman is threatened by a terrible horse symbolizing aggressive male sexuality, which she has feared for thirty-five years along with guilt or "retribution" if she responds. In stanzas 2-3, another woman, a maturer aspect of the dreamer, helps by advising the dreamer to give of herself, to give something "you alone claim." In stanza 4, the dreamer in giving herself loses her fear, and the figure of terror becomes a figure of gentle love.

WOMEN

The poet describes that "provident" trait of women by which, in fearing to produce "wilderness" by making a mistake, they actually deprive themselves and are thus improvident.

Withdrawn in their "tight hot cell," women do not understand life around them ("cattle cropping," "many crops," "wood cleft"); they have no moderation ("Too tense, or too lax," "shout and a cry"); and they make improvident decisions (wait instead of journey, stiffen instead of bend, take life when they should let it go by).

EMILY BRONTË

NO COWARD SOUL IS MINE

The speaker asserts that her soul is armed with faith. God is within, and this is the source of the power. Creeds are powerless to awaken doubt in one who has this secure faith. God's love permeates all things and God endures forever.

REMEMBRANCE

The speaker asks herself is she has forgotten her dead lover (lines 1-8). It is now fifteen years since his death, and life goes on (lines 9-16). All her bliss is buried with him (lines 17-20). Yet she learned, when youth had passed, that existence was precious even without joy. She resisted her desire to join her dead lover. Still, the memory brings an anguish that makes the world seem empty (lines 21-32).

THE OLD STOIC

The speaker scorns riches, love, and fame, and asks for "a chainless soul" and the "courage to endure."

ELIZABETH BARRETT BROWNING

Sonnets From the Portuguese

Mrs. Browning wrote this sequence of forty-four sonnets to express her love for Robert Browning.

1: I THOUGHT ONCE HOW THEOCRITUS HAD SUNG

As the speaker muses upon the past years that had brought her melancholy, she is aware of a shape behind her. In her confusion she thinks first of Death, which she had apparently been expecting, but the shape is really Love.

3: UNLIKE ARE WE, UNLIKE, O PRINCELY HEART!

The speaker and her beloved are unlike. He is bright and attractive; she is poor and tired. Only death can bring two such opposing people into agreement.

6: GO FROM ME. YET I FEEL THAT I SHALL STAND

The speaker now feels her beloved present with her constantly. However far apart they are, he is with her. He is in her acts and in her dreams. He is with her in her prayers.

7: THE FACE OF ALL THE WORLD IS CHANGED, I THINK

Her beloved's coming completely changed the speaker's world, from death to love. Places are loved for his presence, and this music is dear for his presence.

14: IF THOU MUST LOVE ME, LET IT BE FOR NAUGHT

The speaker asks her beloved to love her "for love's sake only," because if he loves her for such things as her look or her way of speaking, this love might go when these things change.

22: WHEN OUR TWO SOULS STAND UP ERECT AND STRONG

Rather than aspiring to a heavenly state, the lovers' two souls should stay on earth, where their two spirits will be untouched by the irritable moods of others.

26: I LIVED WITH VISIONS FOR MY COMPANY

Formerly, the speaker lived only with "visions" instead of real people. These shadows faded. When the beloved came, he made real the splendors that had before been only dreams.

43: HOW DO I LOVE THEE? LET ME COUNT THE WAYS

The speaker describes the fullness of her love. It reaches as far as her spirit can reach, and it includes the simplest daily activities. Her love is free and pure. Its passion grows from the depth of all her experience.

ROBERT BROWNING

A GRAMMARIAN'S FUNERAL

The speaker is one of a group of followers or students who are bearing the body of their master, a famous scholar, to burial. It is also possible to interpret the poem as being spoken by a chorus of admiring disciples.

As they leave behind "the unlettered plain," the speaker asserts that the proper place for their famous master is a tall mountain (lines 1-28). This man had "Left play for work," that is, had devoted himself to acquiring all knowledge available in the commentaries on the real text itself (lines 29-64). The speaker interprets the scholar's motive as an intense preparation for life (lines 65-72).

As the students proceed up the ever-narrowing way, the speaker continues with his praise of the scholar's determination to learn despite disease and failing eyesight. For he knew that, through God's will, his preparations in knowledge would come to fruition in a fuller life. Success in heaven would be the reward for a life immersed in learning (lines 73-110). This aspiration toward the impossible defines the difference between the "high man," who pursues a great (though impossible) thing, and the "low man," who "seeks a little thing to do" (lines 111-124). And so, having pursued knowledge until he died, the great scholar deserves burial on the heights, not on the common plain with the multitude (lines 125-148).

A TOCCATA OF GALUPPI'S

Playing a toccata (a light piece of music requiring technical dexterity to play) by Galuppi brings depressing thoughts of Venice and the meaning of its culture to the speaker (lines 1-9). The speaker then proceeds to reconstruct the life of Venice in the eighteenth century through his interpretation and playing of Galuppi's toccata.

Did young people then spend their time at balls? Was it all flirtation between men and women (lines 10-18)? Galuppi played them grave music (lines 19-21) and gay music (lines 22-24). They applauded both (lines 25-27). Finally, death took these people of Venice (lines 28-30). Then the speaker in a thoughtful mood feels Galuppi's music "creep through every nerve" (lines 31-33). Venice has gone as she deserved with her trivial people.

This is what Galuppi says through his music to the speaker in the poem: Where there is a soul—perhaps the speaker with his attainment has a soul that grows—there is immortality. But the people of Venice were limited to the earth, like butterflies. For these people there was little soul left, if any, when the kissing stopped. The thought of the death of those beautiful women makes the speaker feel "chilly and grown old" (lines 34-35).

ANDREA DEL SARTO

Andrea del Sarto, speaking to his wife, Lucrezia, reveals his theory of art, his background, and his relationship with his wife.

Andrea reveals that he is dependent upon his wife and will do as she wishes, accepting even her fickleness and her directions for his painting (lines 1-32). Talking to his wife, he thinks of a picture he could paint, "All in a twilight," that would represent his own life, which he has come to accept fatalistically (lines 33-52). He then discusses his own art and his theory of art in general. His painting, though technically superior to that of many contemporaries, is spiritually inferior, for the others have aspired to a higher achievement than he (lines 53-99). Specifically, Raphael cannot reproduce an arm as well as he, and yet the material improvement destroys the spiritual quality (lines 100-117). If Lucrezia had inspired him, he suggests that they might have achieved greater things together. Yet he admits he lacks the will to achieve greatly, and so relapses into his fatalism (lines 117-144). He is now afraid to stir abroad to face the visiting Paris lords because, long ago, when he was in Paris, where he sometimes painted greatly, he had betrayed King Francis' trust for the call of Lucrezia (lines 145-174). He recalls that at one time he was capable of challenging Raphael himself, though he does admit that Raphael has "the soul" (lines 175-197). As Lucrezia listens absentmindedly and uncomprehendingly, Andrea pleads with her to give him more attention (lines 198-207). He feels guilty, and he pleads for her love, but the Cousin whistles and she is ready to go (lines 208-221). So Andrea must work supposedly to pay off the Cousin's loans, but before he returns to his painting he dreams of the great pictures of the Virgin he might paint, though he returns as always to the thoughts of money (lines 221-242). He is finally resigned to the facts of his life, he says, and yet he aspires to hope that perhaps in heaven he may be counted as one of the great painters (lines 244-263). Here and now, he accepts his inferior position with Lucrezia even as the Cousin calls (lines 264-267).

CALIBAN UPON SETEBOS

Caliban, a monster emerging into primitive powers of reasoning, speculates upon the nature of his god, Setebos, whom he models after himself.

Caliban sprawls at ease in the muck and muses upon Setebos (lines 1-23). He thinks: Setebos made most things we know (but not the stars) because of some feeling of being ill at ease, like a fish that wants to live out of the water in warmth, but can't (lines 24-43). He seemed to make everything "in spite," and "in envy, listlessness, or sport" made creatures that resembled Him, "Worthy, and yet mere playthings" (lines 44-65). Taking a drink he has made, Caliban imagines that he wants to be a bird, can't be, and so, having the power of Setebos, makes one. He would treat his creation capriciously, mainly to show his power. To Setebos (lines 66-97) such conduct has no moral implications: He is strong and therefore rules, as Caliban decides, for a whim, to attack a crab or give it two worms (lines 98-108).

Although His creatures may in some ways be better than He is, they are nevertheless completely dependent upon Him, as a pipe is dependent upon the person who blows it (lines 109-126).

Perhaps above Setebos is a supreme power, the Quiet. Perhaps Setebos looks upon this higher power, and in envy tries to imitate in earthly creations what He cannot achieve in the heavens, where the Quiet is beyond joy and grief. Setebos imitates the Quiet as Caliban in his monstrous way imitates his master, Prospero (lines 127-169).

Setebos made creatures weak so that He might vex them. He created things for His pleasure, whatever that may be, and for no other reason, as Caliban on a comfortable and idle summer day might make a thing for no purpose but pleasure (lines 170-199). Setebos is terrible too, for a wave tore down a fence Caliban had made (lines 200-210).

Caliban is awed by the force in a meteorite, and, looking at a fossil newt, he wonders how he can please Setebos and so prevent himself from being turned to stone. But there is no way to find what pleases Setebos. It is better not to try to outguess Him (lines 211-240). Things will continue in this way—unless Setebos overthrows the Quiet or perhaps evolves into the higher being (lines 241-249). Caliban believes that there is no future life and that in this life Setebos plagues those that seem too happy but at times helps the overburdened (lines 250-262). He therefore pretends that he is miserable and allows himself to be happy only when he thinks Setebos cannot see him. He hopes to propitiate Setebos by suffering and sacrifice. Perhaps someday Setebos will be conquered or will grow old (lines 263-283).

A storm comes and the superstitious Caliban cowers in fear, promising penance for his thoughts (lines 284-295).

"CHILDE ROLAND TO THE DARK TOWER CAME"

The knight tells of his strange and terrifying experiences in his search for the Dark Tower.

At the direction of the old cripple, who "lied in every word," Childe Roland turned on "that ominous tract" toward the Dark Tower, relieved that, after many years of searching, an end or purpose has come to him (lines 1-24). In a mood of bitterness, like a dying man who perceives that his friends are already preparing for his death and who does not want to disappoint them, the knight, "quiet as despair," turned from the highway to the path the cripple pointed out (lines 25-48).

As the knight started on his way, he suddenly found himself completely alone on the plain (lines 49-54). Everything was ugly; Nature did not seem to care. Grass was sparse. A single horse looked so wretched that it was hateful (lines 56-84). The knight turned from the present to the past, hoping to find refreshment in memories of happier times. Instead, he recalled Cuthbert and Giles, who were disgraced (lines 85-102). Returning to the present, his attention was aroused by a stream, which seemed a very image of death and pain (lines 103-126). Across the stream he found evidence of a mad battle, for the evidence was an area beaten down as though in "savage trample," but there were no footprints leading either in or out (lines 127-138). Further on, the knight found an instrument apparently made for torture (lines 139-144). As he proceeded in the distorted landscape (lines 145-159), a bird flew past, and then he saw that the plain had turned into mountains, "ugly heights and heaps" (lines 160-168). First the knight realized that he was caught, and then he saw that this was the place that he had been searching for (lines 169-186). Now, at first bewildered and overwhelmed by the dark oppression and the memory of the other knights who had been lost on the quest, he grew determined and blew the slug-horn fearlessly (lines 187-204).

FRA LIPPO LIPPI

Fra Lippo Lippi explains his life and his theories of art to the guards who have stopped him on the street.

Having been caught in a compromising situation, Fra Lippo first establishes control of the situation by alluding to important connections (lines 1-31). He then identifies himself as a painter and shows that he has an eye for creating (lines 31-42) before he explains how he came to be in the street. He is here because he was attracted by the girls (lines 43-75). As the guard shakes his head over the monk's activities, Fra Lippo explains that he decided to become a monk when he was really too young to make such a decision (lines 75-105). Under the monks' encouragement, he became a painter, and, with his experiences as a child of the streets, he had learned to judge people's faces (lines 106-162). Although his fellow monks at first praised his realism, the Prior says that the purpose of the artist should be to paint the soul (lines 163-198).

Fra Lippo protests to the guard that spiritual truths are seen in the physical body. He finds at the Medici house where he is now painting that people still criticize him for his realism, and so in sheer rage at these narrow-minded restraints he bursts his bonds periodically. He defends himself by saying that he learned his lesson from the fact that God made woman in the garden (lines 198-268).

Fra Lippo continues with his discussion of aesthetic theory. Since the world is beautiful, the artist is justified in reproducing it. The artist draws our attention to beauties we would not otherwise notice. Furthermore in painting things of this earth, the artist paints the meaning that is here for us to see: "it means intensely, and means good . . ." He strongly objects to using a painting didactically, as with the picture of the martyr being burned (lines 270-335).

Having been carried to a high pitch of resentment, Fra Lippo comes back to the immediate situation and speaks to the guard in a conciliatory tone. Then he goes on to describe the painting he has in mind, which will be a religious subject, though even so his sensuality slips out. He ends on good terms with the guard (lines 336-392).

HOME THOUGHTS, FROM ABROAD

The speaker describes spring in England.

Stanza 1 describes the first leafing of April, and stanza 2 describes the sights and sounds of May—the birds, the blossoming pear tree, and so on.

HOME THOUGHTS, FROM THE SEA

As the poet sails toward Gibraltar, the sights bring to mind great naval victories in England's past. At Cadiz Bay, for instance, an English fleet defeated a Spanish fleet in 1596. With these services that his nation has given him, he asks what he can do to serve England.

MEETING AT NIGHT

The speaker (who is the same as in "Parting at Morning") describes his meeting at night with his beloved. This is the night of love, dominated by the moon, the shadows, and the soft sounds of the meeting.

Stanza 1 describes the journey along the sea in a small boat to the shore, and then stanza 2 describes the trip on land to the door, where the woman awaits, joyous and fearful.

MY LAST DUCHESS

The Duke of Ferrara is speaking to the Count's envoy about his late Duchess and in the account reveals his attitude toward his late wife and also something of his own character.

Having drawn aside the curtain that covers the portrait of "my last Duchess," the Duke begins to explain to the envoy "How such a glance came there." His complaint is that she seemed to rate everybody's gifts and attentions, no matter how trivial, with "My gift of a nine-hundred-years-old name." So, not stooping to explain his resentment to her, he "gave commands;/ Then all smiles stopped together." The concluding lines (lines 46-56) demonstrate the Duke's suave courtesy, his concern with money, and his interest in art.

PARTING AT MORNING

The speaker (who is the same as in "Meeting at Night") describes the sunrise, when there was a "path of gold" on the sea, and now for him (the speaker) "the need of a world of men." From the woman's world in the night of love, he is now drawn back to the man's world of day.

PROSPICE

The speaker as he looks forward (*Prospice* means "look forward") says he does not fear death. He will face this battle against the ultimate terror, and he would not want death to bandage his eyes and let him slip by. For at the worst point the sudden vision will come, and he will be united with his beloved.

RABBI BEN EZRA

This poem expresses an optimistic philosophy of old age through the speech of Rabbi Ben Ezra.

Old age is the best time of life. The speaker does not mean to complain about youth's hopes and fears. On the contrary, he prizes doubt as opposed to the untroubled lives of lower kinds (lines 1-18). Life is not supposed to be all joy and fulfillment. To give is better than to take (lines 19-30). The pain of opposition is the sign of success. Aspiration is marked by failure, for total success means a failure to aspire high enough (lines 31-48). Yet the body does have its use in enabling us to see and know power and love, and we should recognize that the flesh is helpful to the soul in this life (lines 49-72).

After the struggles and confusion of youth, age will help the speaker to see things clearly. He will be able to face the future (that is, death) with more certainty because he sees the past in truer perspective (lines 73-102). Man's lot is to learn from his experiences in this life something of God's ways (lines 103-108).

As youth waited for age, so it is fitting that age waits for death. Age will enable us to judge the true worth of our deeds, freed from the erring judgment of the world (lines 109-135). In the true assessment of one's worth will be included motives and purposes beyond worldly judgment (lines 139-150).

The speaker attacks the hedonist philosophy that sees man like a pot created by the indifferent Potter's wheel of time. The spirit of God and the human soul endure. Matter helps to form the spirit (lines 161-168). What does it signify that earlier lives have faded and that the present looks grim? Man's purpose is not on earth but is to fulfill God's will (lines 169-180). He needs God now as in the past in order that he may fulfill his true purpose, which is to serve as God directs (lines 181-192).

SAUL

David tells the story of how he played upon the harp for King Saul, who had summoned him to play. The King had been troubled by an evil spirit, and David's music and words relieved him.

David arrives and is accosted by Abner (sections 1 and 2). Then he enters Saul's tent (section 3) and finds the king motionless and suffering (section 4). David begins to sing. He sings the gentle song for the sheep (section 5) and the tunes for God's other creatures (section 6), followed by songs of various aspects of human life (section 7). David pauses momentarily at a sound from Saul and then goes on (section 8) with a song of human vitality and achievement, which culminates in praise of King Saul (section 9).

David pauses as Saul, like a mountain down which the snow slides in the spring, gives a sign of self-recognition (section 10).

As Saul now is brought to a mid-point toward the acceptance of life (section 11, lines 134-135), David calls upon his imagination that had sustained him in the past (section 12). With this inspiration he sings of man's spiritual triumph, as seen particularly in the great force exerted by Saul himself (section 13). David pauses in his story a moment to consider the glory and power to which God had inspired him (section 14). Then, continuing his story, David tells of the next stage in Saul's recovery. As Saul shows signs of recovery, David wonders what to do to help him further (section 15). Suddenly he realizes that it is now time for speech, not music (section 16). The nature of God is love (section 17), and so inspired by God's love, David wills to try to raise Saul from his affliction. David's insight into God's love leads to a vision of Christ as the human incarnation of almighty power and almighty love (section 18), and as he leaves Saul's tent, the whole earth is awake and bright with this new law.

SOLILOQUY OF THE SPANISH CLOISTER

The speaker reveals his intense hatred for another monk, Brother Lawrence. His speech marks him as bigoted, lustful, deceitful, and superstitious, while Brother Lawrence is seen as a gentle man of simple, straightforward piety.

In stanza 1 the speaker gives vent to his hatred, and then in stanzas 2 and 3, he recalls Brother Lawrence's gentle conversation and his care about his eating utensils. The expression of jealousy grows more intense as his thoughts turn to sex, first (stanza 4) when he attributes his own sensual pleasure to the mild-tempered Brother Lawrence and later (stanzas 7-8) when he considers sending Brother Lawrence to hell by putting his own "Scrofulous French novel" where the hated monk will see it. Or he will even risk his own soul if he can make a compact with Satan to ruin Brother Lawrence (stanza 9).

THE BISHOP ORDERS HIS TOMB AT ST. PRAXED'S CHURCH

A dying bishop of the sixteenth century gives instructions to his sons for his tomb and in so doing reveals much about himself and his past.

As his sons stand around the dying bishop, he tells them of the envy that Gandolph (a rival priest) felt for him because he (the bishop) had won the girl that was his sons' mother (lines 1-5). The thought of her death leads to the thought of his own death, and then to the subject of the tomb. He had fought with Gandolph over a favorite niche (lines 6-19) and now he is satisfied that from the location he has chosen he can continue to enjoy the beauties of his church (lines 20-25). He wants an elaborate tomb with the lapis lazuli he stole from his own church during a fire poised between the knees of his graven image (lines 26-50). He describes an increasingly expensive and elaborate tomb, with bas-relief of Christian and pagan scenes. Always on his mind is the envy of Gandolph, and he is also always fearful that his sons will not carry out his wishes. He thinks to bribe them by praying to St. Praxed for horses and mistresses for them (lines 51-75).

He suddenly thinks of his epitaph, which must be a choice quotation from Cicero (lines 76-79). Then his thoughts project into the future, when he will lie on his tomb through the centuries, apparently thinking of his body in terms of sculpture (lines 80-90). Various confused images come into his mind (lines 91-101), and then he returns to thoughts of his tomb and, as his sons leave, he realizes they are indifferent to his wishes (lines 102-115) and that his tomb will not be the splendid thing he has wished (lines 116-118). Nevertheless, as he is left alone, he feels the peace of his church and enjoys the envy of Gandolph (lines 119-125).

THE LOST LEADER

The subject is a man who turned from a liberal to a conservative position. The figure is modeled on Wordsworth, but is not intended to represent in detail Browning's view of that poet.

From being a leader of the others, the man in question has sold out for a "handful of silver" and a "riband," unlike other poets who remained true to their original insights (lines 1-16). Nevertheless, says the speaker, we shall go on with other songs. His name will be blotted out. But, after death, when the greatest victories have been won and he has been taught by those he first inspired, the "lost leader" will be "pardoned in heaven, the first day by the throne" (lines 17-32).

UP AT A VILLA–DOWN IN THE CITY

The speaker would like to have a house in the city, where there is activity.
    His villa is on a bare mountain edge (lines 1-10). Houses in the city are neat and regular while at the villa winter stays late and summer comes abruptly (lines 11-25). In the city square a fountain plays on statuary while at the villa there is nothing to see or hear but the cypress, fireflies, bees, and so on (lines 26-37). Though there is much activity in the city (lines 38-54), the speaker must stay at the villa because city living is too expensive.

WILLIAM CULLEN BRYANT

THANATOPSIS

A brooding acceptance of death pervades this poem, whose title means "A View of Death." The poem begins by stating a close relationship between man and Nature. Nature speaks with "a voice of gladness" when man is gay, and with "healing sympathy" for "his darker musings." When the fear of death comes, Nature speaks through her visible forms (lines 1-16). Although (she says to man) you will shortly die and return to the earth that nourished you (lines 17-30), your place is with the great men of the past in the tomb of nature. You will share the fate of the millions who have died and who will die (lines 31-72). Therefore, live in such a way that you will go to death serenely, as if to sleep (lines 73-81).

TO A WATERFOWL

From seeing and thinking about a solitary bird, the poet is strengthened in his religious faith. Just as the bird is directed on its solitary and difficult journey to a summer home and rest by "a Power whose care/Teaches thy way," so "I" (that is, the speaker) will be directed in my lonely journey of life by the same Power.

ROBERT BURNS

A MAN'S A MAN FOR A' THAT

The poet says that true virtue lies in the man himself, not in rank or external trappings.

Despite poverty and obscurity, a man is the real gold. Honesty is better than mere show. The independent man laughs at the fool called a lord whom hundreds worship. Though a prince can make a knight or a duke, he is powerless to make an honest man. The time will come when "sense and worth" will be rewarded and all men will be brothers.

ADDRESS TO THE DEIL

The speaker addresses the devil in a bantering tone.

After hailing the devil (stanzas 1-2), the speaker acknowledges his power as evidenced in eerie noises (stanzas 3-8). The devil has strange spells and powers that affect the evil wizard and the ordinary farm wife alike (stanzas 9-14). Then the poet alludes to the devil's conduct in the Garden of Eden, his torment of Job, and his repression by Michael (stanzas 15-19). He concludes with the desire to cheat the devil, and yet he wishes that Nick might mend his ways and possibly escape from hell (stanzas 20-21).

ADDRESS TO THE UNCO' GUID OR THE RIGIDLY RIGHTEOUS

The speaker addresses the bigoted people who criticize other people's frailties.

He accosts the settled and comfortable pious ones and proposes to defend those guilty of folly and sin (stanzas 1-2). Consider the different circumstances, you pure ones, he says. Consider the quickened pulse that even you feel at times, in order to have some idea of the "ragings" in the blood of others (stanzas 3-4). Under changed conditions, "Social life and Glee" become "Debauchery and Drinking." He admonishes the virtuous Dames that they should remember that they have never been tempted as "poor Frailty" has (stanzas 5-6). Therefore they should look upon their fellows "gently," for one cannot know their motives nor their regrets (stanza 7).

HOLY WILLIE'S PRAYER

This is the prayer of a hypocritical Calvinist.

He praises God for his power in sending one to heaven while he sends ten to hell, and he blesses God that he now stands as one of the saved, "A burnin' an' a shinin' light." Despite his just deserts, he is a "pillar in thy temple." He claims to stay away from drinking and swearing, but he has to confess that he succumbs to "fleshly lust" where the girls are concerned. Thus afflicted, he prays God's blessing on the chosen ones, and he asks a special curse for Gawn Hamilton, who dared to ridicule the chosen ones, and also he asks for a curse on the presbytery at Ayr, and on Aiken (Hamilton's defender). He concludes with an appeal for blessings for "me and mine."

TO A MOUNTAIN DAISY

On turning down a mountain daisy with his plow, the poet compares this fate with that of human beings.

The poet pities the flower which he must crush. This event is not like the touch of the lark. The flower survived the storm to grow in humble beauty. So must man suffer disaster: the maid who loses her virtue, the bard, the person of true worth, even you who now sorrow for the fate of the daisy.

TO A MOUSE

On turning up the dwelling of a mouse with his plow, the poet pauses to compare the condition of mice and men.

The poet expresses his sympathy for the cowering mouse and regrets that it has cause to fear man. He is sorry that he plowed up the mouse's dwelling place, but, he observes, "The best laid schemes of mice and men" often go awry. Still, the mouse is better off than the man, for, whereas the mouse lives only in the present, man looks to the past with sorrow and to the future with fear.

GEORGE NOEL GORDON, LORD BYRON

DARKNESS

The poet describes the world after "the bright sun was extinguished." Darkness has come upon the world. Everything is dead or dying. The poet describes the last days of mankind, when all men have been turned into skeletons and fiends. Wild animals grow subdued, but man grows more terrible than before, turning to cannibalism. Finally, everything is dead. Darkness no longer has need even of the winds and the waters: "She was the Universe."

MAID OF ATHENS, ERE WE PART

The speaker addresses his beloved as he is about to depart. He protests his emotion to her in a series of statements tied together by the metaphor of a holy and sanctified love. In stanza 1 he asks her to hear his "vow." In the next two stanzas the repetition of "By" indicates a series of solemn oaths.

ON THIS DAY I COMPLETE MY THIRTY-SIXTH YEAR

The poet broods upon his present condition and impending death on the battlefield. Since his emotional powers are now gone, he calls upon his spirit to awake and seek an honorable death in a soldier's grave.

SHE WALKS IN BEAUTY

The poet praises the lady for her mingling of dark and light in her appearance. This balance gives her a "nameless grace." In her features he sees goodness, peace, and innocent love.

SONNET ON CHILLON

The poet observes that Liberty is "Brightest in dungeons," because when her sons are imprisoned "Their country conquers with their martyrdom." Chillon is therefore a holy place because here Bonnivard was imprisoned for his defiance of tyranny.

STANZAS FOR MUSIC (THERE BE NONE OF BEAUTY'S DAUGHTERS)

The speaker describes the "magic" of a woman.

The first stanza describes the magic of the loved one's voice, as though it had the power to calm the ocean and still the winds. The second stanza compares the gentleness of the ocean and the moon to the submission of the lover's soul before the beloved.

STANZAS FOR MUSIC (THERE'S NOT A JOY)

The poet laments the passing of youth and its joy. With the passing of youth the heart's "tender bloom" also fades (stanza 1), and the few who survive this time are without proper direction (stanza 2). The soul grows cold, and under the surface glitter lies the "worn and gray" interior (stanzas 3-4). If the poet could weep as he once wept, his tears would seem sweet (stanza 5).

THE DESTRUCTION OF SENNACHERIB

Byron expanded the brief Biblical account of the attack by Sennacherib, king of Assyria, upon the Jewish people (see II Kings 19:35). The power of God smote the heathens, horse and rider alike, without the Israelites having to raise a hand.

THE PRISONER OF CHILLON

Bonnivard, the prisoner, tells the story of his imprisonment. The poem describes a mental state induced by long imprisonment. Byron's approach makes his point about liberty by showing the terrible effect of long imprisonment upon a man's spirit.

The three imprisoned brothers are the last of a family of seven— a father and six sons—who have refused to submit to tyranny. Though the three brothers try to comfort one another in their dungeon, their voices eventually take on "a dreary tone." Bonnivard describes his two brothers. The younger one was his father's favorite, naturally handsome, gay, and generous. The other one was a hunter and fighter, who languished under imprisonment. His brothers died, leaving him alone. For a while Bonnivard's mind went completely blank in "A sea of stagnant idleness," until a bird brought him back to consciousness with its song. But then it flew away, leaving him lonelier than before.

Being now free to roam the dungeon, Bonnivard could climb to the window and look out. The sight depressed him further, for it reinforced his own solitude and confinement. Finally, he is released, but ironically he is half-sorrowful because the years have made him accustomed to his dungeon.

WHEN WE TWO PARTED

The speaker recalls a parting with his love, when the chill of that event foretold the sorrow of the present. He shudders now when he hears her name, and he will grieve at her forgetfulness and deception.

THOMAS CAMPION

MY SWEETEST LESBIA

In a *carpe diem* ("seize the day") love poem, the poet calls for his beloved (Lesbia, after the Roman Catullus' mistress) to "live and love" now before death, the ever-enduring night.

Stanza 1 calls for love despite the reproof of the "sager sort," because the movement of time marked by "Heaven's great lamps" is swift. Stanza 2 says that if all loved as the poet, there would be no wars, that they are "fools" who waste their "little light" in not loving. Stanza 3 expresses the poet's wish that even at death he be surrounded with love—not "mourning friends," but lovers and "sweet pastimes," especially Lesbia.

WHEN THOU MUST HOME TO SHADES OF UNDERGROUND

The poet, complaining at unrequited love, imagines his beloved after death in Hades telling about her love.

In stanza 1, all gather admiringly to hear her stories of love. Stanza 2 describes her telling of all the honor given her beauty—banqueting delights, masques, revels, tournaments. By contrast, in the last line, she did dishonor to the poet, "didst murther" him by not returning his love.

THOMAS CAREW

A SONG (ASK ME NO MORE WHERE JOVE BESTOWS)

The poet praises the beauty of his beloved by comparing her with five beautiful things that have become part of her: the rose, her beauty (stanza 1); golden atoms, powder in her hair (stanza 2); the nightingale, her voice (stanza 3); meteors, her eyes (stanza 4); and the immortal phoenix, her bosom (stanza 5).

JOHN CLARE

I AM

The poet makes his statement of misery and isolation.

I am (I exist), he says, and yet I am alone, consumed by woes. I feel that I am tossed in the meaningless sea of my life, and I long to be with God and sleep an untroubled sleep.

SECRET LOVE

The speaker says that he hid his love until his senses became oversensitive.

He tried to avoid the memory of her (stanza 1). He met her in the summer, when she was a part of summer's beauty (stanza 2). He hid his love, and the breeze, the bees, the flies, and even the silences haunted him. Nature could not find out that the answer nature was seeking was secret love (stanza 3).

ARTHUR HUGH CLOUGH

QUA CURSUM VENTUS

The title means "as the wind blows." Clough describes the estrangement between himself and a friend by the analogy of two ships at sea.

Two ships lie becalmed at evening. In the night with the rising wind they sail without realizing that they are getting even further apart. With the dawn, each is far from the other. Each must now go its own way, never to join again until they are united at the port which has been their common goal.

SAY NOT THE STRUGGLE NAUGHT AVAILETH

This poem is a counsel of courage to those who may doubt the ultimate victory of a cause.

The poet first states that the struggle may be going better than it seems to be and that, "but for you," the comrades may now be victorious (stanzas 1-2). The full power of the ocean lies "Far back," not in "the tired waves, vainly breaking," and though at daybreak the sun seems to rise slowly in the east, the west is already bright (stanzas 3-4).

SAMUEL TAYLOR COLERIDGE

DEJECTION: AN ODE

The poet laments the passing of his poetic inspiration.

In his depression the poet wishes that the wind might inspire him (lines 1-20), for he perceives that "in our life alone does

Nature live" and states his present conception of philosophic idealism (lines 21-58). It is joy that is the secret of life and inspiration, and now that joy has gone the poet has only "abstract research" as a substitute for "My shaping spirit of imagination" (lines 59-93). He listens to the roaring wind, which brings grim sounds to mind (lines 94-125). He concludes on a quieter note, hoping that the unnamed lady will be free of such nightly vigils as this (lines 126-139).

KUBLA KHAN

In general, Coleridge seems to be evoking the mystery of the creative imagination.

Kubla Khan decrees that a "pleasure-dome" be built, with a large walled-in area containing trees and gardens bright and sweet-smelling (lines 1-11). From the chasm that runs across a "cedarn cover" a fountain bursts, from which flows the sacred river that meanders until it reaches the immense caverns and noisily sinks into the "lifeless ocean" (lines 12-30). The shadow of the "dome of pleasure" and the sounds are impressive. The speaker recalls the vision of the Abyssinian maid which was so inspiring that, if he could remember it, he could recreate in song the beauty and the mystery of the pleasure dome, and all would wonder at his inspiration (lines 31-54).

THE RIME OF THE ANCIENT MARINER

Coleridge's glosses outline the main story line and some points for special emphasis (see, for example, his second gloss for Part the Second). Coleridge summarized the story as follows: "How a Ship having passed the Line was driven by storms to the cold Country towards the South Pole; and how from thence she made her course to the tropical Latitude of the Great Pacific Ocean; and of the strange things that befell; and in what manner the Ancyent Marinere came back to his own Country."

Three important themes explored in the poem are social relationships, the Christian idea of sin and suffering, and the supernatural or spiritual world. The poem begins with emphasis on accepted social functions: a wedding is in progress. The Mariner begins his tale: the ship leaves amid the cheers of the crowd. In Part

II the question of the Mariner's acceptance or rejection by his fellows arises. After his fellow sailors die, he is alone except for the spirit-crew. His loneliness or isolation is perhaps his greatest misery. Six stanzas from the end he comments on the importance of walking "together to the kirk/With a greatly company!−" The Christian theme of sin and suffering is brought out by the Mariner's fate. He sins by thoughtlessly and cruelly killing the albatross, one of God's creatures. For this sin, "Instead of the cross, the Albatross/About my neck was hung." Then follows the suffering and the complete spiritual isolation until, through suffering, he learns to bless the water snakes "unawares." He learned with his whole being the meaning of love.

Coleridge was also creating a world beneath our apparent world, like the spirit that drove the ship. This world exists in the poem side by side with the world of ordinary social relationships and religious traditions and may even at times impinge upon our everyday lives.

WILLIAM COLLINS

ODE TO EVENING

The poet invokes the spirit of evening and describes her appearance and influence in various places and various seasons.

The poet opens with an appeal to "chaste Eve" to teach him to write in a way that will fit in with the evening stillness (lines 1-20). This appeal modestly hopes that music or song may soothe the ear of evening as her "springs and dying gales do" (lines 1-4) now when the sun sinks splendidly into the water (lines 5-8). All is now hushed except for the bat and the beetle (lines 9-14). In this evening still-ness, the poet calls upon evening to teach him how to compose (or sing or write) a soft strain fitting to the still and dark surroundings (lines 15-20).

The next eight lines describe the coming of evening through mythology and personification. The rising of the evening star shall be the signal for the "shadowy car" of evening to be prepared by the fragrant Hours, the elves, the nymphs, and the thoughtful Pleasures (lines 21-28).

The poet calls upon evening to lead him to a heath, where there may be a lake nearby or a noble building or fallow upland fields (lines 29-32).

When inclement weather confines him, the poet wants to be in a hut on a mountainside that overlooks the "wilds, and swelling floods," and the hamlets, and that hears the bells from the spires and sees the "dusky veil" of evening spread over all (lines 33-40).

So long as Spring brings rains and Summer brings the time for outdoor evening play; so long as Autumn brings falling leaves and howling winter frightens the shortening evening; then so long under the forest hut shall Fancy, Friendship, Science, and Health acknowledge evening's gentle influence (lines 41-52).

ODE TO SIMPLICITY

The poet addresses Simplicity as the chief inspiration for his poetry.

Simplicity expresses the "genuine thought" of Nature and nurses Fancy, the babe of Simplicity or Pleasure. Simplicity comes disdainful of ornament, arranged simply "In Attic robe" (lines 1-12). By "the honeyed store" of Hybla, by the nightingale, and by the river Cephisus (in Attica), the poet pleads for Simplicity to aid him, for even the most beautiful flowers need Simplicity to arrange them (lines 13-30). While Rome admired virtue, Simplicity inspired her poets, but she sang alone to one famous poet and then she turned from Rome, fleeing "her altered land." No longer are the passions subject to Simplicity. Weak poetry means only Love. For you, Simplicity, have left us, and no more will you bless "the servile scene" (lines 31-42).

Though written with taste and genius, a work is cold without Simplicity, which alone can "raise the meeting soul." Others may ask for the aid of taste and genius. The poet seeks only the simplicity of Nature (lines 43-54).

ODE WRITTEN IN THE BEGINNING OF THE YEAR 1746 (HOW SLEEP THE BRAVE)

The poet praises the brave dead who lie blessed by their country. Spring shall "deck their hallowed mold richly." They shall be grieved for by "fairy hands" and "forms unseen," and Honor and Freedom shall do them homage.

HART CRANE

REPOSE OF RIVERS

The river speaks, thinking back over the course that brought it to the repose of the sea.

Not until old age had brought it to the sea could the river reflect upon the events of its passage. Then it remembered its origins among the "slow sound" of willows and the seething marshes, the alcoves that drew it almost into hades, the black gorge, the pond it fled from, the ugly city, and the monsoon at the gulf.

It was when the river reached the "wind flaking sapphire" of the sea that it knew real repose—"willows could not hold more steady sound."

The Bridge

This sequence of fifteen poems in eight sections is Crane's attempt to find vitality for the modern world by relating it to the traditions of America, from the voyages of Columbus, through Indian culture, to the modern age symbolized dominantly by the figure of Brooklyn Bridge, and on to a vision of a great new age in the future.

1: PROEM: TO BROOKLYN BRIDGE

The proem announces the basic theme of the sequence of fifteen poems that compose *The Bridge:* to see in the aesthetic form or "curveship" of Brooklyn Bridge the ability of the poet's civilization to free him from a confining, oppressive existence.

Stanzas 1-3 depict three delusory promises of freedom from confinement and oppression: gulls, daydreams of office workers, and cinemas. The gulls soaring above the "chained" bay water "forsake us" and are as "apparitional" as the daydreams of office-workers who see themselves as out sailing while they go about their work. The "elevators drop" both gulls and sailing to dull reality. The cinema's "flashing scene" also is never revealed.

In stanzas 4-9 the poet looks to "Thee," the bridge, as a more stable symbol of freedom. He attempts to deify the bridge. From it come "guerdon," "accolade," "reprieve and pardon," "harp and altar," and "eternity." But the heaven offered by the bridge is obscure.

So in stanzas 10-11, the poet stands in the darkness of the bridge and prays that this symbol of our technical, industrial culture may become deified: "lend a myth to God."

2: AVE MARIA

Columbus on his way home from the discovery of America describes his voyage as a spiritual quest. The title alludes both to Columbus' ship *Santa Maria* and to the religious invocation ("Hail Mary").

In stanza 1, Columbus faces Spain and invokes the presence of two men who helped him on his quest—Luis de San Angel and Juan Perez. He tells them he is bringing them back Cathay (an earthly paradise).

In stanzas 2-3, Columbus thinks back on the voyage—a quest for truth that brought him to what he thought was "Chan's great continent" of Asia (actually the West Indies). In stanzas 4-5, he considers the hardships encountered so far and those yet to come—from Indians, deaths at sea ("floating in a casque"), "hurricanes," "Bewilderment and mutiny," and "shadow."

In stanzas 5-8, even under the "tempest-lash," Columbus has faith in his vision. He is not bringing jewels back to Ferdinand of Spain, but he is bringing the vision of joining East and West ("eastern shore" and "western sea"). He hopefully looks through the dark waters to see the "prow free."

In stanzas 9-15, Columbus praises God ("Te Deum laudamus"), who is seen as the Absolute behind this "parable of man" ("Word," "Elohim," "Crown," "Hand of Fire"). Columbus' voyage is a spiritual voyage ("knowledge," "beyond desire," "in the/trembling heart").

3: THE HARBOR DAWN

In the first poem in the section "Powhatan's Daughter," a modern man establishes links with his American past, idealized as Pocahontas ("to merge your seed—with whom?").

In stanzas 1-4, the man awakening from his dreams at dawn hears the noises of the modern city along the harbor. In stanzas 5-9, in his state midway between dreaming and waking, the man addresses his beloved beside him, asking her to lay her arms about him before day arrives. The woman merges with the idealized Pocahontas (as the epigraph and the marginal notes indicate), "the woman with us in the dawn."

4: VAN WINKLE

In the second poem in the section "Powhatan's Daughter," the poet uses Rip Van Winkle as a symbol of how memory works to lose one in time. (In a letter, Crane described Van Winkle as the guardian angel of the protagonist's journey into the past. The marginal notes tell that, in the background, the idealized daughter of Powhatan, "time's truant," also links the past and present.)

In stanza 1, the poet begins traveling in the modern city, "Far Rockaway to Golden Gate." In stanzas 2-4, he travels back in time to recall historical figures he learned about in school—Pizarro, Cortez, Priscilla, Captain John Smith, and Rip Van Winkle. In stanzas 5-9, memory takes the poet to scenes of childhood play and relationships with his father and mother. In stanza 10, the figure of Rip Van Winkle has blended with modern man to take a trip in the city.

5: THE RIVER

In the third poem in the section "Powhatan's Daughter." the scenes of the Mississippi River Valley seen through the eyes of hoboes and train passengers express the spirit of the American past.

Stanzas 1-2 give a view from the train window of the slogans of the year. (Crane described the scene as a "burlesque on the cultural confusion of the present.") Stanzas 3-5 present three hoboes along the tracks who wander to Ohio to Indiana to Cheyenne to Louisiana to Booneville. In stanzas 6-10, the poet reflects that the hoboes in their "empire wilderness of freight and rails" parallel the experiences of the pioneers. He thinks that the hoboes "touch something like a key" by being in touch with the land itself, as were the "redskin dynasties" and the pioneers with "axe and powder horn." In stanzas 11-12, the poet asks the Pullman breakfasters to lean from the windows and join the hoboes in knowing the Mississippi River Valley. For the train passengers too "feed the River timelessly."

Stanzas 13-20 describe the River with its one passion to flow till it reaches its "biding place," the Gulf—symbolic of a merging with God ("Jordan," "Passion," "hosannas").

6: THE DANCE

The fourth poem in the section "Powhatan's Daughter" tells of the poet's union with Pocahontas and of her symbolically becoming modern America.

Stanzas 1-3 describe the land of America as the Indian maiden, Pocahontas. Stanzas 4-7 tell of the poet's union with the Indian maiden ("bed of leaves") and of her death ("crescent die"). In stanzas 8-11, the poet makes a journey to a place where there is to be a ritual dance. In stanzas 12-20, the poet becomes the Indian mythical hero Maquokeeta, and is burned at the stake in a ritual death dance. In stanzas 21-26, he is resurrected and reunited with Pocahontas, who has become America ("bride immortal in the maize," "singing tree," "slope and vineyard").

7: INDIANA

The fifth poem in the section "Powhatan's Daughter" describes the transfer of the vitality of native tradition from Indian to white culture, as a prairie woman expresses the hardships, failures, and restlessness of American life.

In stanzas 1-7, an old pioneer mother bids goodbye to her son going off to sea. She recalls that she and the boy's father had once been "Prodigal" and pioneered for gold in Colorado, where her husband died.

In stanzas 8-11, the mother tells how on the "long trail back" to Indiana a heroic Indian squaw restored the woman's hope by giving a look of love.

In stanzas 12-16, the mother tells her son to remember her and to come back to Indiana.

8: CUTTY SARK

In the figure of ships, the poet considers past and present in terms of dreams, fulfillments, and failures.

In the first part of the poem, the poet hears a derelict sailor tell of his sailing experiences and his love for the sea. The poet sees the "frontiers gleaming of his mind" and connects him with the Ideal of the quest ("Atlantis Rose"). In the last part of the poem, the sailor leaves and the poet walks toward the Bridge with a vision of successful clipper ships set against the failures of ships sunk and missing.

9: CAPE HATTERAS

The poet takes Whitman as his model and inspiration to envision cosmic evolution moving mankind to that glorious age when the human soul reaches divinity.

In stanzas 1-4, the poet considers that modern America neglects infinity, as Whitman saw it. Instead, the airplane ("eagle") has become the symbol of conquest of time and space.

.Stanzas 5-10 describe the airplane as man's embodiment of conquest ("Iliads"), a conquest that has brought war's destructiveness. Man's concept of "infinity's dim marge" is the plane in space. The upshot of it all is a plane crash, a "beached heap of high bravery!"

In stanzas 11-17, by contrast, Whitman had a concept of transcendence and "living brotherhood." It was he who first sang the theme of the Bridge, the "Years of the Moderns," and saw beyond the "sesames of science" to transcendent experience ("endless terminals").

10: SOUTHERN CROSS

The first poem in the section "Three Songs" idealizes an as yet nameless woman, who eludes the poet.

In stanzas 1-2, the poet tells of his desire for the Woman of the South, not imaginatively ("wraith") but actually ("utterly"). The woman is nameless, but she is associated with divinity through the Southern Cross and idealized as Eve, Magdalene, Mary, Venus, and Hero of Abydos (epigraph).

The rest of the poem describes the poet's search as futile. The woman, again identified with God in her namelessness, eludes him ("derision," "Insolence," "phantom").

The Bridge

11: NATIONAL WINTER GARDEN

In the second poem in the section "Three Songs," a striptease dancer expresses the "burlesque of our lust." Yet it is through Magdalene, as the redeemed prostitute or woman of flesh, that we are drawn back "lifeward."

Stanzas 1-3 describe the burlesque dance. It is lustily watched but unsatisfying, for it is a cheap substitute for the idealized woman ("someone else," "cheapest echo").

In stanzas 4-6, the dance continues with hints that this dancer is a distortion of womanhood ("sandstone grey," "silly snakes," "fakes"). The watchers leave without sexual satisfaction ("fleshless").

In stanza 7, though woman as purely sexual may be a burlesque of the ideal woman, sexual love is a way to love and life.

12: VIRGINIA

In the third poem in the section "Three Songs," a man idealizes his girl friend, who works in the Woolworth Building ("nickel-dime tower").

In lines 1-6, the man waits for his Mary who retains her virginity, as the title suggests, by "smiling the boss away," primarily for the financial reason of her "Pay-check at eleven."

In lines 7-14, the lover looks forward to Saturday, when Mary gives time to him.

In lines 15-25, he mentally asks her to let down her "golden hair" for her idealized princely lover, as did Rapunzel in the fairy tale. The girl is also idealized as the Virgin Mary (see title and "Cathedral Mary").

13: QUAKER HILL

The poet describes the degeneracy of modern American life in contrast to the serene, holy life of the Quakers.

Stanzas 1-2 describe the serene Quakers with their holy perspective. Stanzas 3-5 describe the Quaker meeting house. Its windows are like eyes looking at the countryside with a stare of death. The weekend golfers travesty the "Promised Land." The meeting house

The Bridge

itself has become a roadhouse, and the woodlice eat at the furniture. In stanzas 6-8, the poet looks to his American forerunners to guide him, for modern commercialism has severed his cultural birthright. The "slain Iroquois" can guide him better than the Yankees. And, especially, like Emily Dickinson and Isadora Duncan, we must create love out of our despair.

14: THE TUNNEL

The poem describes a subway ride under the river, which suggests death, descent into hell, purgatorial ascent, and rebirth. (Crane described the poem as a "kind of purgatory.")

In stanzas 1-3, the protagonist prepares to take the subway as the "quickest promise home." In stanzas 4-5, he enters the subway with the "other faces, also underground." Stanzas 6-11 picture the subway experiences. The noises and fragments of conversation are like "phonographs of hades in the brain." In stanzas 12-13, the poet has a vision of Poe, who died in Baltimore in ugly circumstances, like the subway's ugliness. In stanzas 14-15, the subway disgorges passengers and then dives under the river.

In stanzas 16-18, the poet asks if the Daemon takes us home. The Daemon is both the evil spirit of the subway taking us underground and the divine spirit of Columbus ("Genoese") leading to "some Word that will not die," to a rebirth such as Lazarus had. In stanzas 19-20 the poet stands looking at river and harbor, having emerged from his purgatorial "Hand of Fire" (see end of "Ave Maria").

15: ATLANTIS

The poem uses the image of the mythical lost city to bridge reality and myth. (Crane said that in this poem "the Bridge becomes the symbol of consciousness spanning time and space.")

In stanzas 1-2, the poet looks upward by moonlight at the arc of the Bridge. He sees the arc as binding all the world ("all tides," "seven oceans"). In stanzas 3-7, the poet's vision moves beyond present universal love, and the Bridge blends past and future ("Tomorrow into yesteryear"). Voyages and conquests of the past join in the Bridge as "Vision-of-the-Voyage" ("Tyre," "Troy," "Jason," "Cathay").

The Bridge

In stanzas 8-12, the poet invokes the Bridge as symbol of transcendent meaning ("Cognizance," "Myth," "Deity's glittering Pledge") with Love as the leading force—"unspeakable Thou Bridge to Thee, O Love."

Voyages

In a sequence of six poems, Crane uses the dominant image of the sea as woman to make sea voyages through love, life, and death. The sea as universal life-death principle symbolizes the speaker's relationship to both the life-wish and the death-wish. The sea as woman presents life-wish and death-wish in terms of transcendent and sexual love.

I: ABOVE THE FRESH RUFFLES OF THE SURF

In his thoughts the speaker warns the carefree children on the beach that the sea is cruel.

They can play on the beach, but must not trust themselves to the "caresses" and "breast" of the sea, for the "sea is cruel." The use of feminine imagery suggests the danger of growing up to adult love.

II: AND YET THIS GREAT WINK OF ETERNITY

The transitional opening "And yet" leads to a qualification of the sea's cruelty described in "Voyages: I." The sexual imagery of the first poem is extended to present the sea as a voluptuous goddess who can free the speaker and his lover from the fate of the sea.

In stanza 1, the sea is personified as a voluptuous goddess with "undinal vast belly," losing the speaker in "wrapt inflections of our love." Stanza 2 presents the sea as a form of impersonal justice as she "knells" and "rends" all but the lovers. In stanza 3, with hope for lovers offered, the speaker calls upon his lover, "O my Prodigal," to love, "to complete the dark confession" of the sea. Thus they can perhaps rise above the cruel fate of the sea in "one floating flower" of love from the union of "sleep, death, desire." In stanza 5, the speaker prays to the seasons and the waves to indeed reconcile in them both time and eternity—"earthly shore" and "paradise."

III: INFINITE CONSANGUINITY IT BEARS

A voyage into love is described as a sexual union with the sea.

Lines 1-14 describe the union in images of closeness: "consanguinity," "no stroke/Wide from your side," "Light wrestling . . . with light," "Star kissing star," "wave on wave." Lines 15-18 describe this union as a shedding of death which leads to a "single change" which rises above song. Line 19 is a prayer for such a voyage into love.

IV: WHOSE COUNTED SMILE OF HOURS AND DAYS

Union in love is described as an exalted, supreme experience.

Stanzas 1-2 define love as containing all reality. Love is a "smile of days and hours," "a spectrum of the sea," a "circle" that bridges no greater love than this mortal love flowing immortally, "All fragrance" and all "claim." In stanzas 3-4 all possibilities for the speaker, "All bright insinuations," are fulfilled in this joining of "Mutual blood," which is universal in containing the "secret oars and petals of all love."

V: METICULOUS, PAST MIDNIGHT IN CLEAR RIME

The exaltation of the lovers is slashed away and they return to the voyage to death.

The moonlight becomes a "white blade" to slash away the lovers' former triumphs. The "cables of our sleep," the exalted and delusionary love-sleep, are "filed." With delusions gone, the lovers' communion with one another is gone and they "never quite understand." They become aware of nothingness: "that godless cleft of sky/Where nothing turns." After their sea-love illusions of "drifting foam" and "ghosts," they resume their separate voyages, "the long way home."

VI: WHERE ICY AND BRIGHT DUNGEONS LIFT

The poet celebrates the lost vision of transcendent love. Though such love was impermanent and the sea brings ultimate destruction, man has triumph by refusing to deny the glory of the vision he had.

In stanzas 1-3, the fading vision leaves the speaker a swimmer in "icy and bright dungeons," a "derelict and blinded guest." But, in stanzas 4-8, he still sees in the universality of the sea, with its "rivers mingling toward the sky/And harbor of the phoenix' breast," a relic of hope, "some splintered garland." In holding to this glory of "Creation's blithe and petalled word," he has a remembered vision that, though impermanent, is "unbetrayable." He has a triumph that lasts beyond the "farewell."

RICHARD CRASHAW

ON OUR CRUCIFIED LORD, NAKED AND BLOODY

The poet laments the crucifixion of his Lord, but sees the blood flowing from His side as a royal garment which robes Him with the best garment of all, Himself.

THE FLAMING HEART

The devout poet praises the mystic St. Teresa for her suffering and love. He sees Teresa's book and a painting of her being accosted by an angel who kindled her heart to ecstasy with a flame-tipped spear.

In the first part of the poem (lines 1-58), the poet extolls Teresa by suggesting that the painter made a mistake. Since Teresa is superior to the seraph (lines 1-36), the painter should transpose the seraph and the woman—give him the veil, her the spear (lines 37-42). The veil can cover his embarrassment that she outdoes him (lines 43-46), while her effect on her devotees is like seraphim being shot into the heart (lines 47-58).

In the second part of the poem (lines 59-108), the poet rhapsodizes on the excellence of Teresa with her flaming heart. In lines 59-68, he reverses himself from section 1—lets the seraph keep the spear that Teresa may have only her flaming heart. For, in lines 69-84, with her flaming heart as symbol of love and martyrdom, she has all love. She can live in her book and bring "mystic deaths" to those "wise souls" who will be "love-slain witnesses." In lines 85-108, the poet asks Teresa to extend her love and suffering to purge him and to bring him to mystic death of self.

WISHES TO HIS (SUPPOSED) MISTRESS

The poet describes his unknown, ideal mistress, "That not impossible she."

In stanzas 1-5, until that "divine/Idea" appears in some real woman, the poet will describe her for us. Stanzas 6-35 give a detailed description. In her physical appearance (6-22) and her behavior and inner life (23-35) she is beautiful, natural, virtuous, graceful, and happy—"In her whole frame/Have Nature all the name,/Art and ornament the shame." Stanzas 36-42 proclaim that if Time knows of such a woman, this poem is for her.

E. E. CUMMINGS

A WIND HAS BLOWN THE RAIN AWAY

A man's desolation over a lost love is expressed through the main image of an autumn wind blowing through leafless trees.

Lines 1-3 present the image of bare trees and sky in autumn. In lines 3-8, the poet identifies himself with the autumn wind which maybe also "did love somebody." In lines 9-13, both wind and poet are left with death, "doom's integration." Lines 13-17 return to the opening image of bare trees against the sky.

ANYONE LIVED IN A PRETTY HOW TOWN

The poem is a love story about noone and anyone.

Stanzas 1, 4, 7, and 8 tell the life story of two unpretentious people, "anyone" and "noone," who met, loved, lived, and died in harmony with themselves, life, and the cycling seasons and the universe ("yes," "spring," "stars"). Stanzas 2, 5, and 9 tell by contrast the life stories of the self-important "someones" and "everyones" in the "how town" (method, not meaning) who lived busy but meaningless lives ("isn't," "nevers," "slept"). Stanzas 3 and 6 tell of the children in the middle who early guessed "anyone's" and "noone's" secret of happy love and life, but forgot as they grew up and became "someones" and "everyones."

BUFFALO BILL'S DEFUNCT (PORTRAIT VIII)

The poet states the fact of Buffalo Bill's death and recounts his achievements as a circus performer. He then states his attitude toward Buffalo Bill ("a handsome man") and finally asks Death what his attitude will be toward his "blueeyed boy."

CHANSON INNOCENT ("IN JUST-SPRING")

The poem expresses the joy of spring.

The spontaneous joy of early spring and childhood is seen in the world of pleasure ("mud-luscious"), of pals (as "eddieandbill" united in one word), and of games. The post-childhood spring is a more adult fertility season with the "baloonman" becoming a faun ("goat-footed") and "Man" emphasized by capitalization.

I THANK YOU GOD FOR MOST THIS AMAZING

Joy of life is expressed through response to a day in nature.

In stanza 1, the day is alive, natural, and infinite. In stanza 2, the effect on the poet is rebirth. In stanzas 3-4, the five senses become keenly alive and especially focus the joy of the day on the poet's relationship to another person, "You."

Childlike phrasing suggests a child's spontaneous happiness and acceptance of life (trees with spirits that leap greenly, sky with blue true dreams, exclamation "yes" for affirmation of life, "sun's birthday").

O SWEET SPONTANEOUS

A vital relationship to life must be spontaneous and natural, not academic or abstract.

In a metaphor of a woman sexually attempted by the men, earth does not yield her meaning and vitality ("gods") to the philosophers, the scientists, or the religions. She answers these sterile, bawdy methodologists with their opposite: spring—the spontaneous, natural expression of the rhythmic cycle of death and life.

PITY THIS BUSY MONSTER, MANUNKIND

Scientific "progress" is satirized as a disease that deforms mankind into a "monster."

The poet depicts how the excesses of the artificial world of "made" ("deify," "ultra-," "hyper-") have violated the living world of "born." Man is left without a goal or a wish ("unwish") and without a self ("unself"). He has but one thing to do: depart for the "universe next door."

PLATO TOLD

The poet points up man's slowness to learn the lessons of war.

Wise and good men (Plato, Jesus, Lao Tsze), World War I (Sherman), the ordinary citizen (I, you, we) "told him" of war, but he didn't believe. He believed only when wounded by war itself—when Japan (Nippon) fired back at U.S. the steel acquired from U.S. (a bit of the old 6th ave. el.).

POEM, OR BEAUTY HURTS MR. VINAL

The poet burlesques dead language as a sign of a dead culture, especially the patriotic, the commercial, and the artistic.

Allusions from patriotic songs ("let freedom ring"), advertising slogans ("If It Isn't An Eastman . . ."), and literature ("O World O Life") are used by the poet to protest that "certain ideas gestures/rhymes" have been used to the "moment of dullness." The poet sardonically sings, "America, I love you," accusing a hundred million Americans of being spiritually dead in this crass culture ("gelded," "vacant eyes").

SINCE FEELING IS FIRST

In love, "feeling is first," not formalism and intellect.

Images of emotion and vitality ("kiss," "fool," "spring," "blood," "flowers," "laugh") are posed against images of formalism and intellect ("syntax," "wisdom," "brain"). The reason is given in the last two lines: life, of which love is an expression and which includes death, is a whole, not an incidental "parenthesis" or a "paragraph."

SOMEWHERE I HAVE NEVER TRAVELLED

This tender love poem shows the power of a woman over the man who loves her.

Images of strength and delicacy are joined in the woman to move the man. Her "most frail gesture" and her "slightest look" and "wish" express the power of her "intense fragility" to sway him at will. She can open him as spring opens a rose or close him as snow closes a flower. The nature images suggest the vitality of their love (spring opening the rose, hands like rain).

THE HOURS RISE UP PUTTING OFF STARS

In a cycle of life in the city from dawn to night, men fail to live the beautiful lives possible to them.

Dawn comes with "light" and "poems," but the waking city goes forth to "murder dream." The day holds mostly ugliness and unhappiness ("digging bread," "brutal faces"). The frail man has frail dreams only, and not fulfillments. The city's day closes "with death." Night completes the cycle "scattering poems."

WHEN GOD LETS MY BODY BE

The poet at death will achieve immortal return to earth by growing into particular items in nature. (The sense units may be clarified by reading the poem as rhymed couplets.) His eye shall return to the world through tree and fruit (lines 1-4). His lips shall return to maidens through a rose (lines 5-8). His fingers shall return to his love through birds (lines 9-12). His heart, meanwhile, shall be one with the sea (lines 13-14).

WHEN SERPENTS BARGAIN FOR THE RIGHT TO SQUIRM

Nature is posed against modern customs to show how nonsensical these customs are.

Stanzas 1-3 suggest a condition of things in nature separated from their essential qualities and unable to function freely—serpents bargaining for the right to squirm, the sun striking for wages, the oak begging permission from the birch to grow an acorn. Stanza 4 says that society is incredibly awry for binding man with similar restrictions that prevent his natural functions.

SAMUEL DANIEL

CARE-CHARMER SLEEP, SON OF THE SABLE NIGHT

The poet seeks sleep as an escape from the cares of the day.

In lines 1-4, he asks sleep to relieve his languish from the cares of the day. In lines 5-8, he says that day is time enough to mourn the misfortunes of his youth. In lines 9-12, he wishes his sleep not to give him the additional grief of dreams of "day desires" that the morrow would only leave unfulfilled ("liars"). Nevertheless, in lines 13-14, he wants sleep to take him away from the "day's disdain."

LET OTHERS SING OF KNIGHTS AND PALADINS

This sonnet is in the convention that a poet's verses are the most enduring monument to the beloved's beauty. The poet rejects the "imaginary" subjects of the past of "knights and paladins" to write of his beloved's beauty for "time to come." His verses are his monuments, his "arks" and "trophies" to preserve her name from "old age" and "Time's consuming rage" and to show that the poet also "lived and loved."

WALTER DE LA MARE

REMEMBRANCE

The speaker's "remembrance" of someone "of all most dead to me" gives him a sense of detachment from all things around him. The natural setting is a backdrop for a "dreamer in a dream"—a sky, tranquil but forlorn and edged with lightning; a sea, infinite and profound; elms against bright stars. In his dreamlike remembrance, he has "Not wonder, worship, not even peace," but only pure memory.

THE GHOST

A man, believing a dead loved one has returned to him, opens the door to find the "sweet cheat gone."

Stanzas 1-3 give a dialogue between the yearning man and someone once beautiful, now returned from the grave to knock on the door. In stanzas 4-5, with "hope-wearied hand" he opens the door only to find "vacancy," "vast sorrow," and all an illusion.

THE LISTENERS

The poem creates a mood of vague and unfulfilled purpose.

The traveler has apparently come to the house because of some obligation, but the "phantom listeners" only "Stood listening." Feeling their presence, he strikes the door and says, "I kept my word." The spirits are left in the silence.

THOMAS DEKKER

SWEET CONTENT

The contentment of the poor is better than the misery of the rich. With the rich man's wealth go the "mind perplexed," "tears," and misery ("punishment"). But the poor man, in his honest labor and in his patient bearing of the burden of want, has "golden slumbers" and contentment.

EMILY DICKINSON

A NARROW FELLOW IN THE GRASS

The poet describes the movement of the snake through the grass and its effect upon her.

Stanzas 1-3 describe the sudden, brief appearance of the snake, "narrow Fellow in the Grass." Stanzas 4-5 tell the effect. Though the speaker feels "cordiality" for several other creatures of nature, seeing the snake makes her feel a "tighter breathing" and "Zero at the Bone."

A ROUTE OF EVANESCENCE

The poet develops an image, apparently of a hummingbird—the "revolving Wheel" of its wings, its dominant colors of green and red ("Emerald" and "Cochineal"), its sudden movement among the blossoms, and speed so great that delivery of mail from Tunis could be made in a morning.

AFTER GREAT PAIN

To describe the "formal feeling" that follows great pain, the poet uses images of heavy immobility: "like tombs," "like a stone," and "lead." She also expands her phrase "formal feeling" with "The Nerves sit ceremonious," "a Quartz contentment," and the description of freezing (line 13).

BECAUSE I COULD NOT STOP FOR DEATH

The poet describes dying and immortality in the dominant metaphor of a carriage on a journey.

In stanza 1, Death, accompanied by Immortality, stops to pick up the speaker in a carriage. In stanzas 2-4, they journey, leaving earthly life behind them ("labor," "leisure," "children," "grain," "setting sun"). In stanza 5, they pause before the grave ("swelling of the ground"), and stanza 6 depicts the speaker "centuries" later, speaking from "eternity."

ELYSIUM IS AS FAR

One's happiness ("Elysium") is dependent upon the good fortune of a friend.

As a friend in the next room waits for some news or decision that will determine his good fortune, the speaker waits with fortitude the "coming foot" or opening door that will let him know the outcome.

HOPE IS THE THING WITH FEATHERS

The poet uses the dominant metaphor of a bird to describe hope. Hope, perched in the soul like a bird, sings unceasingly (stanza 1). It is undismayed by the "storm" of trouble (stanza 2). Though it has sung to the poet in her dire need ("chillest," "strangest"), it has never asked anything for itself.

I HEARD A FLY BUZZ WHEN I DIED

The buzzing of a fly accompanies the stillness and isolation of dying.

In stanza 1, the dying speaker, hearing the fly buzz, thinks of the stillness in the room as a lull between storms. In stanza 2, the attendant living people begin to resume normal living, with their crying stopped and breathing firm. In stanza 3, the dying person releases her hold on life, and, in stanza 4, she hears a fly buzz as she dies.

I LIKE A LOOK OF AGONY

The apparent paradox of line 1 is explained in the rest of the poem. The poet is looking for truth (line 2) in contrast to evasion (line 3) and pretense (line 4). Death is "Impossible to feign"; the evidence of anguish is real (lines 5-8).

I LIKE TO SEE IT LAP THE MILES

Once the subject is seen as a steam locomotive, the poem becomes clear as an extended metaphor, the train being described as though it were a horse. The poem gives a sense of the train's speed (lines 1-2, 13), power (lines 4-5, 16), noise (lines 11-12, 14), and punctuality (line 15). The poem also gives an idea of the train's course through valleys and mountains and its superiority to "shanties by the sides of roads."

I NEVER SAW A MOOR

The poet knows what heather and a wave are like without having seen the moor or the sea (stanza 1). She is just as confident of the existence of God and of Heaven, though she has not seen them (stanza 2).

I TASTE A LIQUOR NEVER BREWED

A happy experience of nature is described in the dominant metaphor of drunkenness.

Stanza 1 tells of the precious nature of the drink. Stanzas 2-3 describe the drunken actions and inordinate consumption of the drink, involving air, dew, summer days, blue skies, bees, flowers, and butterflies. Stanza 4 tells of the excitement in heaven over the "little tippler."

MUCH MADNESS IS DIVINEST SENSE

To the "discerning eye," what the majority consider madness is actually "divinest sense" and what they consider sense is "starkest madness." Yet the majority enforces conformity to its mistaken notions on pain of being rejected as mad.

SUCCESS IS COUNTED SWEETEST

Anything that we greatly desire is understood best in failure. To have fought and been defeated is the way to understand success completely.

THE BRAIN IS WIDER THAN THE SKY

The power and scope of the brain can be seen by how easily man grasps within his comprehension the sky (stanza 1) and the sea (stanza 2). Such a brain has its greatness and its strength in its affinity with divine power—"just the weight of God" (stanza 3).

THE BRAIN WITHIN ITS GROOVE

Though the brain normally runs "evenly and true," once it swerves, it is as difficult to restore it to order as it is to put back flooding waters that have overrun the countryside.

THE BUSTLE IN A HOUSE

Grief over the death of a loved one is described in the metaphor of housework. The common, matter-of-fact images ("bustle," "sweeping up," "putting away") give a sense of routine and restraint, a determined effort to control the emotions which are under extreme tension.

THE MURMUR OF A BEE

The poem is in praise of the life-giving mystery of God, the Creator.

Stanza 1 states that the creation, such as a bee (also "red upon the hill" in stanza 2, and daybreak in stanza 3), is hard to understand ("witchcraft," "easier to die"). But stanza 2 asserts there is no doubting ("sneer") that "God is here"; it is simply beyond the "will" of man to explain existence ("That's all"). Only God (stanza 3), the "Artist, who drew me so," can explain.

THE SOUL SELECTS HER OWN SOCIETY

The soul is independent and highly selective in her friendships. Neither worldly position ("Chariots," "an Emperor") nor numbers ("ample nation") influence her decision, which, once made, is inflexible ("like stone").

THERE'S A CERTAIN SLANT OF LIGHT

The way the light slants on a winter afternoon "oppresses," gives a sense of "despair," which pervades all of nature with a suggestion of death. The feeling has mystical overtones, as of a divine communication ("heavenly hurt," "inspired affliction").

JOHN DONNE

A HYMN TO GOD THE FATHER

This is a confession of sins, which, though serious in tone, contains a number of puns on the poet's name. The sins include the original sin in birth (lines 1-2), the kind of sin that continues despite guilt (lines 3-4), the sinful influence on others (lines 7-8), the sin which was given up only after long years of indulgence (lines 9-10), and the sin of spiritual fear (lines 13-14). All these sins are redeemed by God's Son, however, and with this knowledge, the poet says, "I fear no more."

A NOCTURNAL UPON ST. LUCY'S DAY

The poet uses a series of images of "nothingness" to express how meaningless his life is since the death of his beloved.

St. Lucy's Day is the dominant image. Falling on December 23, it was considered the shortest day of the year and the beginning of winter. Thus the day is for the poet the time of the year most bereft of life. Other images of nothingness can be seen in "epitaph," "every dead thing," "grave/Of all, that's nothing," and "Of the first nothing, the elixir grown." In the last stanza the poet bids lovers enjoy their summer while they have it, while he looks to "prepare towards her" and join his beloved in death.

A VALEDICTION: FORBIDDING MOURNING

The lover in his "farewell" tells his beloved that they should not mourn when separating for a while, because true lovers are indivisible and absence cannot impair this unity.

Four main images develop this idea of unity despite separation: the parting of the soul from the body (stanzas 1-2), the quaking of the earth opposed to the calm of the astronomical spheres, or lovers (stanza 3), refined gold beat to thinness (stanzas 4-6), and the two legs of a draftsman's compass (stanzas 7-9).

Holy Sonnets

The dominant theme of these nineteen religious sonnets is the poet's plea for God to become pervasive in his life to the exclusion of all else. Other motifs are the poet's search for faith, his sense of sin, and his sense of death.

5: I AM A LITTLE WORLD MADE CUNNINGLY

The poet prays for purging of sin.

In lines 1-4, he says that both parts of himself as microcosm— body and soul—have sinned and must die. In lines 5-9, he prays for God in his macrocosm of new worlds to send new seas of penitential tears to wash away his sins. In lines 10-14, he prays that if fire of purging is required, then he wishes to be burned with piety's "fiery zeal," which alone can heal.

7: AT THE ROUND EARTH'S IMAGINED CORNERS

Anticipating the Judgment, the poet seeks pardon for his sins.

In lines 1-8, he prays for the angels to blow the final trumpets that call the dead and living to be redeemed into heaven. But, in lines 9-14, he realizes that the calling of souls means judgment upon his own sin, and so he asks for a stay of judgment until his sins can be pardoned.

10: DEATH, BE NOT PROUD

Death presents no fear to the poet, for he believes eternal life will destroy death.

Lines 1-4 say that death has no reason to be proud, for it does not really kill others or the speaker. Lines 5-8 describe death as a sleep that gives pleasure and "soul's delivery" to the best men. Lines 9-12 state that many things, such as war, poison, and charms, can produce sleep better than death can. And, in lines 13-14, once we are dead, we shall awake into eternity and so death shall die.

14: BATTER MY HEART, THREE-PERSONED GOD

The theme is the spiritual struggle between man's desire for God's Grace and his sinful nature. Lines 1-8 express this struggle primarily through images of battle; lines 9-14 add imagery of sexual chastity and violation. The paradoxes throughout ("break—make me new"; "love You—betrothed unto your enemy"; "enthrall—free"; "chaste —ravish") emphasize the intensity and complexity of the struggle.

LOVE'S INFINITENESS

The poem is a word play on various meanings of "all your love," developing paradoxes that are resolved only through union of the two lovers.

In stanza 1, the poet argues that if he doesn't have all his beloved's love, he will never have it, because he has done everything possible to attain it. In stanza 2, he argues that if she once gave him all her love and later developed more love, he is entitled to that also as contained in the original gift of her heart. In stanza 3, he states that he does not wish to have all her love, since he wishes more later. But to give her heart later would show that she never gave it earlier. All these paradoxes and "riddles" of love can be resolved if the two lovers join hearts—then giving or taking love becomes irrelevant.

SATIRE III (ON RELIGION)

The poet satirizes those who refuse to make an effort to find truth in religion but accept a corrupt sectarianism.

In lines 1-42, the poet challenges his readers to search for true religion with as much courage as has been shown in war, commerce, discoveries, and duels. In this search the three enemies are the Devil, the world, and the flesh.

In lines 43-79, the poet compares religious preferences to sexual preferences. Mirreus, the Roman Catholic, seeks a woman in ancient rags at Rome. Crantz, the Puritan, prefers "coarse country drudges." Graius, the Anglican, takes the woman picked by his guardians. Phrygius, the alienated, "knowing some women whores, dares marry none." Graccus, the indiscriminant, "loves all as one."

Lines 79-110 offer a vision of Truth on a promontory, attained only by effort and independent thought. That truth is beyond sectarianism, and those souls will perish who choose "men's unjust" systems, rather than "God himself to trust."

SONG (GO AND CATCH A FALLING STAR)

The theme is that beautiful women are fickle. The poet makes statements of impossible actions (catching a falling star, seeing invisible things) and fantastic ideas ("Teach me to hear mermaids singing") to lead us into the most impossible idea of all: that a woman can be both "true, and fair." Satirical references to the falseness of society in the first stanza ("envy," "honest mind") help prepare for the falsity of the fair woman.

SONG (SWEETEST LOVE, I DO NOT GO)

The poet gives reasons why his beloved should not grieve at his absence.

He does not leave her out of boredom or interest in another woman, but as a playing at death (stanza 1). He, like the setting and rising sun, will return, though more speedily (stanza 2). It is natural for good fortune to make time seem brief and bad fortune (as his absence) to make time seem long (stanza 3). Because of their oneness, when she grieves, she hurts him (stanza 4). And they who are joined in oneness can never really be parted (stanza 5).

THE CANONIZATION

The poet uses the special slang meaning of "die" (to perform the sex act) to develop the metaphor that the lovers have become saints.

In stanza 1, the speaker urges an unnamed person to go about his business and stop interfering with his love. He asks in stanza 2, Who is injured by my love? What activities are interfered with? In stanza 3, like flies (which have a short life) and self-consuming tapers, the lovers "die" and rise again, thus giving meaning to death and rebirth of the phoenix from its own ashes. In stanza 4, the lovers' legend will be immortalized in verse because "a well-wrought urn" is as fitting for "The greatest ashes" as an impressive tomb. In stanza 5, the canonized lovers shall be the pattern for all who created their own world and religion of love.

THE ECSTASY

The poet develops two aspects of the idea of the unity of love. First, the union of two souls produces a greater single soul, "that abler soul" (lines 41-45). Secondly, the spiritual union is achieved through physical union (lines 65-70). At first the lovers have only the most tenuous kind of relationship. Their bodies are like "sepulchral statues" while the souls "negotiate." They recognize the union of their souls (lines 1-48). But their bodies are the souls' agents, and until their bodies are joined love ("a great prince") is imprisoned, for men know love through the body, which is the "book" of love (lines 49-76).

THE GOOD-MORROW

The poet develops the idea that love has awakened the souls of the lovers into a larger world which makes them immortal.

In stanza 1, the poet conceives of their former life as childish (lines 2-3) or as a sleep (line 4), which meant that former pleasures were "fancies" or a "dream."

In stanza 2 the poet bids goodmorrow to the lovers' souls, which love has awakened to new and larger lives. Each lover has become a world larger than the new geographical worlds recently discovered.

In stanza 3, the poet sees the face of each lover reflected in the eye of the other, and thinks of the two worlds or hemispheres as having become one. The lovers thus united are immortal. For death (according to contemporary belief) is the result of improper blending of the elements ("not mixed equally"), and the lovers have blended equally.

THE INDIFFERENT

The poet uses the paradoxical idea that constancy in love is a "vice." Venus herself, the goddess of love, has decreed variety in love. Stanza 1 lists contrasting types of women to make the point that the speaker can love any woman, as long as she is not true. Stanza 2 addresses a specific woman, who is guilty of the "vice" of constancy. In stanza 3 the speaker is assured by Venus that the "heretics" (i.e., those lovers who are constant) shall be punished by loving those who are false in love.

THE RELIC

The miracle of love is suggested in the first stanza by the "bracelet of bright hair about the bone," which was intended to bring the souls of the lovers together again at the Judgment Day ("last busy day"). Stanza 2 points out that if the bones of the lovers are dug up, they will become sainted relics because as lovers they wrought miracles. The woman as saint is identified with Mary Magdalen and the man with "something else," which suggests either Jesus, whom Mary Magdalen especially loved, or one of her other lovers. Stanza 3 tells of the miracles they wrought. They loved well and faithfully, and their love transcended sex, somewhat restrained by some recent social "law." The greatest miracle of all was the beloved.

HILDA DOOLITTLE (H. D.)

HEAT

This imagist poem conveys the impression of heat as oppressive by making it a tangible solid.

In stanza 1, the heat is cloth-like, for the wind to rend to tatters. In stanza 2, the heat becomes lava-like, thick enough to mold the shape of pears and grapes. In stanza 3, the heat is as thick as earth, to be cut with a plough.

LETHE

The river Lethe in the ancient Greek abode of the dead gave forgetfulness to all who drank from it. Here the poet describes the desire to forget.

In lines 1-6, in longing to forget, one wants no covering, neither crude nor fine. According to lines 7-14, one wants no living thing at all to enlist the senses or to awaken one, not the sparest thing ("gorse") nor the touch of a lover. According to lines 14-18, the desire to forget has one longing: the "full tide" of oblivion to cover.

PEAR TREE

The poet sees the beauty and fruitfulness of the blossoming pear tree in a dominant image of silver and strength.

The tree (stanza 1) mounts as a great mass of silver. The flowers (stanza 2) are "staunch," silver parted from silver. The "purple hearts" (stanza 3) of this beauty and strength will bring summer and ripe fruits.

ERNEST DOWSON

NON SUM QUALIS ERAM BONAE SUB REGNO CYNARAE

The title means "I am not what I was under the reign of good Cynara," from Horace (*Odes,* IV, i).

A man recalls the experience of having the memory of Cynara come between him and another woman.

Last night the shadow of Cynara fell between the man and woman (stanza 1). As they lay together, the man remembered his old passion (stanza 2). He says that he lived "riotously," trying to forget Cynara (stanza 3). No matter how mad the music and no matter how strong the wine, he is still "hungry for the lips of my desire" (stanza 4).

MICHAEL DRAYTON

HOW MANY PALTRY, FOOLISH, PAINTED THINGS

The poet tells his beloved that through his poetry he will preserve her for posterity.

Lines 1-4 tell of the "foolish, painted" women who will be forgotten because no poet sings of them. Lines 5-8 tell of the poet's giving his beloved eternity. Lines 9-12 claim that future women will see her as their "sex's only glory," because, in lines 13-14, the poet's song will raise her above the ordinary throng.

SINCE THERE'S NO HELP, COME, LET US KISS AND PART

In this love poem, the poet gives up hope of success in love and then seeks once more for his beloved to restore love.

In lines 1-8, he suggests that since "there's no help" for their failing love, they should "shake hands" and part forever, never showing that they their "former love retain." In lines 9-14, he tries once more. He personifies love, dying, "at his last gasp," "pulse failing," and beyond the help of passion, faith, or innocence. Yet it is within his beloved's power to "yet recover" love.

JOHN DRYDEN

A SONG FOR ST. CECILIA'S DAY

In honor of St. Cecilia, patron saint of music and inventor of the pipe organ, Dryden praises the power of music.

Stanzas 1-2 state that the orderly universe was created by heavenly harmony.

Stanzas 3-6 suggest the power of various musical instruments to excite emotions: the harp of "chorded shell" arouses religious awe (3), the trumpet arouses warlike courage (4), the flute and the lute arouse sorrow for hopeless love, while the violin arouses a range of emotions from jealousy to fury (5), and above all, the organ (Cecilia's instrument) inspires holy love (6).

The closing Grand Chorus repeats that the world was begun with music and adds that music will accompany the end of the world.

ALEXANDER'S FEAST; OR, THE POWER OF MUSIC

In honor of St. Cecilia, patron saint of music, Dryden describes the power of music to arouse passion. The situation is a feast of Alexander the Great after his conquest of Persia at which he reportedly was incited by his mistress to set fire to the Persian palaces at Persepolis. In Dryden's poem, the music of Timotheus incites him.

Section 1 presents Alexander sitting at the feast, surrounded by his peers and his mistress, Thaïs.

In sections 2-6, Timotheus arouses various emotions in Alexander through music: godly pride by singing of Alexander's birth from Zeus and Olympia (2), pleasure by singing of Bacchus (3), mournfulness by singing of the fall of Darius (4), love by singing of Thaïs (5), and finally revenge by singing of the Furies, whereupon Alexander seizes a torch to set fire to Persian abodes and temples (6).

Section 7 restates Timotheus' power to "swell the soul, or kindle soft desire," and adds that at last Cecilia enlarged music by inventing the pipe organ.

EDWARD DYER

MY MIND TO ME A KINGDOM IS

The poet expresses the ideal of the contented mind, made such through simplicity and moderate living. Because his own mind is a kingdom, he does not crave "princely pomp" or "wealthy store." He seeks "no more than may suffice" and is content with what his "mind doth bring." Thus he maintains the pleasures of a "quiet mind."

RICHARD EBERHART

DAM NECK, VIRGINIA

The theme is the disparity between war and man's spiritual nature.

Seen from a distance at night, the anti-aircraft fire from the training center presents an illusion of dreamlike beauty that has no "relation to the reality" (stanzas 1-3). The practising gunners also show a disparity in having both knowledge ("expert," "skill to kill") and ignorance of the dreamlike effect (stanzas 4-5). These illusions, quite unlike the fierce truth of guns aiming at death, suggest the "disrelation" war represents to the spiritual (stanza 6).

GO TO THE SHINE THAT'S ON A TREE

The poet urges a perception of nature that leads to man's spiritual unity with nature.

After going to the "shine that's on a tree," the song of the bird, and the earth itself, one may become one ("Be tree") with nature. Then he can be aware of nature's spiritual meaning—"light unseen" and "unheard song."

IF I COULD ONLY LIVE AT THE PITCH THAT IS NEAR MADNESS

The poet longs to live, as he did in childhood, with an emotional intensity beyond complexity and morality.

Stanzas 1-3 praise childhood as timeless, infinite in possibility, egoistic, and amoral. Stanza 4 points out that adulthood with its truth, necessity, and morality means the death of the child's "pitch that is near madness."

SEALS, TERNS, TIME

The poet is drawn by his sympathetic and natural relationship to the seals and the terns to consider the conflict in man caused by his dual nature, the animal and the spiritual.

The seals (stanzas 1-4) suggest that man, also a mammal, in time past came from the sea ("animal soft bonds," "pre-history"). The airborne terns (stanzas 5-6) suggest man's spiritual nature ("spirits," "aspirations," "spirit," "freedom"). Stanzas 7-8 show man in conflict ("pulled back" vs. "enticed") because of his split connection ("balanced on the sea") to the "mammal water" and the "release of the sky."

THE ATTIC

We love an attic because the nostalgic associations, the strange disorder, the broken strangeness, and the isolation provide an escape from the real "world downstairs."

In an attic one sees expressions of real life that he cannot cope with or may not indulge in—evasive dreams, the profound aberration of the world, the need for a citadel from the world, the anarchy and oddness of life, the confusion of the senses, the conquest of time, and the indulgence in chaos without pain of reality.

THE GROUNDHOG

The poet's attitude towards the death of the groundhog is traced in its intellectual-emotional conflict through four stages of the groundhog's decay.

In stage one (June), love conflicts with loathing and in turn both emotions conflict with intellectual control. In stage two (autumn), intellect controls, but with a sense of loss. In stage three (another summer), intellect controls calculatingly, "like a geometer." In the final stage (three years), the poet comes to a spiritual realization of the meaning of death and change in the cycles of man's history, and the emotional repugnance and intellectual questioning of the first part are here reconciled in a total acceptance. The allusions at the end cover a wide range of time, differing cultures, and differing intellectual and emotional attitudes toward life and death.

THE HORSE CHESTNUT TREE

An incident of boys stealing prized chestnuts from high in the tree and being chased by the owner is used to symbolize man's urge to grasp the unknown and unattainable.

In stanzas 1-5, the boys in autumn pick the chestnuts that are "highest up," until the speaker chases them away.

In stanzas 6-8, the poet points out the analogy to man's ambition to attain a "tangible good from the unknown," before death drives him from the scene.

T. S. ELIOT

A COOKING EGG

The poem deals with the disappointments of time, career, and human relationships.

The speaker is a "cooking egg," that is, one not strictly fresh, one affected by age. The epigraph quoting Francois Villon suggests that the speaker, as Villon at thirty years of age, also knows life's disappointments.

Stanzas 1-2 describe Pipit, a childhood love now deteriorated to middle-aged mediocrity. Stanzas 3-6 imply that Honour, Capital, Society, and love have failed the speaker. In stanzas 7-9, he implies that his youthful hopes for a "penny world" to share with Pipit have been destroyed by the "red-eyed scavengers," and he is left with desolate meals at the A. B. C. restaurant chain.

ANIMULA

The title means "little soul" or "little life." The soul is described in an analogy of the growing child. The soul moves farther from God as it grows from birth and is misshapen by time.

Lines 1-15 describe the first stage of the soul. When the infant issues "from the hand of God," it takes simple pleasure in the varied objects and actions around it, confusing reality and illusion.

Lines 16-31 describe the second stage of the soul, when it "issues from the hand of time," selfish and misshapen.

In lines 32-37 the poet asks prayers for five specific people and all of us, whose souls have been misshapen by the hand of time.

ASH WEDNESDAY

The poem traces the progress of the soul from spiritual despair to its rest in God's peace.

Section I gives the first step to regeneration, the contrition of Ash Wednesday. The poet's utter despair ("Because I do not hope") gives him the base on which to "construct something." The "hour of our death" can be the means to a new birth.

In section II, the death of the flesh and the self (fed on legs, etc., "I am forgotten") leads to selflessness, love and the white Lady, as soul mediator, and so out of the desert of the world to the Garden of God. Here the joining of paradoxes (lines 66-88) points to the unity later found in God.

In section III the soul begins its positive progress in the symbol of ascent of stairs. At first the poet can see the "face of hope and despair." By the third stair, he has achieved enough "strength" beyond the despair of section I to begin a prayer.

Section IV describes a condition of suspension between the old despair and the new redemption ("between sleep and waking"). The Lady of section II ("wearing/ White light," "silent sister") blends with Mary to act as mediator and bring renewal ("fountain sprang . . . bird sang"). Whispers come from the yew tree (symbol of immortality) and the end of exile from God is near.

In section V, Christ the Word goes unheard in the world and man's heart. There is need for the Lady ("veiled sister") to mediate for those caught in the conflict between desire for God and inability to surrender to him.

Section VI opens with the "time of tension" between the speaker's death to the world and his spiritual rebirth. At the end, the soul comes to rest in God, as in the phrase from Dante, "his will is our peace."

Four Quartets

Four Quartets is composed of four related poems—"Burnt Norton," "East Coker," "The Dry Salvages," and "Little Gidding." Each of the four is an individual poem, though all are related by common theme and structure.

The common theme is time and timelessness—the meaning of history, the relation between time and eternity, the moment of illumination in which the spirit achieves a timeless insight.

In structure, the five movements or parts of each poem suggest the form of a quartet or sonata. The title of each quartet is named after a place, visited by Eliot, which shows an intersection of time and timelessness.

BURNT NORTON

"Burnt Norton," the first of the *Four Quartets* dealing with time and timelessness, tries to reconcile time with timelessness by seeing men as living both in and out of time through a series of "timeless moments."

The title, the name of a manor house in Gloucestershire that Eliot visited, suggests a significant moment in time. The two epigraphs from Heraclitus are translated: "Although the word (logos) is common to all, most men live as if they had each a private wisdom of his own" and "The way up and the way down are one and the same." They indicate man's relationship to the social world in time and the transcendent world beyond time.

Part I considers the relations of four aspects of time. Added to the usual past, present, and future is possibility, or "What might have been." The body of the section presents an example of a "door we never opened" on the imagined scene in the rose-garden. The conclusion is that past, future, and possibility are contained in the one actuality, the present moment.

Part II adds Heraclitus' concept that all things exist in tension to Eliot's concept of the "still point" where all opposites are reconciled. Lines 50-63 express the Heraclitean perpetual tensions between opposites. Lines 64-71 add the wheel pattern of the "still point of the turning world," which symbolizes the timeless moment without "where" or "how long." Lines 72-84 describe the nature of the timeless moment, with freedom from desires, corruptions, and actions and a presence of grace, transcendence, and intensity. Lines 85-92 point out that these experiences which seem to transcend time can occur only in time.

Part III shows, by contrast, the life with no "point," no center or relationships. Such is ordinary time in this "twittering world" (lines 93-116) The way out is withdrawal beyond the world of time—sense, movement, even spirit—to the still point of no movement (lines 117-129).

Part IV begins the way to resolution by moving through images of death in nature ("black cloud," "clutch," "yew") to the ecstatic light at the "still point."

Part V relates time and movement of works of art—music and words—to the world of time and the still point. The dynamic tensions of time in music and words show that the timeless moments —as the "laughter/ Of children" in the rose-garden—must be realized in time—"Quick/ now, here, now, always."

EAST COKER

"East Coker," the second of the *Four Quartets* dealing with time and timelessness, considers the meaning of time in terms of beginnings and endings. Both are contained in a given moment or event—the beginning and the end, the cause and the consequence, birth and death. The poem unites the two by opening with "In my beginning is my end" and closing with "In my end is my beginning."

Part I shows life as "succession." The end is in the beginning, and all things are subject to change, decay, and death. Lines 1-13 describe all things as rising and falling in ceaseless process of change. Lines 14-51 carry the poet's thoughts back to his beginning with his ancestors in sixteenth-century East Coker in an image of country dancers. Archaic phrases taken from Sir Thomas Elyot's *The Boke Named the Governor* depict dancers moving through time and succession to "Dung and death." The closing "I am here" connects the poet to his historical setting: he cannot escape his beginning.

Part II develops the idea that wisdom is not in the experiences of history but in humility. Lines 52-67 describe the lack of temporal pattern and orderly creative sequence in the universe, whose end can only be destruction of the world by fire and ice. Lines 68-100 describe the lack of meaningful pattern in history. Little can be learned from history, for "the pattern is new in every moment." What is to be learned is humility: for "humility is endless."

Part III directs the way through humility, which is the only way to arrive at meaningful experience. It is the way of darkness, death, agony, and dispossession of self. Lines 101-128 say that the way of darkness and death can be the "darkness of God," as in the experience of St. John of the Cross. Lines 129-147 say that one can get to the timeless moment, as in "Burnt Norton" (echoed in "laughter in the garden"), through the "agony/Of death and birth" or the "way of dispossession."

Part IV, in the two metaphors of a hospital and Good Friday, describes the spiritual death that must precede spiritual birth. Our spiritual disease is our evil nature, the curse we got from Adam, "the ruined millionaire." Friday is "good" because it brings the death which is prelude to resurrection, or spiritual birth.

Part V connects Eliot's art of poetry to the theme of beginnings and ends. Lines 173-190 relate him to the poetic tradition. In every attempt to use words, he must find a new pattern. He cannot emulate preceding poets, but must "fight to recover." So there is "the new beginning," the "trying," in poetry. Lines 191-210 extend the new beginning to wider human endeavor. Beginning and end come together in the "intense moment," when "here and now cease to matter."

THE DRY SALVAGES

"The Dry Salvages," the third of the *Four Quartets* dealing with time and timelessness, develops the idea that timelessness is not a temporal sequence without end, but a qualitative experience to be entered here and now through Incarnation.

Part I presents time through the metaphor of the river as racial experience. Man, in moving from his primitive ancestry, still carries the past with him in "hints of earlier and other creation" in a "time not our time." The underlying sea voice, sea swell, and tolling bell bring in the contrasting timelessness.

Part II shows life as a meaningless sequence in time. Lines 51-86 use the central metaphor of man adrift as a boat to show lack of meaning—"drifting wreckage," "littered with wastage," and having "no destination." Lines 87-125 look for a permanent pattern in the flux—the "sudden illumination." The meaning must somehow come from the pre-history of the human race—"The backward look behind the assurance/ Of recorded history."

Part III uses the main metaphor of a voyager to offer disinterested action as a way of giving meaning to sequence in time, Krishna's principle of disinterested action or detachment from self is one way to break out of the time cycle. A second way is Heraclitus' principle that the "way up is the way down." These principles show that the value of experience is not in past and future, but in quality of consciousness. The voyager is to "fare forward," not into a time sequence, but into a "sphere of being" in which "time is withdrawn."

Part IV is a prayer for all voyagers through time, a preparation for the Annunciation of the next part.

Part V reconciles the disparity between time and timelessness through Incarnation—"the impossible union/ Of spheres of existence." The timeless intersects time in moments of illumination, such as "a shaft of sunlight . . . thyme . . . lightning . . . waterfall . . . music . . . right action . . . significant toil."

LITTLE GIDDING

"Little Gidding," the fourth of the *Four Quartets* dealing with time and timelessness, relates past to present, sin to purgation, beginning to end in a progress to achieve the moment of timeless insight. Setting the scene at the seventeenth-century religious community of Little Gidding allows the poet to reckon the timeless moment between three sets of poles—two times (seventeenth century vs. twentieth century), two wars (Parliamentarian vs. World War II), and two religious views (devout Little Gidding vs. twentieth-century secularity).

In Part I, the time of "Midwinter spring" (lines 1-20) gives the sense of suspension beyond time. The place (lines 21-40) gives a sense of beyond place ("the world's end"). The place as religious (lines 41-55) is the closest to the "intersection of the timeless moment."

Part II considers the ravages of time, change, and death by the four elements that structured the universe in the time of Little Gidding—air, earth, water, and fire (lines 56-79). Then the poet (lines 80-151) undergoes a limbo-like death between two worlds—life and death, hell and purgatory. Walking the streets after an air raid, the poet meets a fire-warden who reminds him of a ghost. The stranger is like a spirit returned from the other world to talk of purgation ("refining fire") from the three gifts reserved for old age.

Part III suggests that purgation might come through detachment or wisdom. The allusion to the mystic Juliana (lines 168-169, 198-199) suggests that the detachment is mystic. The reference to the factions of King and Parliament finally being "folded in a single party" suggests that through wisdom we learn to rise above experience.

Part IV sees fire as purgative as well as destructive (the dove of peace has become the bombing plane). Love also has a dual nature, in devising the torments of the fire which refines. We are left with the choice of the fire of destruction or the refining fire of love.

Part V finally brings us to the insight into the mystic timeless moment. Death is a beginning of life, time is equated with eternity ("to make an end is to make a beginning"). History is a "pattern/ Of timeless moments." Quotations from the mystic Juliana (lines 257-258) and the mystic *Cloud of Unknowing* (line 240) support the idea of mystic wholeness—death and life, purgation and love are reconciled ("the fire and the rose are one").

GERONTION

The speaker characterizes himself and his society as spiritually arid, deprived of God's grace, which is symbolized by the life-giving rain.

The first section (lines 1-16) shows the decay and sterility of modern life ("old man" "dry month," "decayed house," "goat coughs").

In the second section (lines 17-30) the speaker calls for a sign of God's grace, recalling that the greatest sign of all, the birth of

Christ, has been neglected for spiritualism ("dark room") and aestheticism ("bowing among the Titians").

The third section (lines 34-48) indicates that spiritual knowledge is not easy to acquire. Ambitions, vanities, abundance, heroism, fear, virtue, all betray into error.

In the fourth section (lines 49-75) salvation, though possible, does not come through the jaded senses. For all mortal things (senses along with other people—De Bailhache, etc.) face the destruction of nature ("spider," "weevil," "fractured atoms"). With such thoughts, spiritually homeless like "Tenants" of a rented house, Gerontion can only wait for the rain of God's grace, brought by the "Trades," or tradewinds.

JOURNEY OF THE MAGI

One of the wise men who came to the Nativity of Christ relates in old age what the experience meant to him.

The journey itself (lines 1-20) was uncomfortable ("snow," "lack of shelters," "cities hostile") and discouraging ("all folly"). The arrival (lines 21-31) was "satisfactory," a blend of renewal ("temperate," "vegetation," "stream") and foreshadowing of Christ's crucifixion ("three trees," "pieces of silver"). The effect of the experience (lines 32-43) was "bitter agony." The old dispensation was dead for the wise man, but there was no rebirth into a new one.

MARINA

The theme is wondrous renewal of life and hope. Marina is Pericles' daughter, from Shakespeare's *Pericles,* who was born at sea, lost to her father, and then found as a young woman. Pericles here expresses his joy and wonder at virtual rebirth. He is a contrast to Hercules, who, when he regained sanity after killing his children in his insanity, said, as in the Latin epigraph, "What place is this, what country, what region of the world?" The "What" for Pericles means the wonder of a renewed world, for he has had a child come to life. Images of renewal (pine, woodthrush, pulse) dominate, and death becomes "unsubstantial." Pericles resigns his old beaten ship and his old life to live in the new life opening out before him, embodied in his daughter—"the new ships./What seas what shores what granite islands."

PRELUDES

The poet depicts the sordid existence of those in the modern city.

Parts I and II present sordid images of a winter evening and a winter morning in the city.

Part III depicts one of the people whose hands are "raising dirty blinds." Her vision of the street suggests general loneliness and defeat.

Part IV presents another character, who is sensitive enough, "with soul stretched tight," to be constantly affected by the life around him. The standards of the street ("certain certainties") seem the only "conscience" for him and the entire world. In the last seven lines, the poet enters, and is moved to compassion. He is *not* ready to wipe his hand across his mouth and laugh at human suffering in a meaningless world.

RHAPSODY ON A WINDY NIGHT

A man walking at night to his lodgings passes a series of street-lamps. Each lamp provokes his memory to toss up images of his useless, sterile existence. The last lamp at four A.M. reminds him that his present routine life of "bed . . . tooth-brush . . . shoes" is also empty—"The last twist of the knife."

SWEENY AMONG THE NIGHTINGALES

The vulgar Sweeney and his companions at a restaurant party are set against a noble past to point out a debased present.

Stanzas 1-2 describe the repulsive Sweeney. As he laughs, he is silhouetted against the window. Overhead pass the ominous constellations of Death, the Raven, Orion, and the Dog. Silhouetted against the tips of the crescent moon, Sweeney seems to guard the "horned gate," which in Hades is the gate through which true dreams come. It is ironic that it is now the coarse and trivial Sweeney who guards the gate.

Stanzas 3-9 describe Sweeney's coarse companions and their actions. They are the woman in the Spanish cape who tries to sit on Sweeney's knees and sprawls on the floor; the "silent man" who gapes; the "silent vertebrate" who withdraws; the Russian-born Rachel who "tears at the grapes"; the man with heavy eyes; and "someone indistinct."

Stanzas 9-10 provide a background of noble tragedy in contrast to the present coarse trivia. There is the tragic murder of Agamemnon (also, the epigraph from Aeschylus: "Alas, I am struck by a mortal blow within"), the Greek myth of the ravishment of Philomela and her transformation into a nightingale, and the great truth of Christ's death, honored at the "Sacred Heart."

THE HIPPOPOTAMUS

The clumsy, earthy "hippopotamus" (the world) is attractive by comparison to the hypocritical materialism of the True Church.

In stanzas 1-6, the first two lines of each stanza seem to condemn the hippopotamus' activities, while the last two lines of each stanza ironically show the Church hypocritically has engaged in the same activities. Stanzas 7-9 describe the hippopotamus gloriously finding salvation with God, while the Church "remains below" in the "miasmal mist."

THE HOLLOW MEN

Like the horror of life seen by Mr. Kurtz of Conrad's *Heart of Darkness,* so there is horror in a world of hollow men. Unlike the violent Old Guy Fawkes, burnt in straw effigy on November 5, the hollow men are themselves effigies of straw.

In their loss of force and meaning, the empty men contrast with three other kinds of death: In Section I, it is death by violence, or "death's other Kingdom," reached by violent men such as Kurtz and Fawkes. In Section II, it is death by illusion, or "death's dream kingdom," reached by men who wear "disguises." In Section IV, it is "death's twilight kingdom." These hollow men will remain "sightless," unless their only hope appears, Dante's multifoliate rose, which symbolizes death by mystical union with God.

Sections III and V give the futile prayer of the hollow men. Instead of the spiritual rose, theirs is the "prickly pear." Their "Shadow" of reality and their paralyzed force allow them no meaning, and their world ends "Not with a bang but a whimper."

THE LOVE SONG OF J. ALFRED PRUFROCK

The poem, as the epigraph from Dante indicates, tells of a man trapped in the hell of his own character and condition. The narrative line tells of a cultured, intellectualized, sensitive man who is going to an afternoon tea, at which he considers making a declaration of love to some lady. Prufrock struggles with himself psychologically to make or delay making the declaration.

His struggle may be seen as Freudian. The ego is "I," weakly trying to assert itself as an individual. The buried id is seen in the urges to the natural, instinctive life. The dominant force is the super-ego, "You," in conformity to the sterile modern society.

The conflict involves several motifs running through the poem. One is the modern sterile society—the tawdry lower class ("one-night cheap hotels," "men in shirt-sleeves") and the decadent upper class ("talking of Michelangelo," "toast and tea"). Another motif is Prufrock's indecisiveness and his social fear or hypersensitivity ("strength to force the moment," "pinned and wriggling"). Another motif is his sense that he is a product of and a captive of his sterile world ("I have known them all," "would it have been worth it?"). Another is the occasional urge in Prufrock to vital, instinctive life ("ragged claws," "moment of my greatness").

Prufrock is so much trapped by the conflicts growing out of his own character and his sterile society that he does not make his declaration of love. The super-ego dominates at the expense of the ego and the id. Time overtakes his delays ("I grow old") and he misses his chance forever ("will not sing to me"). In the last scene, he has a flash of imagined beauty, vitality, and release through the images of sea and mermaids. Then he wakes from his imaginings to real life ("human voices"), which brings only his psychological or spiritual death ("drown").

THE WASTELAND

The basic theme of the poem is the spiritual sterility and cultural barrenness of the early twentieth century. The poem is built around vegetation ceremonies from Sir James Frazer's *The Golden Bough* and the fertility legend of the Holy Grail from Jessie Weston's *From Ritual to Romance*. The central story in the legend is that of the Fisher King, who rules over a wasteland. He has been wounded in the genitals, and so there is no fertility in the land. The king awaits a Grail knight of purity to heal him and thus bring rain, spring, life after death, fertility to the land, and people. Eliot stresses the sexual theme, using a series of love episodes throughout the poem—Marie as innocent, Marie as romantic, the woman in the boudoir, the woman and the abortion, the typist and lover, the Highbury girl, etc.—all suggesting sexual meaninglessness and so spiritual meaninglessness. Other themes running through the poem are descriptions of the desert rubble, death by water, the swift rush of time, the inconsequential quality of modern business, and the unreality of modern city life contrasted to the wisdom of the ages.

The method of the poem is to use free association. The rich culture of the past underlies images of the present wasteland.

I. The Burial of the Dead.
The title suggests the burial of the fertility god in preparation for rebirth. April, primordially the season of fertility, gives little promise in a sterile society. Young Marie, who should be awakening to fertile love, is caught in arid social life and wintry hibernation, neither "Living nor dead." The prophet sees only "broken images" in a land of no water. The spiritual wisdom of the ages is travestied in a fortune teller. The city is unreal. And there is doubt that the "buried corpse" (an ironic vegetation symbol) will rise.

II. A Game of Chess
The title, taken from Middleton's *Women Beware Women* in which a game of chess is a cover-up for a seduction, suggests that modern love is a game, a meaningless activity. Stanza 1, opening in a boudoir, describes an upper-class love affair in which a neurotic woman can elicit no vitality from her lover. Stanza 2, taking place in a pub, describes a lower-class marriage involving an abortion. In the background are allusions to vital lovers of the past—Cleopatra, Dido, Eve, Philomel, and Ophelia.

III. The Fire Sermon.
The title is taken from Buddha's purgative Fire Sermon and alludes to Augustine's struggle against the fire of passion. The theme is the denunciation of unholy love, which is a corruption of sexuality and symbolically a corruption of spirituality. A series of degenerate, meaningless love affairs is presented: modern lovers by the River Thames, Sweeney and Mrs. Porter, Mr. Eugenides and his homosexual invitation, the typist and her lover, the Highbury girl. In the background are allusions to noble and meaningful loves: Spenser's wedding song, the "coy mistress," the goddess Diana, Philomel, Miranda from *The Tempest*, the Rhine maidens from *Die Götterdämmerung*, and the bisexual loves of Tiresias. A blend

of Buddha's Fire Sermon and Augustine's *Confessions* denounces unholy love at the close of the section

IV. Death by Water.
Water, the symbol of regeneration, can also be a means to death by drowning. Phlebas the Phoenician sailor, Eugenides the Smyrna merchant ("profit and loss"), and Ferdinand of *The Tempest* are related in lines 47-55 of section I and warned by the degenerate fortune teller to "fear death by water," for the degenerate fortune teller could not know that life also comes by water. Here, rebirth is suggested by the sea imagery, which echoes strains in the poem of Ariel's song of transformation, "Full Fathom Five," from *The Tempest*.

V. What the Thunder Said.
This section is a plea for the water of redemption to fall on the wasteland. The thunder speaks and promises rain, but betrays by bringing only a "damp gust." Other betrayals alluded to tell us that we have been betrayed in our quest and the wasteland will not be made fertile. Two such betrayals are that of Christ ("prison and palace," the cock crow) and that of Parsifal's coming to the "empty chapel" but not as far as to free the Fisher King. Neither the Grail Knight, nor fertility, nor the rebirth of the vegetation god will come in our time. The infertile Fisher King sits with the "arid plain behind" and a heap of fragments falls around him. The voice of the thunder tells the only means to rebirth: Give, sympathize, control.

WHISPERS OF IMMORTALITY

The poet contrasts the complete sensualist with the person who tries to see metaphysics beyond the senses.

Stanzas 1-4 describe the sensuous metaphysicians, like John Webster and John Donne, who suffered the anguish of and obsession with death because they believed knowledge came through the senses ("thought," "experience") and that the senses must end in death. They could find no "substitute for sense" to allay the deeper longings ("whispers of immortality," "fever of the bone"). Stanzas 5-8, by contrast, describe Grishkin, a high-class Russian prostitute, who in a life fully devoted to sense, like an animal, completely charms both a social situation ("drawing room") and systems of philosophy ("Abstract Entities").

RALPH WALDO EMERSON

BRAHMA

The poet uses paradoxes here to help the reader understand his concept of the Universal Soul. All actions are incarnations of the same Spirit (stanzas 1 and 3), and all things are reduced to the same ultimate unity (stanza 2). Man, "meek lover of the good," should realize that all other gods and religious beliefs ("heaven") are in reality empty and meaningless.

CONCORD HYMN

The men who fought at the Battle of Concord have long since gone, like the bridge that crossed the stream. Now, a monument ("votive stone") is erected to their memory. The last stanza is a plea to the all-pervasive spirit that "Time and Nature gently spare/ The shaft we raise to them and thee."

DAYS

Lines 1-6 state the poet's idea that the days of our lives offer us the widest variety of goals, from "diadems" to "fagots." Man can choose "after his will." The last five lines give the poet's ironic comment that the typical person ("I") forgets his youthful ambitions ("morning wishes") and takes only small things as his achievement.

EACH AND ALL

Each person, like each object in nature, takes his beauty from his surroundings, his inclusion in "the perfect whole." The peasant, the sparrow, the seashells, and the bride alike take on their individual beauty from the larger scene, from Nature.

GIVE ALL TO LOVE

The poet expresses the paradoxes of love and individualism. He says "Give all to love" but stay "free as an Arab."

One should follow the dictates of love completely (lines 1-17). Love will reward the courageous, who will always grow and aspire (lines 18-25). Yet there is one word of warning: keep free of your beloved (lines 26-33). When she first perceives a joy separate from you, let her be free to go (lines 34-42). Though the knowledge that she now has other interests than you will make you sad, you must know that there is compensation. When a lesser good (half-gods) leaves, a greater good (the gods) takes its place (lines 43-49).

HAMATREYA

Man's pride and greed are eclipsed by the enduring earth. In lines 1-10 the poet describes the possessive attitude of the first settlers of Concord. Owner is followed by owner, each equally ignorant of the true relationship between man and earth, for it is really the land which has the final ownership in death. Earth sings her song of endurance and triumph, which finally (lines 60-63) makes man humble.

ODE, INSCRIBED TO W. H. CHANNING

Above the tumult of wars and ideological conflicts stands the scholar, whose purpose is to see the affairs of men in their true perspective. The poet says that he will not leave his study for the public turmoil (lines 1-11), which produces such monstrosities as the Mexican War, the Fugitive Slave Law, and the proposal to dissolve the Union (lines 12-44). The trouble is that men serve the law of things, not the law of men (lines 44-70). The poet wants everyone to turn "to his chosen work," and "The over-God/ Who marries Right to Might" will eventually cause good to prevail (lines 71-97).

KENNETH FEARING

HOMAGE

In three episodes, the poet expresses his view that the "good," "decent" people do not support the deeper values of human achievement.

The good, decent people in the time of Columbus understood only the gold, not his spirit of exploration (stanza 1). The good, decent people want only the "lighter vein," not a tragic insight into life and character as in *Hamlet* (stanza 2). The good, decent people could appreciate only the pecuniary use of the airplane, not the spirit of discovery and conquest of the Wright brothers.

PORTRAIT

The poet gives a satirical "portrait" of a typical American whose sole identity has been manufactured by others.

All of life's ills are corrected for him in the fashionable mode— poor eyesight, falling teeth, fallen arches, poor golf, the ravages of love, and his will and his funeral. The refrain that his soul is his own is ironically refuted not only by his purchasing his external self from others, but also by his taking his opinions from Lippmann and his spiritual solace from Scotch whiskey.

LAWRENCE FERLINGHETTI

CHRIST CLIMBED DOWN

The poet condemns the contemporary mode of celebrating the birth of Christ.

In stanzas 1-5, Christ climbs down from his cross and runs away from sham as seen in "rootless Christmas trees" (stanza 1), from modernized merrymaking (stanza 2), from affected spirituality as in "Sears Roebuck creches" (stanza 3), from commercialized giving and a fake saint (stanza 4), and from anti-spirituality as in "Radio City angels" at "Midnight Mass matinees" (stanza 5). In the last stanza, Christ awaits an "Immaculate Reconception" or rebirth in the "darkest night" of the individual soul—the time when one most needs a savior.

SHE LOVED TO LOOK AT FLOWERS

Because of her innocence and simplicity, the sailors' girl with the virgin soul has some personal hope.

Originally she was an unsophisticated, uncomplicated maid who would "look at flowers" and "smell fruit" (stanza 1). Then her virgin innocence was blighted by "halfass drunken sailors . . . scattering semen" (stanza 2). Through searching the "lost shores" and "green birds singing" of her ruined past, she grasps some hope and promise (stanzas 3-4).

EDWARD FITZGERALD

THE RUBAIYAT OF OMAR KHAYYAM

As he drinks, the speaker broods on the meaning of life. At times he is hedonistic. At other times he fiercely questions the God who made man so frail and miserable.

Stanzas 1-3. It is dawn, and it is time to drink at the tavern.

Stanzas 4-6. Men of the past are dead, but for now there is wine.

Stanzas 7-12. Time passes; so drink.

Stanzas 13-18. No matter what men's goals or their position in life, death comes to all.

Stanzas 19-20. Then comes the melancholy thought that the flowers and the herbs spring from the bodies of the dead.

Stanzas 21-24. The speaker recommends drink to forget the fact that we may soon join these dead.

Stanzas 25-29. Whether men prepare for today or tomorrow makes no difference, and all the wisest sages have only taught that "I come like Water, and like wind I go," knowing nothing of the riddle of the Universe.

Stanzas 30-34. For all his searching, the deepest questions remain unanswered.

Stanzas 35-38. As the speaker drinks from the earthen vessel, he thinks of the potter and the clay, of God and the creation of man from the earth.

Stanzas 39-40. The speaker thinks of the damned below, whose thirst is quenched by the wine he spills on the ground, and he advises the reader to look devoutly to Heaven, like the tulip.

Stanzas 41-43. Having given up perplexing questions for wine, men can meet death calmly.

Stanzas 44-45. Sardonically, the speaker asks if it were not a shame to remain in the body.

Stanzas 46-48. Furthermore, the speaker says, millions like us have come and will come, and our death is insignificant, for we are but "A Moment's Halt . . . Of Being."

Stanzas 49-53. If you want to find the meaning of existence, the speaker says, you must be quick, for the Power that created us is elusive.

Stanzas 54-60. But life is too short for such speculation. Wine is better than logic, for Wine is powerful enough to refute doubts and arguments.

Stanzas 61-63. The speaker asks why he should stop his drinking for any fear or hope of an afterlife when all we really know is that this life flies.

Stanzas 64-67. We have no evidence for an afterlife. All that we know of heaven or hell is in ourselves.

Stanzas 68-72. For we are but pieces in a game, subject to the mysterious power that orders our fate and moves the universe.

Stanzas 73-74. We are bound by cause and effect in a relentless series of events. The only release is in drink.

Stanzas 75-77. All I really know, the speaker says, is that a desire for the Grape (wine) is the secret of my soul, which is best caught in the Tavern.

Stanzas 78-81. The speaker resents the idea that man is to be held responsible for the weakness his maker created him with.

Stanzas 82-90. The speaker continues the parable of the pots, who talk among themselves about their fate and the relationship between themselves and their maker.

Stanzas 91-99. The speaker's mood becomes melancholy again, and he broods on death, has a passing moment of repentance, and entertains a wish that things might be made different.

Stanzas 100-101. The speaker's last thoughts are of death.

JOHN FLETCHER

ASPATIA'S SONG (LAY A GARLAND ON MY HEARSE)

The song is sung by a rejected sweetheart in the play *The Maid's Tragedy.* The girl, preparing to die in her grief over her lover's falseness, asks that she be adorned with yew (for death), with willow (for sorrow), and with "gentle earth."

PHILIP FRENEAU

ON THE UNIFORMITY AND PERFECTION OF NATURE

The universe is described as ruled undeviatingly by natural law. All nature, in keeping with reason, never deviates from its systematic course (stanza 1). For nature to interrupt its course to perform miracles for men would indicate an imperfection in the "first design" (stanzas 2-4). But, natural law is "constant, still the same," and perfect (stanzas 5-6).

THE INDIAN BURYING GROUND

The poet thinks of the soul of the Indian as still active in the next life.

In stanzas 1-4, the poet states that the manner in which we bury a person indicates our concept of the soul and the next life. The Indian is buried sitting as at a feast, with bow and arrows, ready for a journey. His soul is ready for activity in the next life. Stanzas 5-10 describe the Indian as still active. A "restless Indian queen" often visits the grave, and at midnight the ghost of the Indian still pursues the deer.

THE WILD HONEY SUCKLE

The poet laments the "frail duration" of the wild honey suckle.

In stanzas 1-2, the poet describes the white flower in its quiet retreat away from the "roving foot" and "busy hand" of man. In stanzas 3-4, he laments that the flower is doomed to die as did the flowers of Eden.

ROBERT FROST

ACQUAINTED WITH THE NIGHT

As one "acquainted with the night," the poet has known intense loneliness.

Between the opening statement of line 1 and the concluding

restatement, the poet lists six specific instances of his lonely actions at night: walked out and back in the rain, outwalked the furthest light, looked down the saddest lane, passed the watchman without comment, heard a cry indicating no human companionship, and heard a striking clock suggest that something is wrong.

AFTER APPLE-PICKING

The poet ponders several kinds of sleep as different means of withdrawal from life's ambitions and achievements, symbolized as apple-picking.

In lines 1-6, the speaker, though his life and work is unfinished, refuses to go on. In lines 7-13, he senses the "winter sleep" of death that could follow his apple-picking. He looks through a "pane of glass" (ice) against the "world" and feels the strangeness (compare "through a glass darkly" of I Corinthians 13). In lines 14-36, he goes into a dream sleep in which he nightmarishly relives his life's work. He is troubled by the nice demand of the "great harvest" he desired. In lines 37-42, he ponders which kind of troubled sleep is now to follow his apple-picking. It could be hibernation like the wood-chuck's, which would be temporary withdrawal for renewal. Or it could be some "human sleep," which could be withdrawal to troubled dreaming about the past or permanent withdrawal to "winter sleep."

AN OLD MAN'S WINTER NIGHT

The poem describes the isolation of old age.

In lines 1-14 a forgetful old man is seen as an alien to both the inner rooms of the old farm house and the outer night. Lines 15-17 describe the man as isolated from other people, a light to "no one but himself." Lines 18-23 indicate the man's dearth of belongings as he consigns what he has, "snow" and "icicles," to the broken moon. Lines 23-28 describe the old man as relating to house and country-side in the only way he can—sleeping on a winter night.

BIRCHES

The poem discusses a form of escape that is recreative and temporary, not deforming and permanent. This kind of escape is symbolized by the boyhood pastime of swinging on birch trees.

The first part of the poem describes the effect of ice storms which bend trees down to stay, in contrast to a boy's swinging play, which only takes the stiffness from them.

In the second part of the poem the speaker tells of his wish to escape ("I'd like to get away from earth awhile") and what effect he wants that escape to have on him. The escape is not to be permanent and deforming (as the effect of the ice storms on the trees), but recreative ("begin over") and temporary (not "not to return"). Escape is definitely not to take one permanently away from earth's activities, for "Earth's the right place for love." The speaker wants both "going and coming back," escape from and return to life's usual activities.

DESERT PLACES

The poem moves from the desert places of a winter scene to the speaker's own spiritual "desert places."

Stanzas 1 and 2 describe the snow and night falling fast on a field so that field and animal life disappear. Since the speaker is "too absent-spirited to count" (that is, he lacks spiritual life and so is not a part of life), he is included in the scene "unawares." In stanza 3 the speaker reflects that the scene in nature and in himself will become so desolate as to suggest absence of moral and rational meaning in nature ("benighted," "nothing to express"). In stanza 4 the speaker considers the desolation of stellar spaces, as propounded by the theorists ("they") with their ideas of a non-spiritual universe ("empty," "void of human races"). Finally he considers the great depths of his own spiritual desolation.

DESIGN

The incident of three normally unrelated objects coming together in a pattern of white suggests to the poet some "design of darkness" in nature. It is ironic that three white objects should constitute this "design of darkness."

Lines 1-8 describe the design of the white spider, the white flower, and the white moth associated as characters of "death and blight." Lines 9-12 ask what purpose of power brought these three together, and line 13 gives the answer as a "design of darkness to appall." Line 14 suggests that perhaps there is no design at all in such a small event with such small objects—perhaps, then, no meaningful design or purpose at all in the universe.

FIRE AND ICE

The destructive force of desire and hate is symbolized by two forces destructive enough to end the world—fire and ice.

Lines 1-2 state the basic image of the destructive end of the world. Lines 3-4 tell of the poet's experience with the destructiveness of desire. Lines 5-9 suggest, by understatement, that hate is even more destructive than desire.

MENDING WALL

The spring ritual of mending a wall raises the specific question of what walls are for and the more general human question of why people thoughtlessly follow tradition.

The poet begins by describing the breaks in the wall (lines 1-11) and the process of repairing it (lines 12-22). Then he raises the question of "Why?" since there is no chance of confusing the two properties (lines 23-31). This leads to a direct criticism of the neighbor's traditional belief that "Good fences make good neighbours" (lines 32-38). The neighbor is both thoughtless (lines 38-42) and ignorantly complacent (lines 43-45).

NOTHING GOLD CAN STAY

All good things, symbolized by gold, last but a brief time.

Stanza 1 points out the mutability of nature as seen in the brief hour of the gold leaf in early spring. Stanza 2 points out the mutability of the happiness of man. Man lost the happiness of Eden to grief, and he loses the hope and promise of dawn to day.

ONCE BY THE PACIFIC

The poem expresses a mood of impending destruction in the basic metaphor of a monster with "dark intent."

The waves "thought of doing something" outrageous to the shore. The clouds were "hairy" and had gleaming eyes. The shore was lucky in being backed by cliff and continent. Indeed, the coming night forecast such "rage" that it might well lengthen into an "age" of darkness, or even the world's end ("God's last *Put out the light*").

RELUCTANCE

The theme is the reluctance of the heart, in opposition to reason, ever to be resigned, to accept the end of anything.

The occasion for accepting an end is offered through the symbols of the end of a journey in stanza 1 and the end of a season in stanzas 2-3. The winter's desolation ("dead leaves," "crusted snow") and isolation ("one by one," "others are sleeping") supports an attitude of resignation. When the heart aches to seek, reason (the feet) suggests resignation—there is nowhere to go, nothing to seek. But in stanza 4 the "heart of man" is reluctant ("a treason") to accept the end of anything, such as a "love or a season."

STOPPING BY WOODS ON A SNOWY EVENING

This poem expresses the conflict between man's urge for responsible social involvement ("promises") and his urge for withdrawal ("woods," "sleep").

On one side of the conflict, the associations of darkness ("dark and deep," "darkest") and silence ("the only other sound") with "lovely" suggest a strong urge for withdrawal, possibly for contemplation, or even for nourishing a death-wish. On the other side of the conflict, "promises" (promises are of social involvement, being made to other human beings) do win out, for the speaker does reject stopping ("But I have promises"). The horse who must "think it queer" and the owner in the "village" (a social unit) contrast with the speaker by not being contemplators of woods nor subject to the conflict described in the poem.

THE DEATH OF THE HIRED MAN

A theme statement could be "Surely you wouldn't begrudge the poor old man/ Some humble way to save his self-respect."

The poem centers around the differing attitudes of two people toward a socially unworthy person who has struggled to preserve his self-esteem in the face of a strong sense of inferiority. Mary's attitude is of mercy and tolerance of human dignity, no matter whether a person is irresponsible and selfish. Her attitude is illustrated by her definition of home as something you "haven't to deserve." Warren's attitude is of justice and practicality ("have to take you in").

THE ROAD NOT TAKEN

The poet explores the general nature of choice.

Stanza 1 presents the situation for choice (two roads diverging) and expresses regret over the limitations imposed by choice ("sorry I could not travel both"). Stanza 2 shows the near equality of alternatives in choice ("as just as fair," "equally lay") with only a slight difference ("wanted wear"). In contrast, stanza 3 shows the wide difference in final consequences ("how way leads on to way") growing from the events set in motion. The final stanza brings together the several aspects of choice, emphasizing the regret ("with a sigh," because of the road *not* taken) that will attend the wide consequences ("all the difference") that developed from a slight determinant ("less traveled by").

THE TUFT OF FLOWERS

The poem presents the process of one man's discovering his spiritual brotherhood with other men.

Stanzas 1-5 describe the speaker's depressing sense of the aloneness of all men. In stanzas 6-13 a butterfly leads the speaker to a tuft of flowers left by the first workman. Stanzas 14-21 give the speaker's realization that his and the mower's mutual love for the spared tuft of flowers is evidence of man's spiritual brotherhood ("spirit kindred," "brotherly," "together"). The butterfly suggests the delicate, bewildered, questioning spirit of the speaker and the link of nature along with the flowers that brings the two men together.

TREE AT MY WINDOW

The poem is an expression of a person's inner turbulence. The speaker relates himself to the tree ("never be curtain") in both being tossed by "weather" and in being put together by Fate.

The speaker's emotional disturbance ("inner, weather") is severe. It is "profound" by contrast to the tree's "light tongues"; its occurring turbulently in sleep indicates the cause to be deep in the unconscious; it almost overcomes him ("all but lost"). The poet concludes that it took the imagination of Fate to bring together these two kinds of disturbance—inner and outer.

TWO TRAMPS IN MUD-TIME

By dramatizing opposing attitudes toward work, Frost brings out the idea of combining vocation and avocation.

The tramps are the professionals who do their work for pay (stanza 1); the speaker does his chopping for the pleasure of physical and emotional release (stanza 2). The tramps, in threatening to remove his love by taking his job, parallel early spring threatened by the return of winter (stanzas 3-5). Especially in spring does the speaker love the sheer physical experience of chopping wood (stanza 6), although he agrees that the tramps have an argument when love and need are separate (stanzas 7-8). The speaker removes the threat by resolving that one's goal in life is to make love and need one (stanza 9).

ORLANDO GIBBONS

THE SILVER SWAN

The poet attacks the folly of his age. Like the swan, which according to popular belief sings only while dying, the poet says farewell to a society that has in it more fools ("geese") than wise men ("swans").

ALLEN GINSBERG

HOWL

The poem is a frenzied attack on the squalid American life and culture which have prevented wholesome growth and expression of human personality. The theme is stated in the first line: "I saw the best minds of my generation destroyed by madness, starving hysterical naked . . . " The poem gives a long catalogue of specific expressions of "best minds" being driven to madness by the stultifying, humiliating effects of American society.

ROBERT GRAVES

THE PIER-GLASS

A woman, having only ghosts of a "time-sunk memory," in a desolate house, cries out to see in herself in the mirror some "True life."

Stanzas 1-2 describe her haunting the "Lost manor" with its near-empty room and the cracked mirror. In stanza 3, she cries out for some sign of life—a rat, a fly, a spider. Then seeing herself reflected in the mirror, she asks the mirror to reflect some sign of "True life," not "phantasma."

THE PORTRAIT

The portrait of a woman becomes a medium into which the observer can project his ideal of woman and of himself. Stanzas 1-3 contrast the woman in the portrait with ordinary women; stanza 4 contrasts the observer with ordinary men.

In stanza 1, the woman's voice is genuine; others' voices are false. In stanza 2, she is "invisible," ethereal, or spiritual; others are crude and gross. In stanza 3, she is "wild and innocent" and eternally loving; other women decry her as a witch or a drab. In stanza 4, the portrait caters to the observer's wish to be idealized, to be "unlike those other men."

THOMAS GRAY

ELEGY WRITTEN IN A COUNTRY CHURCHYARD

The poet treats three main themes in harmonious unity: death, the dignity of the common rural folk, and the young, unknown poet who loves man and nature.

As the evening draws on, the solitary speaker reflects that life's sounds and activities no longer have any relevance to the dead "forefathers" of the hamlet, though once they did their work well (lines 1-28). These humble people should not be mocked or despised because they are not famous, for no fame or praise can bring the dead back to life (lines 29-44). These humble people were prevented by ignorance, poverty, and obscurity from affecting and participating in great events (lines 45-65). On the other hand, they did not commit the evil deeds of many famous people, but remained quietly in their "cool sequestered vale of life" (lines 65-76). Yet a "frail memorial" asks "the passing tribute of a sigh" for these unknown dead. These humble words on the tomb remind us that no man leaves this life willingly, and the "parting soul" asks for love and grief (lines 77-92).

Sometimes, speaking of the young poet, a "hoary-headed swain" may tell that he often saw the youth walking in the morning or brooding beneath a beech at noon or roaming near the wood, sometimes smiling, sometimes weeping. One morning he was gone and the next morning he was buried.

The elegy ends with the epitaph of the youth, perhaps the poet himself. The epitaph states that the youth was of humble origin and melancholy spirit. His soul was sincere and he was sympathetic to misery. Beyond that, his frailties and his merits rest with God (lines 93-128).

THE BARD

As Edward I moves with his army through Wales, which he has recently conquered, slaughtering Welsh poets, one such poet rises to accost the conqueror. The poet curses Edward and prophesies his unhappy death. He also foretells the subsequent history of England, culminating in the reign of Queen Elizabeth I.

Strophe 1 of the first section presents the Welsh bard cursing the conqueror, Edward I, and his voice strikes fear into the English army. In strophes 2 and 3 the poet laments the passing of the famous Welsh bards, who now, "a grisly band," join him "in dreadful harmony." In lines 49-100 the dead bards make their statements.

In the second section, strophe 1 foretells the dismal fates of Edward's son and grandson. Strophe 2 describes the loneliness and sorrow of Edward III's death and the frivolous reign of Richard

II, who (strophe 3) was deposed. Then the bard describes the bloody Wars of the Roses between the house of Lancaster and the house of York.

In the third section, strophe 1, the bard is left forlorn when the spirits have concluded their statements. Now the bard's vision turns to the future glory of England. Strophe 2 describes the majesty and glory of Elizabeth. In strophe 3 the bard alludes to Spenser's *Faerie Queene* (line 126), to Shakespeare's tragedy (line 128), to Milton (line 131), and to the lesser poets after Milton (lines 133-134). Then the bard foresees the sun shining once again and, on this note of prophetic triumph, he defies Edward and plunges to his death.

THE PROGRESS OF POESY

The poet writes of poetry (first section) as it is inspired by various sources and as it enriches its subject matter. He then (second section) describes the comfort and inspiration that poetry brings to life, passing from Greece to Rome and then to England. Finally (third section) the poet describes Shakespeare, Milton, and himself.

In the first section, strophe 1 begins with an allusion to Pindar ("Aeolian lyre") and describes the rills, flowers, harvests ("Ceres' golden reign"), and so on—things in nature that are sources of poetry. Strophe 2 states that poetry has the power to calm and subdue men's "sullen Cares/ And frantic Passions." Strophe 3 states that harmony or poetry controls "the voices and dances" as seen in the "rosy-crownèd Loves" paying homage to Venus.

In the second section, strophe 1 states that poetry was given to us to compensate for the ills of life just as the sun was given to dispel the fears of night. Strophe 2 says that poetry brings its inspiration to the most savage regions and brings "Freedom's holy flame." Strophe 3 says that "on Greece's evil hour" the nine muses (the goddesses of artistic inspiration) descended from Parnassus (their mountain) to the plains of Latium (Rome). When Rome declined, the muses moved to England.

In the third section, strophe 1 praises Shakespeare, who received from "the mighty Mother," Nature, the pencil for description and the keys for unlocking the emotions. Strophe 2 describes first the transcendent vision of Milton and then concludes by referring to Dryden, a lesser but nevertheless impressive poet.

Strophe 3 proceeds with the description of Dryden's power to give life to ideas and fire to words. Next the poet refers to himself. Though he lacks the power of Pindar ("the Theban Eagle"), yet he does have inspiration from the Muse, which keeps him distant from the vulgar. Though lower than truly virtuous people, he is, because of this inspiration, far above the so-called great ones of this world.

ROBERT GREENE

SWEET ARE THE THOUGHTS THAT SAVOR OF CONTENT

The poet praises the quiet mind and the simple life.

In stanza 1, the contented thought and the poor estate offer more than a crown or a fortune. In stanza 2, the simple, obscure life with rest, music, and mirth make a contented mind that is its own "crown and kingdom."

THOMAS HARDY

"AH, ARE YOU DIGGING ON MY GRAVE?"

A person is little remembered after he has died.

In stanzas 1-3, the dead girl hopefully asks who is digging on her grave and receives answers to the effect that nobody cares for her enough to come to her grave—lover, relative, or enemy. In stanzas 4-5, she momentarily builds hope on the "dog's fidelity," but the dog's final statement (stanza 6) is an ironic reflection of the responses of lover, relative, and enemy—"I quite forgot it was your resting place."

CHANNEL FIRING

The poem is an indictment of war-making.

In lines 1-9 the dead, awakened by gunnery practice in the English channel, think it is the Judgment Day. In lines 9-24, God corrects their error and indicts the nations for making "Red war yet redder." The dead lay down again (lines 25-32) wondering if the world will "ever saner be." The sound of the guns (lines 33-36), extending back in time from contemporary Stourton Tower to Camelot and Stonehenge, reminds us that man has always warred.

DRUMMER HODGE

It is a sad irony that a man must die and be buried in a strange land, becoming when dead a "portion" of that land he "never knew" when living.

In stanzas 1-2, the drummer Hodge, an English fatality of the Boer War, is buried in the South African veldt, a land strange to him. Stanza 3 points out the irony of his becoming forever a portion of that strange land.

DURING WIND AND RAIN

Time gradually conquers man.

In stanza 1, the people once sang happily, but now only "sick leaves" remain. In stanza 2, they made the landscape attractive, but the years passed like "storm birds." In stanza 3, they lived blithely in summer, but now the "rotten rose" tells of death. In stanza 4, they moved to a new house with "brightest things," but they have since died and rain falls on their tombstones ("carved names").

HAP

The poem is a complaint against the impersonal universe of "Hap" (happenstance, chance) and "Casualty," indifferent both to the good and the bad lot of man.

If sorrow were caused by some "vengeful god" who delighted in man's suffering, the poet could take some grim satisfaction in knowing that the powerful being was unjust (lines 1-8). But the blind indifference of "purblind Doomsters" has made life empty of happiness—joy, hope, sun and rain, and blisses.

IN TIME OF "THE BREAKING OF NATIONS"

The poem asserts that the simple, elemental human processes will endure longer than nations and wars.

Tilling the soil and making love (the man and his horse harrowing clods, the smoke from the couch grass, and the maid and her man) will go on forever though dynasties (compare Jeremiah 51: 20) and wars pass and are forgotten ("fade into night"). Terms suggesting slowness and quietness ("slow silent walk," "old," "Half-asleep," "thin," "whispering") contrast to the implied clamor and violence of nations and wars.

NATURE'S QUESTIONING

The questioning items in nature see their existence as a confused accident, a riddle, devoid of benevolent purpose.

Nature wonders where it came from—from some "vast Imbecility" (stanza 2), from an "Automation" (stanza 3), from some high "Achievement" struggling against Evil (stanza 4). In stanza 5, the speaker says he has no explanation for the senselessness of the universe, but he is aware of the "glooms and pains," and knows that life and death are neighbors.

NEUTRAL TONES

The dead, neutral tones of nature form a background for the dying of love between a man and a woman.

Stanza 1 describes the dullness of sun, sod, and leaves where the man and woman met. Stanzas 2-3 describe the dying love of the couple. Their relationship had become "tedious riddles," some talk about which one of them had lost more by their love, a dead smile, and a "grin of bitterness." Stanza 4 says that the cruel lessons of love the man learned later have stamped on his mind the scene where love died.

THE CONVERGENCE OF THE TWAIN

The sinking of the "unsinkable" *Titanic* is seen as a fated convergence of two halves of a cosmic plan.

Stanzas 1-5 show the *Titanic* as once an object of pride ("human vanity," "Pride of Life"), of strength ("steel chambers"), of opulence, and of sensuous delight. But now this "vaingloriousness" lies ruined at the bottom of the sea. Stanzas 6-11 describe the sinking as the result of a cosmic plan. The force that runs the universe, called "Immanent Will" and "Spinner of the Years," prepared the iceberg as a "sinister mate," so that ship and iceberg were "twin halves of one august event."

THE DARKLING THRUSH

A thrush's singing is a sign of hope in a desolate time.

Stanzas 1-2 describe a scene of desolation. Nature in winter shows only deadness, the nineteenth century just ending is a corpse, and the poet as well as "every spirit" is fervorless. In stanza 3, an aged, gaunt thrush sings with a joy in sharp contrast to the "growing gloom." In stanza 4, because the bleak terrestrial scene offers "little cause for caroling," the poet thinks the bird may know of some "blessed hope" not apparent to the poet.

THE MAN HE KILLED

A soldier considers the irrationality of war ("how quaint and curious") which makes people of common humanity kill each other without adequate reason.

Stanza 1 suggests the probable congeniality of the two men under circumstances other than war. Stanzas 2-3 offer the inadequate reason for killing as no other than the fact of war ("just so"). Stanza 4 points out the common humanity of the men as seen in the similarities of their lives ("just as I"). Stanza 5 suggests the irrationality of the whole situation.

THE SUBALTERNS

The cruelty of nature becomes easier to bear when one realizes it stems from divine law.

The leaden sky (stanza 1), the cold north (stanza 2), sickness (stanza 3), and death (stanza 4) all say they cause suffering to man not out of enmity but out of subordination ("subalterns") to higher law. In stanza 5, the speaker feels that having such knowledge makes life easier to endure.

WILLIAM ERNEST HENLEY

I. M. MARGARITAE SORORI

Though the title describes the poem as an elegy for his sister-in-law, Henley seems primarily interested in identifying the scene he describes with his own death.

As the lark sings and the evening sun lingers in the west, a "shining peace" falls on the old city (lines 1-7). The smoke rises in a golden haze and the spires shine. Shadows come in the valley. Still the lark sings. The sun, having blessed the city, sinks, and the air "thrills" with the approach of night with her "gift of sleep" (lines 8-16).

The poet says that he wants his passing to be like this. When his life is over and his work is done, may there be in his heart the lark singing, and may he be gathered quietly to the splendid sundown, Death (lines 17-23).

INVICTUS

Despite all the blows of circumstance, the speaker asserts his mastery of his soul and of his fate.

GEORGE HERBERT

LIFE

The poet, gathering flowers that soon wither in his hand (stanza 1), realizes that his "fatal day" also will come soon (stanza 2). But the poet does not care that his life is as brief as that of the flowers, if it is also as good (stanza 3).

LOVE (III)

The speaker, invited by Love to the spiritual feast, feels unworthy because of his "dust and sin." But Love tells him that Love "bore the blame" for sin. Thereupon, the speaker does "sit and eat."

THE COLLAR

The poem exemplifies how rebellion against spiritual servitude ("collar") is resolved in spiritual submission and peace. The poet, chafing under spiritual bondage, raves to go forth to recover by "double pleasures" what he has lost in God's service— wine, corn, the year, flowers. He will forsake the "cage," "the rope of sands," the reminders of death ("death's head"), and the fears. But in the last two lines, the ravings grow quiet as God reaffirms the Father-child relationship.

THE PEARL

Using commercial imagery of buying and selling, the poet seeks the kingdom of heaven, the "pearl of great price" for which a man is to sell all that he has (Matt. 13:45).

The poet trades the attractive ways of learning (stanza 1), of honor (stanza 2), and of pleasure (stanza 3) for the "pearl," knowing fully "at what rate and price" he has the love of God (stanza 4).

THE PULLEY

Man's craving for rest is the pulley by which God draws men to him.

Stanzas 1-2 show God at creation pouring on man all blessings (beauty, wisdom, honor, pleasure) except rest. In stanza 3, God explains that if he gave rest man would have all he needed in Nature and would not need God. So, in stanza 4, God says that if the goodness of His other gifts will not lead men to God, "repining restlessness" may.

THE QUIP

Because the poet belongs to the Lord, he is not moved by the temptations of the world.

When the temptations of the world taunt the speaker to take them, he lets the Lord answer for him. The "quip" that the Lord is to give in each case to Beauty, Money, Glory, and Wit and Conversation is to tell them that the poet belongs to the Lord ("I am Thine").

VIRTUE

Three main images are used to contrast the ephemeral though beautiful physical world to the eternal, spiritual existence of the soul.
The beautiful day must die at night (stanza 1). The rose, red and brave, has its root in the grave (stanza 2). The spring, full of both day and roses, must die as music dies (stanza 3). But the soul is as durable as seasoned timber, which neither breaks nor burns easily. The soul will live on though the "whole world turn" to cinders in the fires of the Last Judgment (stanza 4).

ROBERT HERRICK

TO DAFFODILS

The poet laments the transitoriness of life for daffodils and men.
In stanza 1, the poet weeps at the brief duration of the daffodils. He sees them dying before the noon of life and asks them to last until sunset that we may go along with them to death. For, in stanza 2, our hours are as brief as those of the daffodils.

TO THE VIRGINS TO MAKE MUCH OF TIME

In this *carpe diem* ("seize the day") poem, the poet urges young girls to marry while they have their all-too-brief youthfulness.
The swiftly dying flower (stanza 1), the brief duration of the day's sun (stanza 2), the superiority of the time of youth (stanza 3) provide reasons why young girls should "be not coy," but "go marry."

UPON JULIA'S CLOTHES

The poem comments on how attractive Julia is as she walks by—in stanza 1, the beautiful flowing of her clothes as she approaches; in stanza 2, her free vibration after she has passed and the poet turns to look.

RALPH HODGSON

STUPIDITY STREET

Stupidity Street is Hodgson's figure for a society that so mismanages its economy that the trivia of singing birds may be bought in the shops, but no food is available. The untended crops, with the "worm in the wheat," are offered as reason for the lack of food.

TIME, YOU OLD GYPSY MAN

In vain, the poet tries to get time, in the metaphor of a gypsy, not to pass so quickly.

Stanza 1 and 4 give the refrain asking time to linger. In stanza 2, inducements are offered, but in stanza 3 time as a gypsy with a caravan moves on from ancient Babylon, through Rome, through modern London with its St. Paul's Cathedral, lingering "only a moment."

OLIVER WENDELL HOLMES

THE DEACON'S MASTERPIECE

The poet uses the sudden collapse of a one-horse carriage to satirize the downfall of the logical religious system of Calvinism.

Stanzas 1-4 tell of the Deacon's aim to build a carriage with all of its parts equally strong so that it could not break down. The carriage was finished in 1775, the year of the Lisbon earthquake, an event that provoked many arguments in support of the Calvinistic view of God's control of the universe. Stanzas 5-6 tell of the Deacon's building the shay of the best materials possible. In stanzas 7-8 the years pass until 1855 with the carriage "much the same." In stanzas 9-12, on the first of November, just a hundred years to the day, it looks as if the wonderful one-hoss shay will soon be worn out. It is so tightly and equally built throughout that no one part shows more wear than another. Suddenly during the parson's sermon the shay collapses completely. The closing couplet suggests that it is only logical that such a tightly-built logical system should collapse all at once. It did not break down; it wore out.

GERARD MANLEY HOPKINS

FELIX RANDAL

The priest laments the death of his friend and parishioner, blacksmith Felix Randal.

Stanzas 1-2 describe the gradual sickening and dying of the large, hardy man, while the priest ministered to him. Stanza 3 tells how the sick man and the minister become endeared to one another. The priest's words and touch quenched the sick man's tears, which in turn deeply touched the priest, who thus can now deeply grieve that the man's "boisterous years" at the smith's forge are stilled by death.

GOD'S GRANDEUR

The poem expresses the continuing operation of the grandeur of God in nature.

Lines 1-4 describe the grandeur of God pervading the world, and ask why men do "now not reck his rod" (heed him). Lines 5-8 lament that both man and the earth have been corrupted by trade and toil. Lines 9-14 point out that whether man heeds or not, the vitality of nature continues, and the blessings of the Holy Ghost pervade all.

HEAVEN-HAVEN

The images and tone of the poem indicate the reason for the nun's taking the veil. The images of a place of unfailing springs, of no sharp hail, of no storms, of a quiet sea haven suggest her desire for a life with a minimum of stress and action.

HURRAHING IN HARVEST

The poet's "hurrahing" is his celebration of the glory of God seen in the sky at harvest time.

In stanzas 1-2, the poet, moved by the beauty of an autumn sky, looks "Down all that glory in the heavens to glean our Saviour." In stanza 3, Christ is seen in nature as if the hills were his "world-wielding shoulder." Christ was present all the time, waiting only for the beholder to see and to feel.

I WAKE AND FEEL THE FELL OF DARK

The priest, dedicated to God, struggles with self-renunciation. In lines 1-8, he laments the black hours, sights, and ways he must undergo when he awakens at night, and his cries to God, "dearest him," are answered no more than are dead letters. In lines 9-14, he tells the cause of his spiritual-emotional darkness; it is his struggle with self-renunciation: "God's most deep decree." His scourge, thus, is the same as that of the spiritually lost: to be his "sweating" self.

MY OWN HEART LET ME MORE HAVE PITY ON

The poet, struggling to get comfort, finally realizes that comfort cannot be "wrung" deliberately, but must come unexpectedly.

In lines 1-4, the poet resolves to be more pitying, kind, and charitable to his own sad self, his tormented mind. For, in lines 5-8, he can no more get comfort from his comfortless existence than a blind man can find day in the dark or than thirst can become ultimate thirst when everything is wet. In lines 9-14, he advises his soul not to seek comfort deliberately. For comfort must come at God's will, at unforeseen times, as a piece of sky appears unexpectedly between mountain tops.

PIED BEAUTY

The poet praises God for the beauty of his creation, which is "Pied" or "dappled," that is, composed of particularized things of variegated color and form. But God, by contrast, receives ultimate praise, for the beauty of God is beyond the creation he "fathers-forth." The beauty of God, the one unity in a world of opposites and variegation, is not subject to change.

SPRING

The theme is the urgency of one's enjoying his transitory innocence before it sours with sinning. The three dominant symbols of spring, Eden garden, and Mayday all suggest newness of life and sinlessness.

The imagery of lines 1-8 shows the beauty and exuberance of the spring of the year (weeds, thrush's eggs, thrush's song, pear tree, blue sky, and racing lambs). In lines 9-11, this exuberance of spring ("juice," "joy") is identified with earth's and mankind's beginning life ("in Eden garden"). Lines 11-14 urge that since the spring of life, the innocence, the Mayday will "sour with sinning" in "girl and boy," one should have and get while he can and so be worthy of Christ ("maid's child").

SPRING AND FALL: TO A YOUNG CHILD

The theme is that the cause of grief is the Fall and the object of grief is one's self.

The child Margaret, in her youth and innocence ("fresh thoughts") grieving over the golden leaves falling ("unleaving"), is told that as she grows older she will have such grief ("sights colder") that she will have no sigh to spare though whole worlds lie in fallen leaves ("leafmeal"). Yet weeping and wanting to know why leaves fall, she is told that all sorrow springs from the same cause and has the same object. The inner part of man, heart and spirit (not mouth nor mind), has surmised this truth. The cause is the "blight," the Fall of man, which brought death to man as well as to leaves. The object of sorrow is one's self ("It is Margaret").

THE CAGED SKYLARK

The poet celebrates the Christian resurrection of the body by making an extended comparison between the spirit in the body and the skylark in a cage.

Man's mounting spirit confined in the body may sometime find the body to be a drudgery or a barrier. Yet the body ("bonehouse") should not be considered finally as a "prison" or an encumbrance, for the spirit when at its best will be bound to the flesh ("flesh-bound"), that is, at the resurrection of the body ("bones risen").

THE STARLIGHT NIGHT

The God in nature, specifically a starlight night, may be perceived through religious devotions.

Lines 1-7 describe the wonder of the starlight sky in several metaphors: fire-folk, bright cities, diamonds in dim woods, elves' eyes, quickgold on gray lawns, whitebeam and white poplar trees, and doves flying from a farmyard. Lines 8-14 tell that with religious devotions such as prayer and vows one can buy this beauty of nature, which is really the home of Christ, Mary, and the Saints.

THE WINDHOVER

The poem develops the priest-poet's conflict between freedom and ascetic service of Christ.

In the early morning, the priest sees the falcon flying on the wind in great ecstasy and strength as a horseman rides a horse (lines 1-7). The priest, restrained by his ascetic life ("heart in hiding"), is stirred by the contrasting freedom and mastery of the bird. For beauty, valor, act, air, pride all combine in the bird's soaring (lines 7-9). But the bird's mastery and beauty collapse ("Buckle") when the priest compares them to his own God ("thee"). He finds "Christ Our Lord," his own "chevalier" or noble horseman (compare the horse-riding imagery of the falcon), to be "lovelier" than the falcon (lines 10-11). And there is "no wonder" that the priest prefers the restraints of ascetic service of Christ to the freedom of the falcon: the dullest ascetic service ("sheer plod," "embers," both as coals and as prayer and fasting) has great beauty (lines 12-14).

THE WRECK OF THE DEUTSCHLAND

The theme of the poem is that man finds spiritual fulfillment and communion with God through mental and physical ordeal. Part I is autobiographical, dealing with Hopkins' own God-caused suffering, which has been primarily mental. Part II is a narrative of the *Deutschland* shipwreck, expressing the distress of the five nuns, which is primarily physical.

In Part I, stanzas 1-2 describe the poet, in his suffering of "terror" and "fire of stress," almost unmade by the God who made him. In stanzas 3-4, the poet prefers God's face to the "hurtle of hell" and seeks comfort in "Christ's Gift," the Mass or "Host." In stanzas 5-7, he seeks to identify the source of stress that unites man and God: it is Christ's Passion. In stanzas 8-10, this illumination leads to spiritual fulfillment (stanza 8) and to acceptance of God's bringing stress to man. God's purpose is to control man—"wring thy rebel . . . man's malice, with wrecking and storm" (stanza 9) in order to "master him still" (stanza 10), either suddenly as with St. Paul or slowly as with St. Augustine.

Part II, the narrative of the shipwreck, is an example of God's "dark descending," the merciful suffering he brings. Stanzas 11-17 give an account of the wreck—the ship striking the sandbar, the violent storm, the heroism of the sailor, the passengers clinging to rigging. Stanzas 18-35 give the account of the "tall nun" whose call could be heard above the storm, "O, Christ, Christ, come quickly." Stanzas 18-24 recount the exile of the nuns leading up to the call. Stanzas 25-34 express the poet's awe at the majesty of such single love and at the thought of Christ's "royally reclaiming" such a soul. In stanza 35, he prays that the nun in her "heaven-haven" may further God's work upon "English souls."

THOU ART INDEED JUST, LORD

The priest, who has given his life to God's cause, is anguished at his lack of spiritual productivity.

In lines 1-4, he acknowledges God's justness, but claims that his plea is also just: why do sinners prosper but his own efforts prove disappointing? In lines 5-13, he suggests that God is thwarting him since other things which are not spending "life upon thy cause" do thrive: "the sots and thralls of lust" and the fertile plants and birds of nature. In line 14, he prays for his lord to make him productive by sending life-giving rain to his spiritual roots.

A. E. HOUSMAN

ALONG THE FIELD AS WE CAME BY

Life is brief and love is inevitably fickle—"time shall put them both to bed."

In stanza 1, as the two lovers walked, the man heard the aspen prophesying that his lover would die and that he would have another lover. In stanza 2, a year later, the prophecy has been fulfilled. But now he with his new lover hears the sound but not the words of the aspen and fears the ironic obverse of stanza 1—death for him and a new lover for her.

BREDON HILL

A tragedy of love is caused by the death of one of the lovers.
Stanzas 1-4 describe the happiness of the two lovers. In summertime they would lie on Bredon Hill on Sunday morning and, when the bells called them to church, they would talk of the bells ringing for their wedding. Stanzas 5-6 tell that by Christmas the girl, ironically, had gone to church not for a wedding but for her own funeral ("alone," "tolled," "mourners"). In the last stanza the man lingers on Bredon, hearing the bells call, and answering "I will come"—perhaps out of his grief to follow her to death.

COULD MAN BE DRUNK FOREVER

If, stanza 1 suggests, one could continuously escape into the illusions of "liquor, love, or fights," then the routine of life ("rouse," "lie down") would be bearable. But, stanza 2 points out, at times men must see life as it is ("sober") and bear the ill ("hand upon their hearts") of thinking about it.

FAREWELL TO BARN AND STACK AND TREE

The poem gives the barest details of a stark domestic tragedy.
A man says farewell to his friend (Terence) and to the things that have made up his life, such as "barn and stack," "mother," "racing," "fold," and "dinner." He has killed his brother Maurice and so must flee. Motives for the killing are not given, but the poem uses many devices to evoke sympathy—"Farewell," "mother," "she'll be alone," "oh, man," "I wish you luck," and "empty plate."

I HOED AND TRENCHED AND WEEDED

In a metaphor of gardener and flowers the poet offers his products (such as poems, or whatever the hard labor of his life has produced) to society and "luckless lads" like himself.

The public rejects his flowers (stanza 1) as out of fashion ("not the wear"). So he sows them (stanza 2) "up and down" for others like himself. Most are lost (stanza 3) to birds and seasons, but a few persist for those (stanza 4) who come after the poet's death.

INTO MY HEART AN AIR THAT KILLS

The poet laments the lost contentment of the past that can never be recovered. The air from that "far country" is "killing" because he knows he can never have again the "lost content" he once had.

IS MY TEAM PLOUGHING?

After his death, a man is soon forgotten and life goes on happily without him.

In four sets of questions asked by the dead man and answered by his live friend, the dead man hears that life goes on as usual in work (stanzas 1-2), play (stanzas 3-4), love (stanzas 5-6), and friendship (stanzas 7-8). The dialogue builds to the final irony that the friend is now the lover of the dead man's sweetheart.

LOVELIEST OF TREES

The loveliness of blossoms in spring is the occasion for expressing a *carpe diem* ("seize the day") view of life.

Because the cherry tree in bloom is so beautiful (stanza 1), and because life is so short, with twenty years of his Biblically allotted seventy years already gone (stanza 2), the poet will go about the woods to see the lovely cherry blossoms (stanza 3). The brevity of life and the poignancy of its end is pointed out by the change from "bloom" and "Eastertide," the time of rebirth (lines 2 and 4), to "snow" (line 12).

ON MOONLIT HEATH AND LONESOME BANK

The poem evokes sympathy for a young man waiting in jail to be hanged.

The speaker recalls (stanzas 1-2) that nearby a shepherd was once hanged ("Keeping sheep by moonlight" was country slang for being hanged) Now (stanzas 3-6), a man waits in Shrewsbury jail to be hanged at eight o'clock the next morning. The poem does not tell the motive or nature of the crime, but sympathy is evoked by such phrases as "a better lad," "A neck God made for other use," and "as straight a chap." So (stanzas 7-8) the speaker will watch the night and wish his friend a peaceful death as he joins those hanged before him.

ON WENLOCK EDGE THE WOOD'S IN TROUBLE

The universality of human trouble and mortality is expressed through the central image of the wind troubling the woods.

Stanza 1 describes the gale disturbing the woods of the local woods of Wenlock Edge and the Wrekin near the Severn River. Stanzas 2-3 point out that in the same way it "threshed" the woods of the Romans, who built the city of Uricon in the same area ages before, binding Roman and English yeomen in a common fate through "blood that warms" and "thoughts that hurt." That fate, stanzas 4-5 tell us, is to be "never quiet" and to "soon be gone."

REVEILLE

The poem evokes a *carpe diem* ("seize the day") philosophy using the dominant imagery of a traveler breaking camp and marching on a journey.

Words like "Reveille," "Wake," "Up," and "drums" call the lad to explore life "beyond the hills." His blood is a "rover" urging him to other towns, countries, forelands, and belfries. For life is very brief, breath being a "ware that will not keep," and death will allow time enough to rest.

TERENCE, THIS IS STUPID STUFF

By defending melancholy poetry, the poet develops the theme that since life has more ill than good in it, it is best to train oneself to face the ill.

In part 1 (lines 1-14), the friends of the poet (Terence) sitting in a tavern rebuke him for giving them sad poems instead of happy ones. In part 2 (lines 15-42) Terence first offers drink as an escape from the pain of thinking ("hurts to think"), but then says the solution is temporary, for we must "begin the game anew." In part 3 (lines 43-58) Terence argues that since "trouble's sure" in life, he will give wise but bitter advice to help his friends in the "dark and cloudy day." Part 4 (lines 59-62) draws a lesson from Mithridates' sampling poison to make him immune to the poison given him by his enemies. Prepare for the evils in life by feeding on trouble, such as poison or melancholy poems.

THE CHESTNUT CASTS HIS FLAMBEAUX

The poet advises his companion to deal with the hard lot that is man's by stoically accepting it and by drinking ale.

In stanza 1, life is brief ("end of May," "our little store"). In stanzas 2-3 life is futile ("hurled . . . plans to emptiness") and devoid of divine benevolence ("brute and blackguard"). In stanzas 4-5, life is disappointing ("want the moon"). In stanzas 6-7, life is full of endless and inevitable trouble ("from eternity," "shall not fail"). The solution to this hard lot: stoical acceptance ("if we can we must./ Shoulder the sky") and ale drinking.

TO AN ATHLETE DYING YOUNG

Because of the brevity of fame, the athlete is considered lucky to have died so young.

Stanza 1 tells of the time he was carried home amid cheers for winning the race. Stanza 2, by contrast, tells of his being brought home today to death ("stiller town"). In stanzas 3-7 he is considered a "Smart lad" to die before his brief glory fades, his record is broken, and his fame dies.

WHEN I WAS ONE-AND-TWENTY

In light tones, the poet points out that the young learn only by experience the sad truth that the heart is easily broken.

At twenty-one, the poet scoffed at the wise man's warning not to give his heart away. But by twenty-two, he had learned.

WHEN SMOKE STOOD UP FROM LUDLOW

Nature (the blackbird) realizes and man comes to realize that death is better than life.

When the blackbird advised the man working happily ("strode," "whistled") that it is wiser to die because man at last must die, the man threw a stone and killed the bird. Then the man's soul took up the song and, like the bird, sang, "Lie down."

WITH RUE MY HEART IS LADEN

The poet grieves for his young, attractive friends who have died— the beautiful, "rose-lipped" girls and the ambitious, "light foot" boys.

RANDALL JARRELL

A CAMP IN THE PRUSSIAN FOREST

The poet depicts the monstrous crimes of the German concentration camps of World War II, and the torture and slaughter of the Jews.

In stanzas 1-5, the speaker, one of the soldiers who liberated the camp. helps lead the captured prisoners to the road, thinks about the enormities that went on in the camp, and helps prepare a grave for the corpses of camp victims. In stanzas 6-8, he makes a wooden star, probably a Star of David, for the grave of the corpses, but the star is fouled symbolically by smoke which still rises from the crematory chimney. In stanza 9, the soldier laughs hysterically in horror of what men have done to men.

A GIRL IN A LIBRARY

The poet idealizes a girl momentarily sleeping in a college library.

As she takes momentary respite from studying, he notes her essential humanness and identifies her with Helen, Brünnhilde, and Salome in her feminine strength (lines 1-31). He praises her soul over her pedantic assignments as a student (lines 35-52). He sees her dreams as her reality and she herself as a "form of joy" (lines 53-83). He thinks of her as an admonishment to live now, not "to have one's life add up to yet" (lines 84-106). As the girl awakens, the poet reflects on his love for her and connects her with an age-old fertility legend of man and woman (lines 107-121).

90 NORTH

A child prefers the North Pole of death to the meaninglessness and aloneness of living.

In stanzas 1-3, the child in his bed at night imagines traveling by dog sled to the North Pole where he sees frozen children and wonders if his end is to be the same. He welcomes the North, as symbol of the rest of death. In stanzas 4-8, he returns to his actual world of "cold and wretchedness" and finds it meaningless, for he is still alone. The only knowledge he wrings from the darkness of living is that "pain comes from the darkness."

2ND AIR FORCE

A mother views the war machine of the air that has taken her son from her and thinks in bewilderment of what she raised her son for: "The years meant *this*?"

In lines 1-13, the mother thinks "heavily" that her son is grown, and she watches as the bombers ("Fortresses") load war gear and take off to fly through the night on bombing missions. The bombers demonstrate an awful truth: "death is pure." In lines 24-55, the mother thinks of her son standing beside her and then remembers various scenes leading up to this bewildering present in which the bombers now carry her son to death.

THE DEATH OF THE BALL TURRET GUNNER

The outrage of war is depicted through the destruction of a young gunner by aerial combat. The effect is produced by two series of images: birth and sleep.

So young, as if from his mother's womb ("sleep"), the gunner fell (as being born) into the State. He was wrenched ("froze") from the possibilities of human development ("dream of life") almost as if still an embryo ("hunched in its belly," "wet fur"). The next-to-last line is an ironic reversal of "sleep" and "dream": he "woke" to the death of black flak and to "nightmare." The last line is an ironic reversal of the womb and birth imagery of line 1.

THE ORIENT EXPRESS

The poet develops the comparison that a man's view from a train (as it passes through life) is like the view of a child, "hunched shivering/ Under the quilt's many colors."

Stanza 1 points out two views from a strange, or orient, express train: by daylight things are plain and safe; by night there is a "questioning/ Precariousness." Stanza 2 recounts a view of the world as seen in childhood—a cold, lonely world that is a "Gray mask" with nothing behind it. Stanza 3 recounts a view from a passing train. There is a glimpse of people's lives, scenes which are masks with something behind them. Then, in stanza 4, the poet identifies the something behind: "The unknown unwanted life."

ROBINSON JEFFERS

APOLOGY FOR BAD DREAMS

The poem expresses a theory of art, of psychology, and of theology. It gives the poet's reason for creating his poems and the characters he has put in them: they serve as a vicarious means through "imagined victims" of purging the evil ("wolves," "bad dreams") from the unconscious ("from the core").

Part I offers evidence for the evil in man—the brutal beating of the horse, set against the beauty of nature.

Part II traces the source of man's cry for tragedy to his "passionate spirit" ("terror," "desire," "wolves") crowding up from the unconscious. So the need to invent victims (like characters in fiction) rather than to have real ones (like the horse or "your own flesh").

Part III restates that our salvation may come in two ways: (1) by remembered deaths—by not forgetting how liable man is to evil, from the earliest tribe; (2) by imagined victims. After Tamar (an imagined character from a Jeffers poem) goes by, the peace of nature returns to the poet.

Part IV compares the poet's shaping his imagined victims to the ways of the non-human God (a God that is not person, but phenomena). Both the poet and God purge humanity through suffering.

BOATS IN A FOG

The poet sees in the serious business of fishing boats an illustration of the earnestness that makes beauty in man or nature.

In lines 1-5, the poet lists arts such as "Sports" and "antics of dancers" which lack nobility because they lack "bitter earnestness." Lines 6-18 give an illustration of earnestness in fishing boats going about their business. Lines 18-23 reassert that "all the arts lose virtue" against such essential reality, whether the movement of fishing boats in a fog, of pelicans, or of planets.

CREDO

The poet asserts his belief that physical reality is independent of and superior to the reality created by the mind.

Oriental thought conceives only the mental ocean to be real (lines 1-5). But the poet's western thought distinguishes the ocean in the bone vault from the ocean "out there" (lines 6-10). The beauty of physical reality is also superior to the reality created by the mind, since it is "sufficient to itself" and "will remain" after heart and mind have passed (lines 10-13).

GALE IN APRIL

The poet asks how man "with the frail naked nerves" can endure the "Intense and terrible beauty" of life. The conflict is symbolized by the gale that challenges the strongest spirits. The answer is that the strong endure the "torture/ Of intense joy"—that is, the suffering, challenge, and beauty of life—in the knowledge that with death will come "the other beauty," peace.

GRANITE AND CYPRESS

The wind, in the metaphor of a falcon, beats on the sea-cliff and threatens the endurance of the cypresses planted by the poet. But he identifies with the long-lasting granite, that "like me . . . are quiet," and is not disturbed by these forces that shake cypresses or people.

HURT HAWKS

A wounded hawk, tormented by captivity and incapacity, arouses the poet's admiration because the hawk in its beauty and wildness is like the "wild god" of nature.

In part 1, the poet describes a wounded hawk waiting for death to deliver him from his incapacity. The poet admires the proud, fierce, free spirit of the hawk; because the hawk is "intemperate and savage," he is aware of the god of nature. The poet reproaches "communal people" for not remembering this god as hawks remember him.

In part 2, the poet, seeing death as the only redeemer, shoots the hawk to release its spirit ("fierce rush").

LOVE THE WILD SWAN

The poet, in the dominant metaphor of wild swan and hunter, describes the world of nature as more beautiful than a poem ("bullets") can express. No matter, though, whether one hates his verses or himself because he cannot adequately express the beauty of nature, he can love his eyes and his mind that they can perceive the "wild swan."

MAY-JUNE, 1940

The poet is not surprised at World War II about the time of Dunkirk, since he believes that the fall of civilizations is in the nature of things.

In stanza 1, the poet says that the present war was foreseen. He forecasts the degradation and other evils to follow, and he gives a solution to social evils: "be few and live far apart" in the sanity of nature. In stanza 2, the poet asserts that the war's "insanities are normal," and that "death and life are not serious alternatives." In stanza 3 he tells "my dear," probably his wife, not to lament the fall of a civilization since such is a natural event and since perhaps it would be best after all if mankind perished.

PRESCRIPTION OF PAINFUL ENDS

In an inevitably deteriorating civilization, the poet tries through his poems to preserve some value and so "gather the insights" for the future.

Just as Lucretius and Plato in their ages saw their civilizations declining, so the poet sees that his age, like a faltering horse, must fall (lines 1-9). Lucretius and Plato tried to preserve the insights of their ages—"great theory," "cells . . . to hive the Greek honey" (lines 9-13). But the poet's age has only "acids" instead of "honey" and "misapplied science and Christianity" instead of "fine dreams." The little hope left is in the poet, who may "burn off at least the top crust of the time's uncleanness" (lines 14-17).

ROAN STALLION

A woman, repelled by her coarse husband, turns her adoration to a stallion and, seeing it as God, she allows it to kill her husband.

The first scene (lines 1-48) tells of the bringing home of the stallion, of Johnny's coarseness, and of California's lack of love for her husband. In the next scene (lines 48-118), on a trip from home for Christmas presents for the child, California has a vision of the baby Jesus modified by various animal deities. She begins adoring and deifying the stallion her husband has brought home. In the third scene (lines 119-154), after California lusts for the stallion and Johnny says he will show her how the stallion acts, the poet says (lines 155-164) we should break away from corrupt humanness to turn to the nonhuman God of nature. Then (lines 164-245), California, riding the stallion to a hilltop, lusts for sexual relations with it and identifies it with God. In the final scene (lines 246-304), when Johnny tries sexual relations with her again, she flees to the stallion and allows it to kill Johnny before, because of some "obscure human fidelity," she shoots it.

SHINE, PERISHING REPUBLIC

The poet assumes that America is decaying and he denounces love of man as a trap to hold man to the corrupt perishing society.

Stanzas 1-3 use the main metaphors of lava (1), rotting fruit (2), and a meteor (3) to describe the decay of a nation as a function in the cycle of history.

In stanzas 4-5 the poet advises his children not to become personally involved in the declining society. They can remove themselves from the thickening centers, the cities (4), and not be trapped by love of man, so dangerous a trap that it even caught God (5).

THE BLOODY SIRE

Ironically, the poet says to let the war continue, since mankind is in need of new values and since historically all values have been produced through violence. He lists such values as the fineness of the wolf's tooth, the antelope's fleet limbs, birds' wings, hawk's eyes, the beauty of Helen, and Christ. While he disparages the war makers ("play," "blasphemies"), the poet sees that out of the very evil of their violence may come new values for a society whose wars are evidence that new values are needed.

THE PURSE-SEINE

The purse-seine catching sardines becomes to the poet a symbol of Progress and of the cities which trap mankind.

Stanza 1 relates the incident of catching the sardines. Stanza 2 tells of the scene's beauty and terror to the poet. Stanza 3 compares the mass of trapped fish to the mass of people in a city "locked all together into interdependence," which, as a seine, will result in "mass-disasters." Stanza 4 ironically labels the process as "Progress" and gives it as reason for the poet's troubled verse, even though he knows "that cultures decay."

TO THE STONE-CUTTERS

The theme is the solace ("honey of peace") man gets from his works of art (marble and poems) even though they, along with man, are destined to oblivion.

The stone-cutters "fighting time" with durable stone are fore-defeated because the ravages of time will "scale" and "wear" their work (lines 1-5). The poet too builds mockingly, because man, earth, and sun will die (lines 6-8). Yet the labor of the artist does have a justifiable purpose, since works of marble have endured and poems have given peace (lines 9-10).

BEN JONSON

EPITAPH ON ELIZABETH, L. H.

The poet writes an elegiac epitaph for an unknown woman, giving only her first name, Elizabeth. He praises her for her exceeding beauty and virtue and for having no fault worth mentioning.

IT IS NOT GROWING LIKE A TREE

The poet uses images of oak and lily to assert that perfection in life and man is more likely to come in small measures rather than in large. The oak with its bulk and long life is not as beautiful as the short-lived lily.

SONG TO CELIA

In a tribute to the beauty of his beloved, the poet compares her, in stanza 1, to a drink better than wine or the nectar of the gods, and, in stanza 2, to a rosy wreath which draws life ("could not withered be") and fragrance from her.

JOHN KEATS

BRIGHT STAR

The speaker wishes that he were as steadfast as the bright star. He does not want to be "In lone splendor" like the star as it watches the oceans or the new-fallen snow. But, "still steadfast," he wants to lie upon his lover's breast, to live forever in a "sweet unrest" and hear her breath—"or else swoon to death."

LA BELLE DAME SANS MERCI

A haggard knight tells his tale of love and despair.

The pale knight, "loitering" on the hillside, tells of how he met a beautiful lady who took him "to her elfin grot." He was convinced that she loved him and he comforted her as she wept and sighed. Then, in a dream, he saw death-pale kings and princes and warriors, who warned him that the beautiful lady without mercy had him "in thrall." He awoke from this dream to find himself "On the cold hillside," alone.

ODE ON A GRECIAN URN

The poet examines two scenes on the urn: a scene of "wild ecstasy" (stanzas 1-3) and a religious sacrifice (stanza 4) Stanza 5 states the theme that the urn tells us that "Beauty is truth, truth beauty"—a statement that has been variously interpreted, but in general seems to mean that art, being unchanging, has the quality of eternal truth. Stanzas 2 and 3 develop the idea that the imaginative world of the urn (melodies, lovers, boughs) is always at the highest pitch of existence since it cannot change or fade. Ordinary ecstasy is followed by pain and disillusionment, but art captures and holds the beauty and the pleasure at the most exquisite moment.

ODE ON MELANCHOLY

There is a mysterious connection between pleasure and sorrow: "in the very temple of Delight/ Veiled Melancholy has her sovran shrine." Therefore, the speaker says, do not seek to escape "your sorrow's mysteries" in forgetfulness (Lethe) or death (stanza 1). Instead, when melancholy comes "from heaven," "feed" upon the beauties of nature or upon your mistress' eyes (stanza 2). You know that, even as you take pleasure in her beauty, your joy will turn to melancholy because the beauty and the joy will pass (stanza 3).

ODE TO A NIGHTINGALE

The poet evokes a mood dominated by the attraction of death in the face of misery. His mood leads him into the contemplation of beauty and the immortality of beauty. The poem is given a cyclic structure in the allusions to daylight (lines 1-2), night (line 35), and midnight (line 56).

In stanza 1 the poet makes a close connection between pain and dying (lines 1-2) and the merging of his consciousness in the bird's happiness (lines 5-10). As he listens he wishes for a wonderful wine that will enable him to "fade away into the forest dim" and leave the dismal and painful world (stanzas 2 and 3). Next, the poet's thoughts turn from wine to poetry, which will be the vehicle for his escape. From heaven, where the Queen-Moon (symbol of beauty) is on her throne, comes the light for the dark world (stanza 4). In the dark, the poet guesses what beauties of summer are about him (stanza 5). Listening, he recalls that he has earlier expressed the attraction of death for him. Now it seems especially sweet to die—except for the thought that, in death, he could no longer hear the nightingale (stanza 6). The bird is immortal, for its song was heard in ancient times and in "faery lands" (stanza 7). Finally, as the nightingale's song fades, the poet begins his return to reality. The fancy releases its hold, and, now questioning the reality of his experience, he relapses into an uncertain state between waking and sleeping (stanza 8).

ODE TO PSYCHE

The poem praises Psyche, the "latest born . . ./ Of all Olympus' faded hierarchy." Keats makes Psyche (the soul) the symbol of the mysterious growth of the human soul through the agency of pain. She becomes the object of worship by the creative imagination.

The speaker recounts how, perhaps in a dream, he came upon two fair creatures lying in a quiet embrace. They were Cupid ("winged boy") and Psyche. In the third stanza he addresses Psyche as the "loveliest vision far" of all the old goddesses, the fairest despite the fact that, being the "latest born," she has no shrine or ceremonies devoted to her. But, says the speaker, let me take the place of the choirs and prophets. The speaker exclaims that he will be "thy voice, thy lute. . . ." Then, in his mind he will create a temple for Psyche, and it shall be beautiful as any natural setting. In it will be all the beauties that Fancy can create and all the delight that can be attained by thought.

ON FIRST LOOKING INTO CHAPMAN'S HOMER

The speaker uses the analogy of traveling to describe his experience of reading poets, particularly Homer.

The speaker has traveled much "in the realms of gold." He has often heard of a "wide expanse" ruled by Homer, but he never had been there until he read Chapman's translation. Then he felt awed, like an astronomer discovering a new planet or like Cortez (it was really Balboa—a notorious historical error by Keats) when he discovered the Pacific.

PROEM TO ENDYMION (LINES 1-33)

A thing of beauty is forever a joy, with increasing loveliness. It will provide "sweet dreams" and "quiet breathing." Therefore, we bind ourselves to the earth in spite of all worldly evils, for a spirit of beauty "moves away the pall/ From our dark spirits." Such "Shapes of beauty" are the sun, the moon, the daffodils, the rills, and the forest brake (thicket). So, too, the grand stories of the "mighty dead" and "All lovely tales" come to us from heaven.

These "essences" do not remain with us briefly. Rather, as the trees that "whisper round" become (by association) as dear as the temple itself, so do "the moon," "the passion poesy, glories infinite" stay with us to become a light. And they are "bound to us so fast" that in joy or gloom "they . . . must be with us, or we die."

THE EVE OF ST. AGNES

As explained in stanza 6, "The Eve of St. Agnes" is based upon the legend that if young virgins observe the correct ceremonies on St. Agnes' eve, they will "have visions of delight." In this poem Madeline is the maiden whom Porphyro, her lover, comes to adore and then impulsively carries away with him.

It is a cold night, and the aged Beadsman has "harsh penance" to perform (stanzas 1-3). In the midst of the revelry in the hall, Madeline's thoughts turn to the legend of St. Agnes' Eve, and she is hardly aware of the activity around her (stanzas 4-8).

In the meantime, Porphyro, his "heart on fire/ For Madeline," has come to this house of his enemies for a sight of his beloved. An old woman, Angela, helps him, though she is reluctant and fears for Porphyro's safety. When she tells him of Madeline's purpose to follow out the legend, Porphyro suggests that the old woman take him where he can see Madeline. As she expresses shock at this suggestion, Porphyro protests that he has no lustful intentions. He concludes by threatening to shout and arouse his enemies against him if she does not agree. So Angela agrees to take him to a closet in Madeline's chamber (stanzas 9-20).

Having been taken to the closet by Angela, Porphyro waits. Now Madeline enters the chamber and kneels in prayer. She undresses, and, going to bed, falls asleep. Porphyro emerges from the closet and sets a table by her bedside. He sets out rich and exotic delicacies and, having prepared the table, calls Madeline to awaken, but her dream is "Impossible to melt" (stanzas 21-31).

Momentarily entranced himself by Madeline's dream, Porphyro finally takes up her lute and plays upon it. Madeline awakes in fear and dismay to the reality of Porphyro's presence. Aroused by her fearful complaint about him, "he arose . . ." and "Into her dream he melted. . . ."

As Madeline expresses fear and regret at the thought of cold reality, Porphyro asks to be "Thy beauty's shield." He urges her to come away with him, and "They glide, like phantoms" through the house and out into the storm (stanzas 32-42).

TO AUTUMN

This is a song—or hymn—of fulfillment. Stanza 1 describes the complete fruition of the vines, the apple trees, and so on.

Stanza 2 expands the personification of the first stanza to enhance our feeling for autumn. The final stanza praises the music of autumn, which has its own fitting sounds.

TO SLEEP

Sleep is addressed as the "soft embalmer" that will "seal the hushèd casket of my soul." The speaker asks sleep, that shuts the eyes in forgetfulness, to come now or when the poem ("hymn") is finished, to save him from the memories and the worries of the day.

WHEN I HAVE FEARS THAT I MAY CEASE TO BE

The poet fears that he will die before all the ideas and visions in his mind are written down. And when he feels that he will never look upon his love again, then he stands alone and all that matters (the writing and the love) sinks into nothingness.

RUDYARD KIPLING

RECESSIONAL

The poet warns, in the form of a prayer, against the "frantic boast" that puts its reliance on war rather than God. Two dominant motifs run through the poem: the vanity of military power and the need for spiritual humility. We must not forget that we must be humble before God, or like the heathen kings and cities of old our pomp and power will fade away.

THE WHITE MAN'S BURDEN

The poet describes the duty of the white man to civilize and care for inferior peoples.

The speaker directs the whites to assume their burden humbly, with no thought of reward except the service itself. He sees the captive peoples as "Half-devil and half-child" who must be treated humanely, gently, and unselfishly by their white leaders, even though these leaders will probably receive only blame, hate, and ingratitude from the "silent sullen peoples."

Those who assume the "White Man's burden," the poet concludes, must put away childish expectations of easy victory and reward, for their manhood will be put to the test.

STANLEY KUNITZ

CARELESS LOVE

The poet personifies the gun to describe the deadly relationship between a soldier and his gun.

In lines 1-9, the lonely soldier caresses his gun as if it were a woman. In lines 10-16, the gun receives and returns the "load of love" like a nymphomaniac, for her deadly enjoyment is inexhaustible.

FATHER AND SON

A man, after searching for his father through a dream landscape and his remembered childhood, finds that his father cannot return to him.

In stanzas 1-2, the son thinks back to childhood, trying to communicate with his dead father. He wonders how to "bridge the chasm" and tell the father what has happened over the years. In stanza 3 the poet calls the father to come back from the pond (where he probably drowned himself). The son would be instructed in the father's "gentleness" so that "between two wars" he can be a child, a brother, and a friend to those in need.

In stanza 4, the son is thrust back upon himself, for his father offers only the "white ignorant hollow of his face."

THE SURGEONS

The poet offers love between two people as the only means of preserving the human being whom the monstrous modern world is destroying.

The dominant figures of diabolical operating surgeons show how the corrupt modern world is maiming and dehumanizing the human spirit. The surgeons, decreeing that certain persons are to be destroyed, perform their operations. They cut dreams out of the brain, anesthetize passions, squeeze out sympathy. The poet's answer is love. He tells the "dear girl" to lie down with him and asserts that he believes "In love."

WALTER SAVAGE LANDOR

MOTHER, I CANNOT MIND MY WHEEL

This is the statement of a disillusioned girl. In her pain, she recalls the basis of her belief in her lover: he had praised her eyes and her lips.

ON HIS SEVENTY-FIFTH BIRTHDAY

The poet states that he was peaceful in temperament, that he loved Nature and Art, and that, having lived fully, he is now ready to depart.

PAST RUINED ILION

After stating that verse gives immortality to Helen and Alcestis, the poet asserts that, after the gay and the proud have disappeared, the name of Ianthe will live on.

ROSE AYLMER

In this little elegy, the poet asks what do all the advantages of birth ("sceptered race") and personal charm matter now that Rose Aylmer is dead. All he can do is to "consecrate" to her a night of grief.

SIDNEY LANIER

THE MARSHES OF GLYNN

The poet tells of the "greatness of God" as seen in the marshes in the county of Glynn on the southeastern Georgia coast.

Lines 1-17 describe the glooms of the live oak trees, which attract lovers and which offer a place of prayer to "the soul that grieves."

Lines 18-34 describe the dusks of the marshes as signs of approaching death ("scythe of time"), which brings no fear to the poet. Rather, in lines 35-64, he is drawn to the marshes. Where the marshes, the sea, and the sky meet, his soul seems suddenly free from fate and sin. In lines 65-105, in the joining of the marshes with sea and sky, the poet sees a symbol of the way his soul is joined to the "greatness of God." The marsh-hen from the sky builds on the watery sod, and the sea floods in till the "sea and the marsh are one." Such an infusion of the "Vast of the Lord" is beyond our "waking" knowledge.

THE SYMPHONY

Lanier said of this poem: "I personify each instrument in the orchestra, and make them discuss various deep social questions of the times, in the progress of the music." The poem indicts "Trade"—industrialism, the factory system, and all competitive business.

In lines 1-84, the strings, led by the violin, speak against the evils of Trade. In lines 85-210, the flute says that Nature calls upon man to love Nature and to love his neighbors—the poor laborers which Trade oppresses. In lines 211-252, the clarinet, speaking as a woman, indicts Trade for driving women into ways of shame. In lines 253-325, the horn speaks as a knight to defend the "Fair Lady." In lines 326-334, the oboe, like a "large-eyed child," speaks against Trade for mistreatment of children. In lines 335-368, the bassoons, as wise old men, say that only Love can remove the evils of Trade, and they foresee the coming of Love in society.

PHILIP LARKIN

DECEPTIONS

Pangs of disillusionment may be suffered by victimizer as well as victim.

In stanza 1, the poet sympathizes with the woman who, after she was raped, felt, as described by Mayhew, inconsolable grief like a scar that would not heal or a drawer full of knives. In stanza 2, the poet asserts that the attacker also felt sufferings afterward, those of finding that the experience gave him no fulfillment.

POETRY OF DEPARTURES

The poet points out the urge to liberation which is expressed in certain everyday clichés about "departures."

We can identify with such audacious, elemental moves as are expressed in "He chucked everything" and "He walked out on . . ." But, in the final stanza, the poet reverses the viewpoint, for actually to walk out on undesirable conditions is "artificial" and a "step backwards."

TOADS

Toads are used as metaphors for the two conditions that prevent the poet's having a free, swashbuckling existence: comforts and inhibitions.

In stanzas 1-6, he laments the bourgeois comforts and security that require the "toad work" to bind him instead of his being like those people who "live on their wits." In stanzas 7-9, he acknowledges an inner toad of inhibition which prevents his getting goods by "blarney."

D. H. LAWRENCE

BAVARIAN GENTIANS

Gentians, an autumn flower, are used as a symbol of the unity of the death or winter aspect of the natural cycle with the life or summer aspect. Persephone, Greek goddess of the seasons, brought summer and life for eight months, and then allowed four months of winter and death as she descended to Hades to be wife of Pluto. The poet here celebrates the dark aspect of the natural cycle, seeing the dark blue gentians of beginning autumn as torches to light his way following Persephone to the "marriage of the living dark."

SNAKE

A man regrets that his education drove him to sin against the lordliness of nature when he tried to kill a snake. In stanzas 1-5, the poet, coming upon a snake drinking at a water-trough, reveres it. In stanzas 6-11, education conflicts with love of nature. Education tells him to fear and kill the poisonous snake, while at the same time he deeply honors it as a guest from the "secret earth." In stanzas 12-14, education wins and the poet throws a log at the departing snake. In stanzas 15-18, he has deep remorse for the "mean act" sprung from his "accursed human education," and he must expiate his sin against "one of the lords/ Of life."

DENISE LEVERTOV

PLEASURES

The poet expresses her love for making unusual objects reveal their concealed beauty. Such discovered secrets satisfy a deep human need, as they fill the "hungry palm."

SOMETHING TO WEAR

A woman through meditation draws beauty from her environment. Like a cat sitting or a woman knitting something to wear to meet another, the thinking poet amid the surrounding clamor makes art and beauty ("stars drumming and poems/ leaping").

THE INSTANT

The "instant" is a moment of enlightenment that occurs when early morning mists clear away to reveal a distant mountain peak with its background of legend. During an early morning search for mushrooms, the view is impressive enough "for a lifetime's look."

C. DAY LEWIS

DO NOT EXPECT AGAIN A PHOENIX HOUR

The lover tells his beloved that the ecstatic joy and passion of early love will grow into a more steady, productive maturity. Stanzas 1-3 tell her not to expect the continuance of the ecstasies of new love—"phoenix hour . . . hot blood . . . lark's ascending . . . spring . . . heatwave." But (stanza 4) the young love will silently grow into rich maturity, described in the imagery of fruitful lands.

NEARING AGAIN THE LEGENDARY ISLE

The poem is a variation of the story of Odysseus and the sirens, adding the theme that age and experience bring disillusionment.

In stanza 1, Odysseus' mariners, returning later to the sirens' isle, wonder what made it so beguiling before. In stanza 2, they see the sirens as cheap ("chorus girls"), old ("past their prime"), and ugly ("paint is wearing thin"). In stanza 4, the mariners themselves are worn ("stripped") and jaded ("mock the theme-song"). Stanza 5 summarizes: sirens are not effective with the "evening skies" of age.

THE CONFLICT

The poet issues a call to take sides in the conflict. Stanzas 1-4 tell that, in the challenging times, the poet sang to keep his "courage up" as the bird makes its "natural answer" or flies high on its own private spirit. He was at peace. But, in stanzas 5-6, neutrality is impossible when there is an important conflict ("two massing powers," "two worlds strive"). Uninvolvement ("innocent wing") or a "private" peace brings destruction ("shot down"). Stanzas 7-8 insist that the "advance of life" calls for united social action ("common," "single") to move from the old life ("where we used to build"). Not to take sides is to die ("only ghosts").

VACHEL LINDSAY

ABRAHAM LINCOLN WALKS AT MIDNIGHT

In a time of war, the poet visualizes the ghost of Abraham Lincoln unable to rest until peace comes. For Lincoln had devoted his life to guiding a "sick world" from war to peace. The mourning figure of Lincoln walks sleepless at midnight in his home town of Springfield, Illinois (stanzas 1-4). He is kept from his sleep by war as peasants, warlords, and dreadnoughts fight (stanzas 5-6). Not until a "spirit-dawn" and a "white peace" come will Lincoln be able to sleep (stanzas 7-8).

THE CONGO

The structure in each of the three sections of this "Study of the Negro Race" makes a shift from a modern scene to the Congo jungle, using for transition the refrain couplet "THEN I SAW THE CONGO . . ."

Part I, "Their Basic Savagery," begins with reveling Negroes in a saloon (lines 1-11), and shifts to savagery in Africa (lines 12-51). Part II, "Their Irrepressible High Spirits," begins with a dance in a gambling hall (lines 1-5), then shifts to a cake-walk in a "Negro fairyland" (lines 6-56). Part III, "The Hope of Their Religion," begins with a Negro revival meeting (lines 1-13) and shifts to a Congo Christian paradise with the witch-men and Mumbo-Jumbo dead and with the Apostles and angels ministering in a "new creation" (lines 14-47). The Mumbo-Jumbo refrain, representing the basic savagery and superstition of the race, is in the first section dominant, in the second subject to derision, and in the third fully defeated by religious hope.

HENRY WADSWORTH LONGFELLOW

HYMN TO THE NIGHT

Night brings peace. When one feels "the calm, majestic presence of the Night," he hears "the sounds·of sorrow and delight" (that is, human experience) and learns that others have borne burdens similar to his. Then peace comes, as to Orestes after he had been pursued by the Furies.

NUREMBERG

Nuremberg's glory was created in the paintings of Albrecht Dürer and the poems of Hans Sachs.

The poem opens with a description of Nuremberg, its historical past, and the importance of art in the city (lines 1-20). In the old time, "when Art was still religion," the immortal Dürer toiled and made the city fairer (lines 21-28). The Mastersingers amid their humble work wrote poetry (lines 29-36). Among these was the famous Hans Sachs. Though his home has now become an ale house in these degenerate times (lines 37-46), he made his city famous by singing the "nobility of labor" (lines 47-52).

THE ARSENAL AT SPRINGFIELD

The poet combines images of sacred music and war to attack war-making.

Stanzas 1-8 compare guns in an arsenal to an organ, and then describe the sounds of war-making as travesties of organ music and of the "celestial harmonies" of nature. Stanzas 9-12 assert that if half the power and wealth given to war-making were devoted to "redeem the human mind from error," then instead of war we would have the peace of Christ and "holy melodies of love."

THE JEWISH CEMETERY AT NEWPORT

In the first half of the poem (lines 1-28) the speaker is impressed by the cemetery. The mysterious quiet of Death in this scene recalls the ancient history and teachings of the Jews. Then the speaker abruptly turns to the bitter thought of the long persecution of the Jews by the Christians, during which the Jews were sustained by "All the great traditions of the past." But, the speaker concludes, once dead the nations never rise again.

THE TIDE RISES, THE TIDE FALLS

The traveler (probably a man approaching the end of life) comes to the town at twilight (stanza 1). During the darkness the sea erases his footprints on the sands (stanza 2), and by morning the traveler has gone, never to return (stanza 3). Throughout (as with a man's life and death), the tide rises and falls.

RICHARD LOVELACE

TO ALTHEA, FROM PRISON

The poet, in prison, uses three main sets of images to express the idea that he is free in spite of walls and bars.

In stanza 1, when he has the love of Althea, the poet is freer than the birds. In stanza 2, when he has companionable drinking ("cups"), he is freer than the fishes. In stanza 3, when he can praise his king, he is freer than the winds. In stanza 4, these three— love, companionship, and loyalty to the king—combine to make the poet free in love and in soul, and so as free as the angels.

TO LUCASTA, GOING TO THE WARS

A conflict between love and honor is resolved by making honor a prerequisite to love.

In stanzas 1-2, the poet asks Lucasta not to think him unkind and unfaithful in leaving her to chase his new mistress, war. For, in stanza 3, he considers love possible only through honor.

AMY LOWELL

PATTERNS

A woman walking in her garden and grieving over the death of her fiancé in war protests against the patterns that have constricted her life. Five dominant restraining patterns are depicted: formal gardens, stiff apparel, sexual restraint, control of grief, and war.

In stanzas 1-2, her passion and softness as a woman war against the formal patterns of garden and costume. In stanzas 3-4, her erotic desires war against sexual restraint, as she imagines a scene in which her lover surprises her bathing in the fountain, pursues her, and embraces her. In stanzas 5-6, her grief at the recent message announcing the death of her fiancé wars against the social demands for control of grief. Stanza 7 gives the climactic protest against the pattern of war which took her fiancé from her and doomed her to a lonely future.

ROBERT LOWELL

AT THE INDIAN KILLER'S GRAVE

The poet considers the despoilations the moderns have made of the relics of the Pilgrim fathers buried in the cemetery.

Smoke from the factories settles upon the graves, the subway burrows underneath, the tall buildings of Mammon cluster around, and the only gesture of reverence to the Pilgrim tradition is that a "public servant putters . . . and paints the railing red." The poet wonders "Who has sowed the dragon's teeth?" and poses his own salvation through Mary and her Son.

CHILDREN OF LIGHT

The poet condemns America for the evil which was in it from the beginning and which continues today.

Our fathers were evil: they built on the bones of the natives, they were "unhoused," and the light they spread was the "Serpent's" (lines 1-5). Today we are evil and outcast: our houses built on the rock (Matt. 7:24) are "riotous glass," our altars are "empty," and we are sons of the exiled murderer Cain (lines 6-10).

COLLOQUY IN BLACK ROCK

Against a background of jackhammers jabbing the ocean, the poet has an ecstatic vision of salvation from death through Christ the kingfisher (fisher of men).

In stanzas 1-3, the Hungarian workmen dig in the black mud at Black Rock to build a church for the martyr Stephen. The poet has two conflicting responses: his heart beats faster, and he thinks of death. All the central images relate to Black Mud as death: workmen giving their blood in Black Mud, the martyr Stephen stoned to death, House of the Savior hanged to death, our ransom "the rubble of his death." In stanza 4, out of the image of mud as death, Christ rises to save from the black water as fisher of men, "wonder of the world." In each stanza the heart beats faster until the mystic experience ("on fire") occurs at the end.

CONCORD

We have fallen so far from the promise of our heritage that we seem beyond salvation.

"Ten thousand Fords" search for a tradition at the shrine of the Minute Men, the Irish Catholics, Walden's "fished-perch," and the Unitarian Church. But "Mammon's unbridled industry" has become so monstrous that the poet wonders how the "white spindling arms" of the crucifix will ever transfix the spread of this evil.

FOR THE UNION DEAD

The poem condemns the lack of public service and human values today in contrast to the unselfish public service of the Union dead.

The public service is illustrated by the public Aquarium (stanzas 1-3), and especially by the monument to Colonel Shaw and his Negro regiment, who died in keeping with the Latin epigraph, "They relinquished all to serve a public thing" (stanzas 6-13). The deterioration of human values is seen in the excavations for the parking lot (stanzas 4-5) and in commercialism, the nuclear blast, and the wrongs to Negroes (stanzas 14-17)—in short, a "savage servility."

IN MEMORY OF ARTHUR WINSLOW

After reviewing his New England heritage and finding that his forbears found no peace in God, the poet seeks his own salvation in Mary and the blood of Christ.

In memory of his grandfather's death (section 1), his burial (section 2), and the poet's return five years later (section 3), the poet recounts a heritage of ambition and achievement. There were the Winslows, Mathers, Pilgrim preachers, the fishing boats, the slave traders, the governors, the silversmiths, and especially the wealth of the grandfather. In section 4, the poet reaches the conclusion that the heritage was without faith—that neither the clippers, the slavers, the father, nor the grandfather reached "the haven of your peace." The poet prays for Mary and the blood of Christ to save him from spiritual death, like Lazarus, and to save him from the hell of his heritage, like the other "Lazarus who was poor."

MR. EDWARDS AND THE SPIDER

Jonathan Edwards is presented as discoursing on spiders, his symbols for man's helplessness in the hands of God and for his torments in hell. The thought of the poem expresses Edward's Calvinistic theology—original sin, predestination, the utter insignificance of man, and the absolute sovereignty of God.

Stanza 1 points out man's inevitable death and destruction. The spiders "purpose nothing" and drift in one direction, to the sea, where they die. Stanza 2 shows man's helplessness against the power of original sin—"treason crackling," "losing game," "sickness past your cure." Stanza 3 shows man's helplessness before God, who "holds you to the pit of hell." Stanza 4 describes the casting of the soul into hell, "the bowels of fierce fire," "the sinner's last retreat." Stanza 5 tells of the especially fierce hell fire reserved for Josiah Hawley, Edward's cousin who led the faction that got Edwards dismissed from his pastorate. Hawley's punishment is to be eternal and he is to be aware—"To die and know it."

THE DRUNKEN FISHERMAN

Using the central metaphor of the saving Christ as the Fisher of Men, the poet seeks his salvation from the present that has violated its heritage, "the glory of past pools."

In stanzas 1-2, the poet fishes for trout "in this bloody sty," with the threat of God's justice ("Jehovah's bow") upon the evil "worm." Stanzas 3-4 link the fishing of his Nantucket whaling ancestors to the spiritual corruption of the present. Life and fishing was once good ("rabbit's foot," "Life danced a jig," "conscience clean"). But now God threatens to "undo/ Man and Creation" in this "pot-hole." In stanza 5, the poet seeks his own salvation from this "dynamited brook" by catching Christ, the Man-Fisher, who will drive back the evil "Prince of Darkness."

WATER

A man and a woman recall the breaking up of their relationship. As they observe the sea-scene before them, the details suggest the decay of their own relationship ("stuck . . . trapped . . . rotting . . . usual gray . . . tearing away . . . mermaid clinging") till "the water was too cold for us."

WINTER IN DUNBARTON

As the winter cold has frozen the poet's cat, so materialistic corruption and spiritual sterility have killed our world.

Stanzas 1-4 describe the cold, the death of the cat, and the "corruption" from industry's "coke-fumes." Stanza 5 extends the materialistic corruption to the grandfather who cheated Charlie Stark and indicts the spiritual barrenness of the father. All that Christ meant to the poet's father was a broken image, "the bronze-age shards."

ARCHIBALD MACLEISH

ARS POETICA

The "art of a poem" is described as three characteristics leading to the summarizing phrase "A poem should not mean/ But be."

First, a poem should be beyond rational expression, "Dumb" and "wordless": like the act of touching "a globed fruit" or "old medallions," or seeing "a sleeve-worn stone" or "flight of birds," a poem should communicate with "mute" significance (lines 1-8). Second, a poem should be beyond rational space-time existence, "motionless in time," like the moon climbing into the sky even though no eye can mark its passage (lines 9-16). And third, a poem should correspond or "be equal to"; that is, a poem should not try to state what is "true," but use symbols which communicate true emotions—such as the two symbols for loss ("grief"), the empty door and fallen leaf. Lines 23-24 summarize that a poem should "be."

"NOT MARBLE NOR THE GILDED MONUMENTS"

The poet, talking to his lover, rejects those praisers of women (such as Shakespeare in Sonnet 55, from which the title of the poem comes) who boast of immortalizing the beauty of their beloved through immortal verse.

In stanzas 1-2, the poet says of the immortalizing praises of women, "These were lies," because the women praised were not immortalized since they are now dead. In stanzas 3-5, the poet asserts that he will not try to force his verse ("words," "line," "beat") to say men will forever remember his beloved's beauty, but the poet will say that her beauty will die and be forgotten. In stanza 6, he says that a "dead man's voice" praising a "dead girl" is a vain affirmation. Therefore, in stanzas 7-8, he will not speak of "undying glory" of "dead women," but he will affirm her beauty now in a moment of time—"Look! It is there!" His affirmation of just this moment has the effect of making the girl immortal ("Till the world ends").

SPEECH TO A CROWD

The poet's speech to all of us ("the crowd") is that instead of seeking meaning in life from various advice-givers, a man must believe in himself and take the pleasures of the world as it exists.

Stanzas 1-3 list various "awaiters of messages"—Christians ("crib in a manger"), ancient Greeks ("oracles"), moderns ("transoms," "Miss Lonely-Hearts"). These, however, receive no help: "There is only earth and the man!" Stanzas 4-13 advise man to look at the world, to see its wonders (the sun, women with lovely breasts), and to take them. Self-confidence will do it: "Tell yourselves there is sun and the sun will rise." As long as man waits for "messages out of the dark," and does not take the world, he will be poor.

THE END OF THE WORLD

The incident of the top of a circus tent blowing off to reveal the starless dark is used as an allegory, as the title indicates.

"Quite unexpectedly," at the end of the world, members of society will be living lives like the trivial routines of circus performers (lines 1-8), in sharp contrast to the sudden stark spread of infinity which shows "nothing—nothing at all" (lines 9-14).

THE LEARNED MEN

The poet questions what intention God had for man's use of his mind.

Stanza 1, including the title, describes the minds of the "learned men," which like horse or ox grow "great in girth" and become dispassionate. Stanza 2 describes the speaker's mind, which like a country hog grows thinner as he grows older, harassed by external circumstances ("flea and dog") and by his own inner turmoil ("love and rage"). Stanza 3 states the poet's inability to let his mind, like that of the learned, grow fat in "sweet content." For the poet's mind, in stanza 4, has remained inquisitive and always unsatisfied ("waste by wanting still").

YOU, ANDREW MARVELL

The poem describes the swift coming on of night, suggesting the passing of a day and possibly of a life.

The speaker lies at noon somewhere in the Western Hemisphere (on the shore of Lake Michigan, according to MacLeish) and feels the night coming on from the "under lands" halfway around the world. He feels the night approaching country by country from near Persia, westward to Spain, across the sea (Atlantic Ocean), and towards the speaker's position "here face downward."

The allusion of the title to Andrew Marvell suggests his famous "To His Coy Mistress" and emphasizes the swift passing of time and of life. "Noon" may be seen as the prime of life, and the "shadow of night" as death. The closing lines of "To His Coy Mistress" ("We cannot make our sun stand still/ Yet we can make him run") may also be implied by the imagery of the poem: as the penumbra of the night moves country by country "up the curving east," of course the sun moves on down the west, thus being made to "run."

LOUIS MACNEICE

BAGPIPE MUSIC

In a rollicking, bouncing poem, MacNeice depicts economic break-
down in England and its special effects of the lower classes.
The working-class speaker wants luxuries—"limousine . . . tiger
rugs . . . bank balance . . . sugar-stick." But the economy is beset
by such evils as low morals ("maidenhead," "sober"), "overpro-
duction," state welfare ("on the parish"), government panaceas
("Herring Board," "grants"), and low wages ("blow the profits").
Any hope of a meaningful existence is "no go."

SUNDAY MORNING

In vain, man tries to give spiritual meaning to Sunday morning by
means of secular activities.
    In lines 1-10, people try to "abstract this day" and make it serve
as an "eternity" to the week of time by "practicing scales," tinker-
ing with a car, or taking an outing "beyond Hindhead." In lines 11-
14, the church spire and bells tell that there is no secular escape
from "weekday time."

THE SUNLIGHT ON THE GARDEN

The poet is glad for what life offers, even knowing time will inevitably take all away.
    We cannot arrest or catch the fading sunlight (stanza 1). The
things we value—freedom, sonnets, birds, dances—are compelled by
the earth, or the grave, to end (stanza 2). Ambition ("flying") and
social protest ("Defying") will end, for, like Antony in *Antony and
Cleopatra*, "We are dying, Egypt, dying" (stanza 3). Still, the speaker
is glad for what life offers—its good and its bad, such as "rain" and
"sunlight," and its human companionship (stanza 4).

CHRISTOPHER MARLOWE

HERO AND LEANDER

Marlowe's account of the two lovers is composed of two sestiads or cantos paraphrased from a version by the Greek Musaeus of the fifth century A.D. Marlowe's poem is noted for its mythological allusions and its sensuous, erotic passages, which relate it to Ovid's account of Hero and Leander in *Heroic Epistles*. The poem is also noted for its mock-heroic and other comic elements—for instance, the hints that Hero is not the virgin that Leander thinks she is, Leander's not knowing what else to do after he has embraced Hero, Hero's screaming when she sees Leander naked at her door, and the slapstick flight of Hero from Leander in her bedroom.

In the first sestiad, lines 1-50 give a description of Hero, "So lovely fair . . . Venus' nun." Lines 51-90 describe "Amorous Leander, beautiful and young." Lines 91-130 show Hero at the Feast of Adonis at Sestos stealing the hearts of men, who, denied, die of grief. In lines 131-198, Hero and Leander meet in Venus' temple, which is decorated with many scenes of the gods making love. There they fall in love at first sight. In lines 199-328, Leander pleads with Hero to "Abandon fruitless, cold virginity." In lines 329-358, when Leander tries to embrace her, she modestly eludes him and suggests, through a slip of the tongue, that he come to visit her. In lines 359-384, when she is ashamed at her slip and vows chastity, Cupid requests the Fates to let the two lovers enjoy one another. The Fates refuse. Lines 385-484 tell why the Fates oppose Love. When Jove interfered in one of Mercury's love affairs, Mercury complained to Love who made the Fates fall in love with Mercury. He asked them to banish Jove, and refused the love of the Fates. So they abhorred both Mercury and Love.

In the second sestiad, lines 1-86, Hero leaves Leander, but he soon visits her. They begin caressing eagerly, and then she insists on preserving her virginity. In lines 87-135, Leander leaves with her hair ribbon and her ring of chastity. In lines 136-226, though rebuked by his father, Leander is mad for Hero and leaps into the Hellespont to swim to her, arriving with the help of Neptune. In lines 227-334, Hero, seeing Leander naked at her door, runs from him to hide in bed, where they finally make love.

THE PASSIONATE SHEPHERD TO HIS LOVE

In this pastoral lyric, the lover, as shepherd, invites the woman, as shepherdess, to "live with me and be my Love." His inducements are the various pleasures of the shepherd's landscape (stanzas 1-3), natural clothes and adornments (stanzas 3-5), and the dancing and singing of shepherds (stanza 6).

ANDREW MARVELL

THE GARDEN

The garden is a symbol of the contemplative life as opposed to the active life.

The first part of the poem (stanzas 1-4) sets the Quiet and Innocence of the Garden against the vain activities of ambition (stanza 1), of rude society (stanza 2), and of love (stanzas 3-4).

The second part of the poem (stanzas 5-8) shows the happiness of the contemplative life. In wondrous contemplation, the mind finds happiness (stanzas 5-6), the soul finds release like a bird (stanza 7), and the lost innocence of Eden returns (stanza 8).

Such a life gives a sense of timelessness, using for its clock the herbs and flowers and the seasonal sun (stanza 9).

TO HIS COY MISTRESS

In this *carpe diem* ("seize the day") poem, the poet's acute sense of the brevity of life leads him to urge his mistress to make the most of life and love.

In lines 1-20, the poet tells how leisurely he would love her if they had world enough and time to do so. With world enough, she could be by the Ganges River in India and he by the Humber River in England. With time enough, he would allow his slow-moving "vegetable love" to spend at least an age to adore each part of her beautiful body and heart.

But, in lines 21-32, the poet warns that time moves fast like a "winged chariot," that the next life is like vast deserts, and that no loving is done in the grave.

So, in lines 33-46, the poet pleads urgently for pleasure and love now. Rather than languishing and letting time crush the two lovers, he urges that they seize the day. Like "birds of prey," they should devour time, and they should hurl all their strength and sweetness like a ball at the "iron gates of life." Thus it will be they who will make time move ("make our sun . . . run") rather than the other way around.

GEORGE MEREDITH

LUCIFER IN STARLIGHT

Lucifer, the symbol of defiance, rises from Hell and looks for further prey beyond earth. Instead, he has to sink back, for he finds himself controlled by "The army of unalterable law."

THE LARK ASCENDING

The speaker describes the lark flying and singing as an analogy to the poet.

As he rises, the lark sings, and his notes spread like ripples of water. As he flies even higher, he reaches further and further and he turns this ecstasy into sound. He wants all to hear his spontaneous song that says "That he is joy." He proceeds in his free and unrestrained song, and the best in us responds to him (lines 1-64).

His song does not leave the earth, but includes earthly things, and we shall know the bitter side of things in hearing the song (lines 65-86). Unlike the bird, we lack the power of combining truth and music in a song "free of taint of personality" and therefore able to be truly representative of humanity (lines 87-100).

We have on earth men who, because of their strength and because they love the Earth, provide substance for song. This truth is heard in the bird's song and so human life is showered down in the song. The lark goes higher and he finally disappears, "and then the fancy sings," that is, the imagination takes over when the actual song leaves off (lines 101-124).

EDNA ST. VINCENT MILLAY

EUCLID ALONE HAS LOOKED ON BEAUTY BARE

Beauty is equated with a sense of infinity.

The poet praises Euclid for conveying this sense of infinity ("nothing," "nowhere") through his pure mathematical reasoning. Such an elevated experience ("holy, terrible day") is not for people of trivial sensibilities ("geese"). To noble people ("heroes"), it gives a feeling of freedom ("From dusty bondage"), of "Beauty," and of strength ("massive sandal set on stone").

GOD'S WORLD

The poet expresses her ecstatic love of nature during an autumn day.

She personifies (stanza 1) the "World" of wind, mist, woods, and crag, and she aches to clasp it to her. This particular day (stanza 2) elicits almost more emotion than the poet can stand. One more falling leaf or the call of a bird would be unbearable.

JUSTICE DENIED IN MASSACHUSETTS

The "justice denied" is the execution of Nicola Sacco and Bartolomeo Vanzetti, supposedly convicted with insufficient evidence for political reasons, for robbery and murder. To present this injustice as evidence of a blighted society, the poet uses the symbol of farmlands.

Lines 1-22 call upon the workers to leave the once productive "gardens" (American society), for they are now unfruitful—sour, grown with weeds, the beneficent sun gone, the hay-rack empty. According to lines 22-29, what we have inherited from our forefathers ("splendid dead")—literally, our valuable traditions—has been overwhelmed by evil. So, in lines 30-36, nothing remains but to wait for death and to hand on to posterity a "blighted earth."

OH, SLEEP FOREVER IN THE LATMIAN CAVE

The poet laments the "hot and sorrowful sweetness" of mortal love, because of which one "wanders mad." In the classic myth the poet draws from, Endymion, mortal lover of Artemis, goddess of the moon, is doomed to sleep forever in Mount Latmos.

In lines 1-8, the poet tells Endymion that he can lie oblivious of Artemis in her troubled condition after the love episode. But, in lines 9-12, Artemis suffers an "altered state" since her immortal nature was joined by the mortal "dust" through Endymion. And Artemis (lines 13-14), being unfit for mortal love with its intensities and disparities ("hot and sorrowful sweetness") and being unable to die or sleep as Endymion, "wanders mad."

ON HEARING A SYMPHONY OF BEETHOVEN

A Beethoven symphony gives the speaker escape from the real world of "excellence and peace."

This imaginatively-created world is thought of as an enchanted city with "towers" and a "rampart." The sleeping "scullions in the fairy-tale" suggest the enchanted Sleeping Beauty. The enchanted world of music gives meaning for mankind instead of chaos ("plausible," "purpose"), magnanimity instead of sordidness ("spiteful," "rude"), and a sense of life instead of death ("let me live"). Time and death do not exist in enchanted lands, only under the "aging sun."

PITY ME NOT BECAUSE THE LIGHT OF DAY

The heart is to be pitied because it is slow to learn that love is fleeting.

In lines 1-8 the poet asks not to be pitied because she is victim of the transitoriness both of nature ("light," "field," "moon," "tide") and of love ("man's desire"). For, in lines 9-12, her mind has always known that love is as fleeting as the things of nature. In lines 13-14, it is her heart she asks pity for, because it is slow to learn this transitoriness.

RENASCENCE

The poet relates an experience of spiritual death and rebirth ("Renascence"). Stanzas 1-5 describe the death of a soul too small to bear infinity. Stanzas 6-7 give the prayer for rebirth. Stanzas 8-11 describe the rebirth with a soul large enough to grasp the Infinite.

In stanzas 1-2 the speaker thinks she is bounded by finite perceptions of mountain, wood, island, and sky. Then, in stanza 3, she is suddenly appalled by a sense of infinity. In stanzas 4-5, in her infinite knowledge she feels the sufferings of all people ("All sin," "fierce fire," "starving," "screams"), but with a soul too small to bear such "awful weight," she craves and finds death.

In stanzas 6-7, soothed by the "pitying rain" and remembering the beauty of earth after a shower, she prays God for a "new birth."

In stanzas 8-11, she is reborn, was "dead and lives again," with a soul large enough (not "flat") to know the infinite God in nature ("see Thee pass," "on Thy heart").

SPRING

The poet is disillusioned because April's law of life does not apply to man.

April and spring promise hope and new life in "leaves opening" and the "smell of earth," and in proclaiming that apparently "there is no death." But the poet knows not only that man dies and is "Eaten by maggots" but that life itself has no purpose or promise ("nothing," "empty cup").

WHAT LIPS MY LIPS HAVE KISSED

This is a nostalgic lament for the passing of love and youth.

In lines 1-8, a woman is stirred, as by ghosts, to remember the men she has loved. Her memory of specifics is vague, but she feels intensely ("quiet pain") the loss of the loves once experienced and now gone forever. Lines 9-14 express her consequent bitterly lonely condition in metaphors of bird, tree, and winter. Once in summer the birds sang in the tree. Now the tree stands alone in the winter.

JOHN MILTON

HOW SOON HATH TIME, THE SUBTLE THIEF OF YOUTH

Though feeling the pressure of time and having made no apparent achievements, the poet shows his willingness to rest in the Divine Will.

In lines 1-8, the poet, made aware of time's swiftness by finishing his twenty-third year, laments that he has achieved nothing that can be seen outwardly—no "bud or blossom." Though he may be inwardly mature and ready to achieve, yet this "inward ripeness" can not as readily be seen in him as it can in other people. Yet, in lines 9-14, he is content to let time and the will of heaven join—to let God, his "great Task-Master," direct his destiny.

IL PENSEROSO

This poem extols the life of contemplation in contrast to its companion poem, "L'Allegro," which extols the life of gay sociability.

In lines 1-10, the poet drives Joys away. In lines 11-60, he calls for Melancholy to come with Peace, Quiet, Fast, Leisure, and especially Contemplation. In lines 61-120, the poet woos Melancholy through evening and night, first in nature (woods, moon, evening sounds), then in scholarly studies in a lonely tower. In lines 121-176, he asks to go with Melancholy during a rainy morning. When the sun gets bright, he wants to dream by some hidden stream and to seek a religious cloister.

L'ALLEGRO

This poem extols the life of gay sociability in contrast to its companion poem, "Il Penseroso," which extols the life of contemplation.

In lines 1-10, the poet drives Melancholy away. In lines 11-39, he calls for Mirth, to come with Jest, Jollity, Sport, Laughter, and Liberty. In lines 40-90, Mirth is to conduct him through the pleasures of nature, including pastòral love. In lines 91-152, Mirth is to lead him to the social festivities of the village—such as dancing, telling of tales, the theatre, and music.

LYCIDAS

The poet laments the death of his fellow student, Edward King, who died when his ship foundered. The poem is a pastoral elegy in which Milton and his friend King (Lycidas) appear as shepherds.

After calling upon laurels and myrtles in honor of his friend (lines 1-14), and after invoking the muses for inspiration (lines 15-

22), the poet describes the former happy companionship of his friend and him (lines 23-36) and the consequent mourning of nature at Lycidas' death (lines 37-49). The poet is then moved to blame the muses for allowing the death, but realizes that not even their presence at the scene of the wreck could have saved Lycidas (lines 50-63). Such fatalism leads the poet to doubt the value of fame and achievement, when the "thin-spun life" can be so easily cut by the fates, but Phoebus tells him the reward of achievement is in heaven (lines 64-84). Various mourners associated with water pass by, notably Neptune, who finds no reason for the ship to sink in a calm sea (lines 85-107), and St. Peter, who mourns the loss of Lycidas because a corrupt clergy needed him (lines 108-131). The poet calls for nature's flowers to deck the hearse (lines 132-150), thinks of Lycidas' body washed in the seas (lines 151-164), and tells the shepherds not to weep because Lycidas has become immortal with God and the saints above (lines 165-185). His song ended, the poet-shepherd departs to "fresh woods and pastures new" (lines 186-193).

METHOUGHT I SAW MY LATE ESPOUSED SAINT

The poet, lamenting the death of his wife, had a vision of her return.

In lines 1-4, he imagined her return like the ancient Greek Alcestis, who went to death and returned to save her husband. In lines 5-12, though she was "veiled" to the blind poet, he fancied her face as shining with "Love, sweetness, goodness." In lines 13-14, the poet sank to grief as the vision fled.

WHEN I CONSIDER HOW MY LIGHT IS SPENT

The poet, lamenting the limitations imposed on him by blindness, finds absolute repose in the Divine Will.

In lines 1-8, the poet fears God will call him to account for not using his abilities, even though he is blind and tries to serve God. In lines 8-14, Patience replies that God, being self-sufficient, does not need man's labor. The best service to God is patience ("yoke," "stand and wait").

MARIANNE MOORE

IN DISTRUST OF MERITS

The poet distrusts the traditional merits of war; the real merit of fighting is to teach us to conquer the evil within us that causes war. In stanza 1, the poet states that fighting is not for "medals and positioned victories," but against the "blind man" who enslaves and hates. Stanza 2 calls for Jew and Christian to "be joined at last" not in hate but in love. Stanzas 3-5 assert that the real fight is against the disease of "Self," from which comes the lack of trust that produces hate. Stanzas 6-9 point out that the fighting, the bloodshed, and the dyings will not be wasted if they "can teach us how to live"—to conquer the evil within us that causes war.

POETRY

In answer to the objection to "all this fiddle" of poetry, the poet agrees that poetry must be genuine, but that genuineness also includes the imaginative.

In stanzas 1-3, the poet defends the "place for the genuine" in poetry. When poetry becomes derivative to the point of being unintelligible, we do not admire it, as illustrated by several other unintelligible actions: "the bat/ holding on . . . elephants pushing . . . immovable critic . . . baseball fan . . . school-books." Stanzas 4-5 point out that these phenomena are important but they cannot be expressed by "half poets," who are imitative and ungenuine. Genuine poetry is both real and imaginative: "imaginary gardens with real toads in them."

THE MIND IS AN ENCHANTING THING

In expanding her description of the mind as "an enchanting thing," the poet uses a series of metaphors to explain this enchantment as being due to the many aspects of the mind in action.

The mind is many-faceted, like a "katy-did wing" (stanza 1). It is exploratory in feeling its way like an "apteryx-awl" (stanza 2). It is unequivocal and certain in using memory, like the "gyroscope's fall" (stanza 3). In its conscientious inconsistency it is like the dove-neck "animated by sun" (stanza 4). In piercing illusions, it "tears off the veil" (stanza 5). The final stanza reiterates the dominant conception of stanza 1: as the "iridescence" of the dove-neck, the mind is many-faceted.

THE STEEPLE JACK

The poet, viewing a seaside town, sees a resemblance to the work of the painter-engraver Dürer. (Dürer's use of sharp detail, his ability to fuse disparate things, and his concern with unusual angles of perspective would have given him a "reason for living in a town" with "so/ much confusion.")

The confusion is composed of such things as marsh grass, schoolhouse, post office, hen-houses, a schooner. Central to the perspective are a steeple-jack on the church steeple and a danger sign which the steeple-jack has placed by the church. The poet sees the danger sign as doubly disparate: that these "simple people" should need a danger sign, and that the church, which carries the sign of hope, should be marked by a danger sign.

TO A STEAM ROLLER

The poet addresses a steam roller, personifying it as one who tries to remove all fine distinctions in aesthetic judgment and to reduce everything to a "close conformity." It crushes "all the particles," the "Sparkling chips," down to the "parent block." Such a heavy-handed trait makes the steam roller the opposite, or "complement," of the delicacy of a butterfly.

WHAT ARE YEARS?

The poet paradoxically sees mortality as the way to immortality.

Lines 1-10 describe mortality ("innocence . . . guilt . . . naked . . . courage") as elusive and paradoxical ("resolute doubt," "dumbly calling," "deafly listening"). Lines 11-25 state that this paradox leads man to accept his mortal state as a means of eventual spiritual renewal, as the sea is renewed by surrendering to the storm, and the caged bird through "his mighty singing" transcends his prison to attain pure joy. So, in lines 26-27, mortality is the only avenue by which immortality (pure joy) and eternity can be reached.

WILLIAM MORRIS

THE DAY IS COMING

The poet addresses a song of Socialist prophecy to England. There will be a time of social and economic equality. Men shall live decently and work in happiness and security. The arts and other aspects of culture shall flourish. People have only to say "WE WILL IT" to bring such a beautiful day into being.

THE DEFENCE OF GUENEVERE

Guenevere speaks in her own defense as she is about to be burned at the stake for adultery.

In a mood of defiance combined with shame, Guenevere begins her statement (lines 1-10). Although such great lords as those she faces must be right in their accusations, she asks them to suppose that they had to choose between two cloths, one meaning heaven and one meaning hell, in complete ignorance (lines 11-39). She did not understand the meaning of her own action in choosing Lancelot until he went away and she had time to think (lines 40-45). She cries out that Gawaine (her accuser) lies. After a brief inward struggle, she throws off her shame (lines 46-60).

At Lancelot's appearance at Arthur's court, Guenevere says, she was overcome by him. In her confusion, she chose between Arthur, who cared little for her, and Lancelot, who loved her greatly. She asked herself if she must give up love forever. So, still resisting, she finally gave herself to Lancelot (lines 61-141).

Guenevere now appeals to Sir Gawaine's pity, but, when he turns away (lines 142-165), she resumes her account. At his castle, Guenevere says Mellyagraunce had accused her of false conduct because of blood stains found in her bed. Guenevere held that it was beneath her dignity to defend herself against this charge. Lancelot came to her rescue and killed Mellyagraunce in combat, thus proving the charges against her were false (lines 166-220). Guenevere warns her present accusers to take warning from this example and proceeds to demonstrate her innocence by appealing to her own beauty (lines 220-241). Lancelot had come to her room, she says, at her invitation. She was lonely and depressed, and he helped her pass the night until confusion entered (lines 242-276). Guenevere breaks off abruptly and once again protests that she speaks the truth. Then she falls silent. Suddenly, Lancelot arrives to rescue her (lines 277-295).

THE HAYSTACK IN THE FLOODS

This is the tragic story of a woman who, along with her lover, has been captured by their enemy.

As she faces the present disaster, Jehane thinks back to when the capture had occurred. She had been riding in a wretched state with Robert and his men in dangerous territory. They came upon the enemy, Godmar, who barred their way with thirty men, twice their number (lines 1-38). Robert tries to reassure her, but she sees her alternatives as returning to Paris to face shame and death or to live sinfully with Godmar (lines 39-59). Robert's men refuse to support him, and he is captured. Godmar says he will spare Robert's life if Jehane will sleep with him; she refuses. She threatens Godmar if he rapes her, and he threatens to take her back to Paris. Still Jehane refuses. Even as Jehane and Robert try to kiss each other, Godmar seizes Robert and kills him (lines 60-151). Then Godmar takes the broken Jehane to his castle (lines 152-160).

EDWIN MUIR

THE HORSES

The people whose mechanized civilization was destroyed by war prefer primitive rebeginnings to the return of the "old bad world."

Lines 1-15 describe the seven-days' war that "put the world to sleep." Lines 15-30 assert that the people do not want the return of the destroyed world. Instead they return to primitive methods of life, rejecting tractors for oxen. Lines 31-53 tell of the coming of the horses, who bring their "long-lost archaic companionship" as if from Eden to help the people begin again.

THOMAS NASHE

A LITANY IN TIME OF PLAGUE

In a time of plague, the poet is moved by the imminence of death and calls upon God's mercy. He bids farewell to earth's joys, for life is uncertain (stanza 1). Nothing can prevail against death—the gold of the rich man (stanza 2), the beauty of the most beautiful women (stanza 3), the strength and swords of heroes (stanza 4), wit or art (stanza 5). Therefore stanza 6 calls for men of each class or "degree" to turn their thoughts from earth to heaven.

WILDRED OWEN

ANTHEM FOR DOOMED YOUTH

The dominant metaphor of a funeral service is used to lament the "doomed youth" who die in war.

Stanza 1 asks what are the funeral bells for the dead, and the ironic answer is that the sounds are not religious anthems, orisons, and choirs, but the rattle and wailing of shells. Stanza 2 tells what the "candles" and other items at the coffin will be. They will be the sadness of the loved ones left behind—"goodbyes" of boys, "pallor" of girls, and "tenderness of patient minds."

APOLOGIA PRO POEMATE MEO

The poet gives, according to the Latin title, an explanation for his poetry: he sees God in his soldier-comrades' keeping their beauty and nobility amid the ugliness of war.

Amid the death and horror, the soldiers maintain their glory and laughter (stanzas 1-2), courage (stanza 3), exultation (stanza 4), fellowship deeper than love between man and woman (stanzas 5-6), and beauty in courage, duty, and peace (stanza 7). Only one who has shared their "sorrowful dark of hell" (stanza 8) is worthy of them (stanza 9).

ARMS AND THE BOY

The poem asserts that the boy must be taught to kill, that fighting and killing are not natural to him as to the beasts.

In stanza 1, the boy is shown the killing qualities of the bayonet with its "hunger of blood." In stanza 2, he is given bullets which long to kill and have sharp teeth. In stanza 3, the boy is compared with the beasts. The beasts are equipped by nature for killing with claws, talons, and antlers, while the boy's teeth "seem for laughing round an apple" and his "curls" suggest the child's harmlessness. He is not equipped by nature for killing, and must be taught.

DULCE ET DECORUM EST

The horrible incident of the death of a soldier prepares for the resolution of the poem: "The old lie."

In lines 1-8, the bedraggled soldiers trudge along. In lines 9-16, the gas comes and one man is caught without his mask. In lines 17-28, the poet tells the readers that if they could realize the horrors of war as seen in the gassed soldier, they would not tell the "old lie" of the Latin quotation: "It is sweet and proper to die for one's country."

FUTILITY

The death of a soldier leads the poet to question the worth of human existence.

The sun as life-force (stanza 1) once woke the dead man in his pre-war home life, "Gently," "Always." The same sun (stanza 2) "wakes the seeds" and caused the very beginning of human life ("woke the clay") on the "cold star" earth. Yet, if this dead man grew up ("clay grew tall") only to die in war, then perhaps it is better that life should never have appeared on earth.

GREATER LOVE

An apostrophe to love shows how insignificant is physical love to the sublime love of soldiers who gave their lives for their friends.

Beauty ("red lips," "eye") and kindness are ordinary when compared to the sacrifices of the dead (stanza 1). The grace ("attitude") of a lover is unexciting by comparison with the grotesque positions of death (stanza 2). The lover's voice is not so dear as were the voices of the dead men (stanza 3). Hearts and hands of warriors are in their supreme sacrifice superior to the heart and hands of the lover (stanza 4). The poet concludes that weeping may be in order for the "English dead," but they are beyond human grief.

EDGAR ALLAN POE

A DREAM WITHIN A DREAM

The poet laments that everything in life slips quickly away from him like a "dream within a dream."

In stanza 1, the poet parts from someone with a kiss, saying that with all hope gone, all is a "dream within a dream." In stanza 2, he tries to grasp something from life, but all things slip from him as sand through the fingers. The poet weeps because he can save nothing.

ANNABEL LEE

A few details tell this story of love and grief. Though the lovers were young, they loved with "a love that was more than love." The reference to "her highborn kinsmen" implies a conflict with the girl's family. Stanzas 2-4 say that the seraphs and angels, envying their love, sent the chilling wind that killed Annabel Lee. But their love is stronger than kinsmen, angels, or demons. The speaker feels that Annabel Lee is with him still in spirit (lines 24-27), and in his desire to be near her he returns to her tomb "by the sounding sea."

DREAM-LAND

The dream world of "ultimate dim Thule" is a place "Out of SPACE —out of TIME." Its forms strain the imagination: "mountains toppling . . . Into seas without a shore" and "Seas . . . Surging into skies of fire." Here, in the "unholy" and "melancholy" places, the traveler meets the "Memories of the Past" and the "White-robed forms of friends" long dead. It is a mysterious region, soothing to the sorrowful spirit, which, however, it is forbidden to view except "through darkened glasses."

ELDORADO

The poet describes man's search for the unattainable. Eldorado, meaning "city of gold" in Spanish, was the fabled rich city vainly sought for by the early explorers of the Western world.

The young knight is gay and gallant in stanza 1 as he searches for the fabulous city, but in stanza 2 he turns sad as he grows old and fails in his quest. In stanza 3, he asks the ghost of a pilgrim where to find Eldorado; the ghost replies, in stanza 4, that he must go to the moon and to death. That is, Eldorado is not attainable in this life.

ISRAFEL

Israfel, an angel in the Mohammedan heaven, sings "so wildly well" that he arrests the attention even of the levin (lightning) and the Pleiads. He is inspired in his passionate music by all the beauty and wisdom ("the ecstasies") of heaven (stanzas 3-5). By contrast, the poet lives in this world, where "flowers are merely—flowers." If the poet could change places with Israfel, perhaps the angel might not sing "so wildly well" while the poet might sing "a bolder note."

LENORE

Stanzas 1 and 3 represent a conventional attitude of ritual grief for the death of a beautiful young woman. Stanzas 2 and 4 are the lover's retort. He first accuses the conventional ones of hypocrisy, for in reality they were responsible for Lenore's death with their "evil eye" and "slanderous tongue." He will not mourn, "lest the sweet soul . . . should catch the note." Instead, he rejoices that she is going "to a golden throne."

SONNET—TO SCIENCE

The poet reproaches science for destroying the world of myth and romance.

In lines 1-4, the poet questions science who "alterest all things" and who, with its "dull realities," preys like a vulture upon the poet's heart. So, in lines 5-8, the poet says he cannot love science or consider her wise. Lines 9-14 list some of the specific items of myth and romance driven away by science.

THE CITY IN THE SEA

The poet evokes the grim, triumphant power of death in this mood poem. The city of the dead is completely alien to human life (line 8). An eerie light from the still waters "Streams" and "Gleams." There is no movement in "that wilderness of glass." The waters are "hideously serene." If there is a movement (lines 42-43), it suggests that the city of Death is in itself settling, eventually to disappear (lines 50-51). This image gives a final touch to the ironic power of death, here destroying its own creation.

THE RAVEN

The narrator, grieving over his lost Lenore, shows himself on the verge of mental collapse. When he hears a noise but finds no human being at the door (stanza 4), he imagines that it might be the spirit of his lost Lenore (stanza 5). When the Raven enters, the narrator at first accepts it in a realistic manner (stanzas 8-9), but he soon lashes himself into an emotional frenzy. Each question he asks the bird makes increasingly appropriate the meaningless word "Nevermore." By the end the Raven has become not only the symbol of death but also a symbol of the darkening soul of the bereaved narrator (lines 105-108).

TO HELEN

Helen, an idealized conception, symbolizes peace, serenity, and beauty. Each stanza brings out a different implication. Stanza 1 suggests the nostalgia of a wanderer. Stanza 2 suggests the serene beauty and power of antiquity. Stanza 3 suggests the beauty of art ("statue-like") pervaded by the spirit (lines 14-15).

TO ONE IN PARADISE

The poet tells of his sadness over the death of a loved one. She had been all that his soul desired (stanza 1). But since that dream ended by her death, he cannot go "On! on!" but hovers lifelessly in the past (stanza 2). For his "Life is o'er," and he is like a stricken eagle or a tree blasted by lightning (stanza 3). He now lives only in his dreams of the one who is by the "eternal streams" of paradise (stanza 4).

ULALUME

The speaker recalls the time when he wandered with "Psyche, my Soul" into the gloomy region of Weir (stanzas 1-2). They did not recognize the surroundings (stanza 3), but they did notice the moon rising just before dawn (stanza 4). The speaker believes the light is a good omen (stanza 5), but Psyche is fearful (stanza 6). By this light they come upon "the vault of thy lost Ulalume" (stanzas 7-8), which brings back memory and grief (stanza 9). Then they think that perhaps the light was meant to bar the way from the terrible memory (stanza 10). The poem ends in a question, as though it is doubtful whether the memory of the experience ("the thing that lies hidden in the wolds") is good or evil.

ALEXANDER POPE

AN ESSAY ON CRITICISM

The three parts of Pope's statement of the neo-classic principles of criticism deal respectively with (1) the importance of following Nature and learning from the ancients in forming one's critical judgment, (2) specific principles of judgment and pitfalls to be avoided, and (3) an admonition to use moderation, courage, and learning in forming and stating critical views. Part III concludes with a survey of famous critics.

Part I
It is less dangerous to write poorly than to judge poorly because poor criticism is much more common than poor writing (lines 1-8). Critics are overly partial to their own judgments, though "true taste"

is as rare as "true genius" in poetry (lines 9-18). Although Nature has endowed most with the potential for sound judgment, some are misled by "false learning" and confused by various schools of criticism so that many fools write bad criticism (lines 19-35). There is a breed of writer who is neither wit nor critic. It is very hard to tell just what breed he is (lines 36-45). Pope advises the true critic to assess his own abilities justly and to remain within their limits (lines 46-51).

Nature has fixed limits to all things, including men's abilities. All men should accept the fact that each is limited to his one "science" (lines 52-67). The critic should base his judgment on the "universal light" of Nature. The effect of this invisible but inspiring force of Nature is seen in art, as the soul gives graceful form to the body. Some lack the judgment to control wit properly (lines 68-87). Those rules discovered long ago are Nature put in an order or system that actually comes from Nature herself (lines 88-91). Ancient Greece wrote down Nature's rules, and her critics praised her great virtues, and urged others to try for the same heights. Drawing their rules from the heaven-inspired parts, the ancient critics taught the world how to admire. Later, a debased breed of critics turned from just praise of poets to setting themselves up too high, and became pedantic and dull (lines 92-117).

Prospective critics should form their judgment by carefully studying the ancients, particularly Homer (lines 118-129). When young Virgil applied his great genius to writing, he soon discovered that Homer's rules were the same as Nature's rules, and so he wrote within the limits of classical rules (lines 130-140).

Some beauties in art come by inspiration, not precept. The inspired poet, ignoring the rules, may leap directly to his effect. But moderns should ignore the ancient rules seldom, and then only from necessity (lines 141-168). Some of these "freer beauties" may seem objectionable when viewed in isolation, but if viewed in the total perspective, they are seen to be part of a harmonious whole.

The great writers of antiquity are still praised by the learned, as they have always been praised and as they will be praised in the future. Part I concludes with a plea that "some spark of your celestial fire" may inform the present poet (Pope) "to teach vain wits" a proper humility in their attitude (lines 169-180).

Part II
Pride is the chief cause of "erring judgment." Right reason brings us the "resistless day" of truth (lines 201-214). Limited knowledge

causes us to think we know more than we do. We should go beyond the first artistic attempts of youth, for the further we go, the more challenges we find (lines 215-232).

Critics should judge a work of art as a whole, and should not censure certain parts if the whole is harmonious, for nature attends to the whole (lines 232-252). No piece of art is entirely faultless. We must observe the writer's intention and judge him by that. Judges should not dwell too much on minor faults; most critics judge a work according to one minor point (lines 253-266). It is told of Don Quixote that he discoursed wisely to "a certain bard" upon Aristotle's rules. His pronouncements seemed entirely balanced until he insisted that a combat be staged (lines 267-284). So critics of poor judgment insist upon a part, rather than the total effect (lines 285-288).

Some critics look to extravagant expressions of wit (conceits), but true wit is universal in content and "well expressed." Wit should appear in moderation (lines 289-304). Other critics judge writing by its style. But "False eloquence" is likely to cover a dearth of content. True expression justly reveals and enhances the thought. The style should suit the content, and the writer should be careful to avoid words that are either too old or too new (lines 305-336). Most critics judge a poet by the smoothness or roughness of the verse, even though it may be feeble and trite. Good writing requires art. The sound of the words should echo the sense (lines 337-383). Moderation should govern judgment (lines 384-393).

Some critics praise only certain groups of writers, such as foreign or native, ancient or modern. The standard should be truth (lines 394-407). Some critics echo only the popular mood of the day. Some judge not by the writing itself but by the author. Thus, a servile critic may praise terrible verse written by a lord (lines 408-423).

Other critics err on the side of singularity. Their criterion is that their opinions be different—different from others' opinions and constantly changing, so that their latest opinion is the right one (lines 424-451). Some critics see themselves as "the measure of mankind," and praise those who reflect their own ideas. Great writers (such as Dryden and Homer) have been subjected to petty criticism and have survived to become universally honored, as the sun at first draws up vapors, but then the clouds at last "augment the day" (lines 452-473). The critic should be quick to praise "true merit" in writing, for fame now lasts for a much shorter time than it did formerly. The language in which the poet writes is less acceptable with the passing years, as the colors of a master painter fade and "betray" his great conception (lines 474-493).

The ill-considered use of wit arouses envy. Although this wit is tolerable in youth, it causes a great deal of trouble, like a wife who, being admired, causes much worry and vexation. This wit is feared by the vicious, shunned by the virtuous, hated by fools, and undone by knaves (lines 494-507). If wit suffers from ignorance, knowledge should not also be its enemy. In old times, the victorious received rewards and those who tried had praise. Now, the successful poets spurn the efforts of some of the unsuccessful ones. The worst writers give praise with most regret, for a poor writer is a bad friend. The critic should always endeavor to join good nature and good sense (lines 508-525). If the critic still has a sour temper, he should vent his spleen on the proper objects, like the obscenity, idle luxury, and debased morals of the time of Charles II and the religious scepticism of the "foreign reign," that of William III. These blasphemers should be engaged by the critics. Nevertheless, the critic should be careful not to see vice everywhere he looks (lines 526-559).

Part III
Learning and judgment are about half of a critic's task. He must learn to speak so that he is liked as well as respected (lines 560-565). The critic should speak confidently but without self-assertion, and he should learn from his past errors (lines 566-571). Truths should be taught with due allowance for men's feelings (lines 572-577). The critic should be sparing of advice where there is not enough merit to bother with. He should not be so courteous that he fails to criticize when criticism is warranted, for good writers can best take criticism (lines 578-583). Poor writers become angry at criticism, and it is sometimes best to let the dullards go their way without criticism (lines 584-609). Some critics also are blockheads. Though they have read widely, their heads are full of "learned lumber." They attack everything they read without fear. Good sense speaks with caution, but these fools talk "rattling nonsense" (lines 610-630).

The ideal critic is a man of balance, a learned and humane man (lines 631-642). In ancient Athens and Rome there were a few such critics. Aristotle, studying Homer, discovered the great truths of literary art and persuaded poets to follow his rules of art (lines 643-652). Horace wrote with judgment and grace. Our critics, on the contrary, judge "with fury" but write sluggishly (lines 653-664). Dionysius (of Halicarnassus) points out "new beauties" in every line of Homer (lines 556-666). Petronius Arbiter in his criticism combines "The scholar's learning, with the courtier's ease" (lines 667-668). In Quintilian we find the "useful arms" of criticism (lines 669-674). Longinus is always just in his criticism and is himself an example of the sublime he writes about (lines 675-680). Learning and the arts grew as Rome grew. Then, with the fall of Rome, learning fell. Dullness and the monks finished what the Goths began (lines 681-692). At length, Erasmus appeared and brought back the light of learning (lines 693-696). Under Pope Leo X, the arts once more flourished: sculpture, architecture, music, painting, poetry, and criticism (lines 697-708). Soon the arts were forced out of Latium. Criticism flourished in France, but Britains stayed free of rules and remained "uncivilized." Some, however, recognized the rightness of ancient rules. Among these were Roscommon and Walsh. The latter has given Pope just and helpful criticism. With Walsh now dead, Pope's muse is now content if he reveals their ignorance to the unlearned and causes the learned to reflect on what they know. He is now a balanced and reasonable muse (lines 709-744).

AN ESSAY ON MAN

Pope treats his subject, Man, from various points of view: Epistle I, Man's relationship to God and the universe at large: Epistle II, psychology, which deals with the passions and the reason; Epistle III, the evaluation of society and its present debased condition; Epistle IV, happiness and how to achieve it.

Epistle I
Pope opens with an invitation to St. John (Viscount Bolingbroke) to join him in exploring all the varied aspects of the subject Man (lines 1-16).

We begin, Pope says, by admitting that we can reason about God only from what we know here on earth (section 1). Man should not question his endowments, for he is placed here on earth in a position that is right relative to other things of God's creation, nor should man question the purpose of his being here (section 2). Man is fortunately not endowed with foreknowledge, but he does have hope, like the Indian, who has his vision of heaven (section 3). Man errs in "reasoning pride" when he tries, with his puny mind, to judge the total scheme of things (section 4). Pride says that all things exist for man's happiness. But on reflection, natural evils such as earthquakes and human evils such as a Borgia or a Cataline also raise the question of divine purpose. It is probably better that "all subsists by elemental strife" (section 5). Each creature has been given its proper powers, and man's bliss is to act and be content with the abilities he has been given by a wise Providence (section 6). Man sits at the top of the scale of creation, which ranges from the lowest to the highest in orderly gradation (section 7). All the elements in the mighty order of the chain of being are interdependent. Man in his pride must not strive to break this order (section 8). All things in nature are equally pervaded by the spirit of God (section 9). Man should humbly accept the existing state of things, for "Whatever is, is right" (section 10).

Epistle II
Man should, then, be content to study himself and not speculate on the nature of God. Indeed, man finds himself a puzzling set of contradictions. He studies science and speculates in the highest reaches of philosophy—and finds himself a fool. He should be cautious in his claims to knowledge (section 1). "Two principles" govern human nature: self-love and reason. They are both needed. The one promotes action; "it prompts, impels, inspires." The other exercises restraint and gives directions to otherwise aimless impulses (section 2). The passions are necessary to man, for he is made for action, not for apathy. With due guidance from the reason, the passions "Make and maintain the balance of the mind." Each man has a ruling passion, which can lead to evil or to good, depending upon the ability of reason to lead the right direction (section 3). Do not suppose, however, that, because good and evil seem to be inextricably joined "in our chaos," there is no difference between them (section 4). Though vice is a frightful monster, familiarity with it brings acceptance (section 5). Every man is a mixture of virtue and vice, but Heaven has a single end in view and converts man's frailties into parts of a well-functioning whole. Each person, no matter what his position in life, finds compensations and has reason to be content.

Epistle III
Each thing has its place in "the chain of love"; "parts relate to the whole." Man should not think, in his pride, that all things and all creatures are made solely for his pleasure and use. All are interdependent and all have their special pleasures and functions (section 1). God has endowed all creatures with "honest instinct," which directly and surely governs their activities (section 2). Each creature is linked to the next in a universal order. Each loves itself but also

is attracted to another by sex, and this union in turn leads to the care of offspring. In men, the longer care of offspring leads to peculiarly human virtues (section 3). "The state of nature was the reign of God," when man lived in peace and virtue. In later times man became violent and vicious. But earlier man had listened to the voice of Nature (section 4). Earlier societies operated in liberty and natural law (section 5). The ruler spoke with the voice of Nature and Providence: he was "King, priest, and parent." He lived with true faith and love of God. Then came superstition and tyranny, and dreadful gods and fiends appeared. Tyrants rose to power, but through self-interest of the people the "kings learned justice and benevolence." The "Poet or patriot" rose to bring government into line with nature's laws and the principle of charity (section 6).

Epistle IV
This epistle opens with an invocation to happiness and asks where it is to be found (lines 1-18). The learned cannot point the way to happiness: they contradict each other (section 1). Follow nature, and abide by the "general laws" of "the Universal Cause," which operates for the general good. Order is the law. All men are of different ranks and endowments, but happiness is independent of position (section 2). The good that man can find is summed up in three words: health, peace, and competence (satisfaction of basic needs). Fools say that virtue brings suffering, but their examples show that chance or something else, not virtue, caused the suffering. If the sun is the light of the whole scheme of things, "partial ill is universal good" (section 3). Shall nature's laws be suspended for each individual passing need (section 4)? We want a better world, but we find it impossible to agree on what principle or creeds would make the world better. When we ask that virtue be rewarded in this world, we raise confusing and contradictory prospects (section 5). What better reward of virtue could be asked for than spiritual serenity and joy? To reward virtue with worldly prizes would be foolishness. The difference between a wise man and a fool is much more significant than any external differences in position or dress. Greatness does not rest with those who are "wickedly wise" or "madly great" but with those who gain noble ends by noble means. Fame is empty compared to one's consciousness of true virtue. Superior abilities bring cares, not happiness. Going over the names of the prominent and the great, one can "See the false scale of happiness complete!" (section 6). Virtue is happiness, and we can find virtue (and happiness) by following "Nature up to Nature's God," from which we learn charity

and the relation of the part to the whole. Pope ends with praise of his friend Bolingbroke and a summary of the main ideas of the poem (section 7).

THE RAPE OF THE LOCK

The poem satirizes a society (through two families) that had allowed a minor incident to assume undue importance. A young man had cut off a lock of hair from the head of a society belle. The incident itself and the reaction to it are inflated by the devices of epic poetry. Through this mock-heroic satire, Pope brings the incident into the focus of common sense.

Canto I

The poet sings of "great contests" that arise from "trivial causes" and hopes that Caryl, who suggested that Pope write the poem, and Belinda, who inspired the poem, will read it (lines 1-6). "What strange motive," the poet asks, could cause this assault and violent reaction (lines 7-12)?

The sun opens the sleeper's eyes. It is twelve o'clock. Belinda lies in bed, still sleeping, protected by her sylph, who has brought her a dream of a charming youth, who seems to speak to her (lines 13-26).

Belinda, the "Fairest of mortals," the responsibility of a thousand bright spirits, should believe all she has seen or heard of "angel-powers." Special knowledge is given to maids and children. She should know that innumerable spirits hover around her and make her superior to common mortals with only physical attendants. These attendant sylphs were once women, and now continue the interests they had when mortal. When the proud beauty dies, her soul returns to its original element (fire, water, earth, or air), as its temperament directs (lines 27-66). Each fair and chaste maiden is protected by a sylph, who guards her honor in the face of the most tempting conditions (lines 67-78). Since nymphs are proudly conscious of their beauty and have dreams of rising to high station, such thoughts "early taint the female soul" (lines 79-90). It is the sylphs who cause women to stray. They direct that beau be opposed to beau, as wigs, sword knots, and coaches strive with each other at the sylphs' contrivance (lines 91-104). The speaker announces that "Ariel is my name," Belinda's guardian sylph. Lately he has seen a dire event in her future, though he cannot tell just what it is to be (lines 105-114).

Awakened by her dog, Shock, Belinda opens her eyes and sees a love letter. She reads it, and the vision vanishes (lines 115-120). Belinda is now carefully groomed and dressed by her maid and attendant sylphs (lines 121-148).

Canto II

Belinda issues forth, admired by everyone. She glances and smiles at them all, but gives particular attention to none. Belinda has two locks of hair, which entrap the hearts of all men (lines 19-28). The Baron plans to seize "the bright locks" (lines 29-33). He had prayed early to all the powers that be, but especially to Love, that he might possess the prize. He had built to Love an altar of French romances and had laid on it offerings from "his former loves." Half his prayer is granted (lines 34-46).

Now Belinda smiles and makes the world gay, unaware that Ariel, her guardian sylph, has summoned "squadrons" of his fellows to protect her from impending danger. He addresses them (lines 47-72). Spirits are assigned their special and various tasks, from guiding the stars to guarding the throne (lines 73-90). One humbler task is to watch over and inspire fair maids (lines 91-100). Some dire but as yet unknown disaster hangs over their charge. Ariel assigns special duties, such as caring for the fan or the watch (lines 101-116). He assigns fifty sylphs to protect the petticoat (lines 117-122). Ariel promises terrible punishment for any sylph who fails in his duty (lines 123-136). The spirits descend and tremblingly await "the birth of Fate" (lines 137-142).

Canto III

The scene now shifts to the royal palace at Hampton Court (lines 1-8). Here the heroes and the nymphs come to engage in all kinds of gossip and chatter (lines 9-18).

Evening has come, and Belinda is ready to play ombre (a card game) with the Baron and another young man. Her sylphs watch over her important cards (lines 19-36). Kings, queens, and knaves along with the other cards ("parti-colored troops") are ready for the combat (lines 37-44). Belinda declares spades to be trumps, and the game proceeds. Her "Matadors" conquer the opposition (lines 45-64). Now, the Baron's queen of spades takes Belinda's king of clubs (lines 65-74). The Baron's diamonds attack the enemy, which is overwhelmed like a broken army (lines 75-86). After her queen of hearts is taken by the knave of diamonds, Belinda triumphantly attacks with her king of hearts (lines 87-100).

Pope inserts a mock-moralizing comment on fate and pride (lines 101-104). Coffee is prepared, and Belinda drinks, watched over by her sylphs. Stimulated by the coffee, the Baron thinks of new stratagems for getting the lock (lines 105-124). Clarissa hands the Baron a "two-edged weapon" (scissors), with which he approaches the lock. Ariel tries to warn Belinda, but finds that she is thinking of a lover (lines 125-146). The Baron opens the scissors ("glittering forfex") and (having cut a sylph in two) cuts off the lock (147-154). "Screams of horror" follow this act (lines 155-160). He exults in his achievement, predicting that his fame shall last as long as the various activities he lists. For his steel has conquered her hairs (lines 161-178).

Canto IV
Belinda feels intense rage and despair over the loss (lines 1-10). Ariel and the other sylphs withdrew from Belinda. Umbriel, a melancholy spirit, descended to the Cave of Spleen (lines 11-16). Spleen dwells forever in this gloomy place (lines 17-24). Ill-nature now stands ready at the side of Spleen (lines 25-30). Affectation also is there, to give the various appearances of pride and woe (lines 31-38). Now "strange phantoms," some dreadful, some bright, fly over the palace (lines 39-46). Spleen gives odd shapes and suggestions to the bodies on every side (lines 47-54). Umbriel petitions the Queen (Spleen), who can affect people in various ways, to "touch Belinda" and thus give "half the world the spleen" (lines 55-78). Spleen gives Umbriel a bag and vial that contain the expressions of female emotions (lines 79-88).

Umbriel finds Belinda sunk in Thalestris' arms. He opens the bag over their heads, and the cries of resentment appear. Thalestris fires Belinda's anger. Was it for this loss that you (Belinda) endured all the pains of developing these curls? To avoid infamy, something must be done. Rather than let this prize remain unchallenged, let chaos and destruction fall (lines 89-120). At her insistence, the empty-headed Sir Plume demands the return of the lock. The Baron refuses (lines 121-140).

Umbriel having broken the vial of sorrows, Belinda appears "in beauteous grief" (lines 141-146). Belinda sorrowfully declares that she would have been happier "In some lone isle," away from the court. She asserts that she had been warned by bad omens not to venture out. Now, the other lock hangs without its mate, doomed to a similar fate (lines 147-176).

Canto V

The Baron remains unmoved by either Belinda or Thalestris. Now Clarissa speaks (lines 1-8). Although beauty may attract the attentions of men, beauty is vain without good sense. Since beauty fades, women must "keep good humour," for "merit wins the Soul" (lines 9-34). The hearers ignore this advice. Instead, the lines of battle are drawn between the men and the women (lines 35-44). It was so when Homer described the gods in battle (lines 45-52). Umbriel and the other spirits gladly view the "growing combat" (lines 53-56). Thalestris "scatters death" with her eyes upon various fops (lines 57-66). Chloe kills Sir Plume and then revives him (lines 67-70). Jove decides the battle in favor of the women (lines 71-74).

Belinda throws "a charge of snuff" into the Baron's nose (lines 75-86). Belinda now draws out a bodkin (ornamental hair pin), which had a long history in Belinda's family (lines 87-96). The Baron protests that he does not fear to die. His only regret is leaving her (lines 97-102).

All now cry out "Restore the lock," but, according to Heaven's decree, the lock has disappeared (lines 103-112). Some thought the lock had mounted to the moon, where all kinds of hypocritical, trivial, and useless things are kept (lines 113-122). Actually, the lock rose upward and became a "sudden star" with "a radiant trail of hair" behind. Lovers then mistake the Star for Venus, and Partridge (an astrologer) will see it and make foolish predictions (lines 133-140).

So the poet advises Belinda that she should not regret the loss of the lock, for, after all her beauty has died, her name shall be inscribed among the stars (lines 141-150).

EZRA POUND

A PACT

The poet praises Whitmen, whom he had once "detested," for opening the way to new poetry ("broke the new wood"). The poet feels at one with Whitman ("one sap and one root") in wanting to do new things for poetry ("time for carving").

A VIRGINAL

The poet praises a woman for her "Virginal" influence over him. That is, her presence has given him a sense of brightness and new life that contact with others would corrupt. In lines 1-8 her effect is expressed in images of brightness and clearness. The poet feels he has been covered with a sheath of brightness, which must not be contaminated by the "lesser brightness" of other people. In lines 9-14, the poet uses the dominant image of wind in white birches in spring to express the woman's freshness, beauty, and life-giving effect.

AN IMMORALITY

The poet prefers "love and idleness" (which society considers "immorality") to the fame of doing "high deeds" in distant lands, such as Hungary. His broad experiences "in many a land" have shown him "naught else in living."

BALLAD OF THE GOODLY FERE

The poet uses a ballad form to present a folk-image of a robust and manly Christ.

After the crucifixion, the disciple Simon wonders if they have slain the best companion ("fere") of all. He then recounts several scenes in which Christ showed his mastery over men and events—his capture in the Garden, his scourging the temple, his healing the lame and blind, his facing the crucifixion, his calming the sea. In all, Christ appears as a folk hero—common ("a man o' men"), dauntless ("never a cry"), conquering ("master of men"), and greater than life itself ("no' get him in a book"). The poem ends with Simon's confidence that Christ triumphed over the crucifixion.

CANTO I

This is an account of Odysseus' visit to Hades to ask the blind prophet Tiresias to direct him on his journey. The first part of the poem is translated from Book II, "The Book of the Dead," from the *Odyssey*. The Andreas Divus referred to is a sixteenth-century Latin translator of the *Odyssey*.

Odysseus journeys to Hades (lines 1-18), makes religious offerings, including a sheep to Tiresias (lines 19-27), then drives back with his sword the many souls who crowd forth to drink of the blood (lines 28-41). The soul of Elpenor, killed by a fall at the house of Circe, comes asking for decent burial (lines 42-57). Anticlea, Odysseus' mother, is withheld while Tiresias comes, drinks of the blood, and prophesies that Odysseus will return over the seas, but will lose all his companions (lines 58-67). At line 68 the point of view shifts from "I" to "He," suggesting that the poet as the protagonist of the canto is assuming the energetic spirit of the Homeric hero to begin his own odyssey, by way of Circe, up from the dead to a new poetic life.

CANTO XLV

Pound indicts usury (lending of money with interest; probably also capitalism and obsessive materialism) as a sin against nature and a cause of sickness in society and the arts.

Lines 1-28 show society in general as ailing because of usury—religion, government ("Gonzaga his heirs"), dwellings, craftsmen, farmers, domestics. Lines 28-42 reflect that usury did not produce the great works of arts of the twelfth through sixteenth centuries—Lombardo, Bellini, Angelico, Praedis, and so on. Lines 43-50 give several images to suggest usury as a sin against nature (slaying the child in the womb, lying between bride and groom, bringing whores to the Eleusinian religious rites, corpses at a banquet).

HUGH SELWYN MAUBERLEY

The theme is the alienation of the poet (autobiographically Pound as Mauberley) from modern culture. The poem is composed of two sequences. The first has thirteen parts; the second, entitled *Mauberley*, has five parts.

In the first sequence the poet considers and then rejects the crude culture he is unable to change.

Part I, entitled, "E. P. Ode pour L'Election de Son Sepulchre," describes the poet's career, "out of key with his time," trying to bring beauty out of the non-beautiful, as "lilies from acorns." He prepares, as the title implies in French, to choose a literary tomb.

Part II describes the degenerating influence of the age in demanding from the artist only an "accelerated grimace," "mendacities," "mould in plaster." not the excellence described as "alabaster."

So, in part III, realization for the artist in society is impossible because of the "tawdry cheapness" coming from commercialism ("marketplace" where "the good" is decreed), from newspaper literature ("Press"), and from the democracy that produces knaves and eunuchs, not "god, man, or hero."

Parts IV-V view World War I as an expression of the degeneracy of society. Youth were slaughtered for a diseased culture or went "home to old lies" in a "botched civilization."

Parts VI-VII, entitled "Yeux Glauques" and "Siena Mi Fe'; Disfecemi Maremma," trace the degeneracy from its beginnings with the loss of aesthetic values of the Pre-Raphaelites ("Yeux Glauques," that is, eyes of a Pre-Raphaelite model), continuing through the Nineties, when the artist either collapsed or turned mediocre, as La Pia said in Dante's *Inferno*, in Italian, "Siena made me, Maremma unmade me."

Parts VIII-XI, the first two entitled "Brennbaum" and "Mr. Nixon," give several portraits of poeple who either yielded to or futilely resisted the age. Brennbaum the Jew (VIII) ignores his ancient tradition for elegant conformity. Mr. Nixon (IX) is a literary opportunist who compromises for popular success. The unyielding stylist (X) decays in a decaying country house. The educated woman (XI) is a victim of the sterile traditions inherited from her grandmother. The fashionable literary circles of the poet's time (XII) show him to be utterly unacceptable.

So, in part XIII, "Envoi," the poet makes his farewell in the form of a love lyric based on Edmund Waller's "Go, Lovely Rose." He bids farewell to his decadent age, but he asserts his devotion to the art, "Beauty alone."

In the second sequence, *Mauberley*, the self-exiled poet considers the validity of his withdrawal from his earlier cultural mission and drifts further into artistic revery.

In part I, the poet acknowledges the limitations of his skill. His models of the "firmness" of Flaubert and the objectivity ("Colourless") of Francesca have still not enabled him to reach his Grecian ideal ("Achaia").

In part II, the poet reviews the three years when he had drifted in dream ("Arcadia") amid "phantasmagoria." He was trying to understand his new-found vision of the ideal ("orchid"). But he had been unable to grasp the ideal, "the good" ("TO AGATHON"). Instead he had insensibly ("inconscient," "anaesthesis") engaged in "verbal manifestations" and had been as a stone dog "biting empty air."

In part III, entitled "The Age Demanded," the poet says the age asked more of him than "agility" with words. In his escape into pure artistry ("porcelain revery," "ambrosial circumstances"), he had avoided the crucial issues of the times ("relation of the state," "current exacerbations"). His grandiose enterprises ("imaginary/ Audition") had served to hide his sense of his own inadequacies ("maudlin confessions").

In part IV, the poet's self-exile has carried him to the point of suspension from life. He has drifted to the Spice Islands of his revery (Moluccas), where he is severed from time ("Not knowing . . . day's end") and from awareness ("consciousness disjunct"). The final epitaph to himself as hedonist contrasts with the heroic opening of the first poem in the *Hugh Selwyn Mauberley* sequence.

Part V, entitled "Medallion," represents the one poem that Mauberley wrote. It is his closest to achieving his "fundamental passion" in part III of presenting a series of portraits "in medallion." But the portrait of the woman singing by the piano is bookish and meticulous. Its sterility ironically contrasts with the "Envoi." Mauberley (or Pound) has proved his point: the age is not able to produce poetry.

PORTRAIT D'UNE FEMME

The poet draws a "portrait of a woman" who is utterly unoriginal.

In lines 1-7, the woman is described as like a Sargasso Sea of accumulated debris. She and her mind "have been second always," composed solely of "Ideas, old gossip, oddments" picked up here and there. Lines 7-10 indicate that this condition is not tragic to the woman, because she preferred it to the dullness of marriage with one man. Lines 11-30 show rather that what she gives to others is interesting, though useless and meaningless, because of its very strangeness, like mandrakes and ambergris.

SALUTATION

The poet indicts the "Generation of the thoroughly smug," for they are also "thoroughly uncomfortable."

By contrast, the unpretentious fishermen living without the pressures of respectability ("untidy," "ungainly") are happier than both the poet and his generation. The fish in the lake are happier yet without even the pressures of possessions ("not even own").

SESTINA: ALTAFORTE

In a dramatic monologue at his castle Altaforte, the man whom Dante put in hell because he was a stirrer-up of strife, Bertrans de Born, dramatizes his love of war and hatred of peace. The sestina verse form uses a varied sequence of six words rather than rhyme.

De Born can be happy only "when the swords clash." He likes summer thunderstorms because they "kill the earth's foul peace" and because they are like God's swords clashing. He likes the sun rising crimson because it is the color of blood and its "spears" drive back the peace of darkness. He is eager to be at war again, especially against the troops of the "Leopard," Richard the Lion-hearted. He would "damn forever all who cry 'Peace!'"

THE GARDEN

The theme is the loss of basic human qualities in formal society.

Stanza 1 presents a fluid, feminine image, in a formal setting, of a woman dying from lack of emotion. In stanza 2, the heirs of this aristocratic lady are, ironically, the poor but strong rabble. Stanza 3 points out the contradictions in her station and her character. Her "end of breeding" has resulted not in personal enrichment but in emotional sterility. Though still human enough to want communication, she cannot, because of her station, accept "that indiscretion."

THE REST

The poet advises the artists of America to leave their country rather than give up their threatened integrity.

In stanzas 1-3, the poet addresses the artists who are mistreated in America. They are "helpless," "broken," "thwarted." In stanzas 4-5 he sees their integrity threatened by their being forced into "persisting to successes," "reiteration," and "false knowledge." The poet's advice, in stanza 6, is for them to follow his example and leave the country.

THE RIVER-MERCHANTS WIFE: A LETTER

This poem translated from the Chinese is a love letter in which a young girl tells of her growing love for her husband, who has been away for five months.

She has grown from a childhood playmate (stanza 1), to a bashful bride of fourteen (stanza 2), to a lover who wishes their "dust to be mingled" (stanza 3) and who is sad because of his departure (stanza 4). In stanza 5, the depth to which the girl's love has grown is expressed in the nature imagery (mosses overgrown, falling leaves, paired butterflies) and through her wish to go out to meet her husband.

WALTER RALEGH

HIS PILGRIMAGE

The poet describes his spiritual pilgrimage from death to redemption in heaven.

The poet gathers his equipment for the journey (stanza 1), is anointed with the blood of Christ, and travels toward heaven (stanza 2). In heaven he will join other happy pilgrims tended by saints (stanza 3), and filled with immortality they shall walk the streets of heaven (stanza 4). The poet will be tried for his sins before God's throne (stanza 5), and with Christ as his lawyer he will plead for an "everlasting head" (stanza 6). The last couplet advises all to think about such a pilgrimage.

THE LIE

The poet makes a scathing attack on social classes, institutions, and ideals. He sends his soul to "give the world the lie" and so expose its evil. Very little is spared. Courts are rotten and churches hypocritical. Potentates are strong only by faction. Men of high condition are ambitious and full of hate. Various ideals and conditions are tarnished and not what they seem to be, such as, zeal, love, honor, wisdom, fortune, friendship, manhood, and virtue. The one true and enduring thing would seem to be the soul, for no stab "the soul can kill."

THE NYMPH'S REPLY TO THE SHEPHERD

Ralegh's nymph here gives a cynical answer to the invitation made in Christopher Marlowe's "The Passionate Shepherd to His Love." The nymph refuses the shepherd's invitation to "live with thee and be thy love." She says that truth is not in the shepherd's tongue since "time drives" away the pleasures he offers. Flowers fade, birds cease singing, what is honey in the spring becomes sorrow in the fall. If youth, love, joys, and age were not subject to the ravages of time, then, says the nymph, the shepherd's proposal might move her.

JOHN CROWE RANSOM

BELLS FOR JOHN WHITESIDE'S DAUGHTER

The poem shows adult relatives gaining control over their grief for the death of a girl.

In stanza 1, they find it difficult to accept the contrast between the girl's present "brown study" and the active life they remember in her. In stanzas 2-4, they adjust to the girl's death by recalling the child's past life as an idyllic world of wonder and magic, with talking geese and fairylike "lady with rod." In such a world out of time, they can consider the girl not dead. So, in stanza 5, when the bells call them to the funeral, they "are ready" to accept the girl's death. Instead of being wildly grief-stricken, they can be "vexed" at the girl who seems not dead, but "primly propped" in a brown study.

BLUE GIRLS

This *carpe diem* ("seize the day") poem advises girls to practice beauty in youth, for beauty is transitory.

In stanzas 1-3, the poet advises the young ladies at a girls' college not to be interested in learning but to display their beauty in blue skirts and white fillets about their hair. Stanza 4 gives a particular instance of frail beauty transformed to ugliness.

JANET WAKING

The theme of the poem is a child's awakening to the knowledge of mortality and her refusal to accept the new knowledge ("would not be instructed"). The light tone used to describe the death of the pet hen ("transmogrifying," "old bald head," "purply") is appropriate to Janet's innocence at that time and provides ironic contrast to the serious tone of the last stanza, when she discovers that the hen cannot be awakened from the "forgetful kingdom of sleep."

PARTING, WITHOUT A SEQUEL

The poem dramatizes the tragic-comic effects of a young girl ending an attachment, perhaps her first love affair.

In stanzas 1-3, the girl dispatches a letter, presumably of farewell, to her boyfriend, and feels tragically the "ruin of her younger years." In stanzas 4-5, she seeks solace from her father who, as a "vaunting oak," consoles her rain of tears with talk "low and gentle."

That the effect is not ultimately tragic is seen in various melodramatic and theatrical connotations: the story-book "Parting" and "Sequel," the melodramatic "ruin" and "so richly has deserved," the pretentious "functioner of doom," and the triple rhymes of *bicycle–icicle*. The girl is genuinely moved, but she will soon get over it.

PIAZZA PIECE

The conflict of youth against age is acted out in a scene on the piazza.

In stanza 1, the old man tries to make the young girl hear, but she prefers the young men. The old man knows he must have his "lovely lady" soon or not at all, for the dying roses and the spectral moon tell him death is near.

In stanza 2, the young and beautiful girl, waiting for her "true-love," rejects the "gray man."

THE EQUILIBRISTS

Two lovers try to balance, like acrobats or equilibrists, two opposing attitudes toward love.

Stanzas 1-6 assert romantic, passionate love of the body, but "Honor," the Christian idealization of chastity, comes between the lovers, "cold as steel." Stanzas 7-12 describe the "torture of their equilibrium"—always torn between "fierce Love" and "Honor." Their problem is whether to "ascend to Heaven and bodiless dwell" or take their bodies "honorless to hell." Great lovers, because of their passion and torment, lie in hell. In stanzas 13-14, the poet makes an epitaph for the lovers where they lie in their torment, "perilous and beautiful," untouching in each other's sight.

EDWIN ARLINGTON ROBINSON

CASSANDRA

A modern prophetess attacks contemporary "Dollar" philosophy, and, as with Cassandra of ancient Troy, her prophecies go unheeded. The age is indicted for substituting money values for spiritual values ("Word," "altars," "Trinity"), for ignoring Reason, for thinking that it can ignore the laws of history, and for treading down the "merciless old verities." Is this age, Cassandra asks, going to trade its soul ("all you are") for possessions ("what you have")?

CLIFF KLINGENHAGEN

Amid an affluent life with "soup and meat/ And all the other things," Cliff Klingenhagen takes a drink of wormwood symbolizing the bitterness in life. By such an act, he maintains self-assurance ("only looked at me/ And smiled") and happiness.

CREDO

In a basically meaningless life in which "I cannot find my way" and there is "no star . . . no glimmer," the poet finds some grounds for philosophical assurance. Though slight, like a bar of "lost, imperial music," such grounds are definite enough to give assurance of some transcendent force working in the universe, and the poet feels "the coming glory of the Light."

FLAMMONDE

In the character Flammonde, the poet ponders the psychological twist, "the small satanic sort of kink," that may mar an otherwise flawless man.

Stanzas 1-2 describe Flammonde's character as the epitome of excellence ("royal," "iron," "never doubt," "alert repose," "taste"). Stanzas 3-4 consider his unknown origin and role in life. Stanzas 5-8 point out his powerful influence for good in the lives of others. Stanzas 9-11 ponder his inscrutability and the "kink" that withheld him from his "destinies." Stanza 12 universalizes the theme by observing that each of us has, like Flammonde, his own dark problem ("darkening hill").

HOW ANNANDALE WENT OUT

In a dramatic monologue, a physician explains, to another person or to a jury who could "hang me," his mercy-killing of his friend Annandale.

As attendant physician, the speaker saw Annandale so deteriorated as to be hardly human ("it"), with only pain ahead ("hell"). So "Annandale went out" through the physician's use of a "slight kind of engine" (such as a hypodermic needle). For this action, he believes he should not be hanged, and the listener seems to agree ("I thought not").

KARMA

Moved by the Christmas spirit, a man has a shallow and delusive rebirth ("Karma") of conscience and brotherly love.

In lines 1-8, a Santa Claus ringing a bell aroused pangs of conscience in a man for a ruthless business deal with a friend who would "neither buy nor sell." In lines 9-14, the pangs are seen as shallow and delusive, for, in contrast to the priceless love-gift of the founder of Christmas who "died for men," the man gave but a dime for human charity.

MINIVER CHEEVY

The life and character of Miniver Cheevy ironically demonstrate the futility of romantic escapism.

Miniver's idealization of the past took him through ancient Greece (Thebes), ancient Troy (Priam), the knights of the Round Table at Camelot, and Renaissance Italy of the Medici, while he scorned the commonplace present with its khaki suits and gold. The ironic result of his romanticizing the glorious past is something quite unglorious—health impairment ("grew lean," "coughed"), poverty ("sore annoyed"), futility ("thought and thought"), and alcoholism ("kept on drinking").

MR. FLOOD'S PARTY

Through Mr. Flood, the poet describes the tragic loneliness of old age.

In stanzas 1-2, Eben talks to himself and, sorrowfully aware of his age, drinks alone but pretends he has a companion. Stanza 3 brings out Eben's loneliness, with all his "friends of other days" gone. Stanza 4 tells us that Eben has learned about the uncertainty of life. The "party" continues in stanzas 5-6. Stanza 7 gives us the final statement of Eben's loneliness, old and friendless amid strangers.

RICHARD CORY

Richard Cory's suicide demonstrates that the external appearance of a man may conceal a secret weakness or problem.

Although he had every quality "to make us wish that we were in his place" (good looks, impeccable taste, good manners, riches, adulation), for some reason Richard Cory "put a bullet through his head."

THEODORE ROETHKE

ELEGY FOR JANE

In his tender, loving elegy at the grave of his student, the teacher identifies her with the nature of living things, such as tendrils, wren, sparrow, fern, and pigeon. Even the shade and the mould "sang with her." Still he is aware of the social irrelevance of his love and grief, for he has "no rights in this matter," neither of "father nor lover."

FOUR FOR SIR JOHN DAVIES

The theme of fulfillment of love is developed through the basic metaphor of the dance as used by Yeats and by Davies. Yeats made the dance an image of reconciliation of sense and spirit. Davies' sixteenth-century poem "Orchestra" uses the dance to explain the hierarchic structure of the universe. Roethke's poem moves from an isolated dance at the beginning to a transcendent fulfillment shared by both lover and beloved.

In part 1, "The Dance," the poet is "dancing all alone" with the movements of the universe and of clumsy animals. In part 2, "The Partner," he seeks a human bond and takes a woman partner. Their sexual activity demonstrates that both the "body and soul know how to play." In part 3, "The Wraith," the physical love of the two leads to unity and spirituality, as each becomes the other, and the flesh makes the "spirit visible." In part 4, "The Vigil," they move to a transcendent fulfillment that "outleaps the world," as Dante did by inspiration of his love for Beatrice.

I KNEW A WOMAN

With exuberance and humor, the poet expresses his delight with the energy and loveliness of a woman and with her effect on him.

The dominant images are those of movement: "moved more ways than one," "Turn," "mowing," "light and loose," "circles moved," "how a body sways." The exuberant humor is especially expressed by puns such as "rake," "goose," "knowing" a woman, and by humorous metaphors such as a woman as a "container," nibbling from her hand, love as a "prodigious mowing," and measuring time by how a body sways.

MY PAPA'S WALTZ

A son remembers an evening when his drunken father waltzed him about the kitchen and carried him off to bed. The experience had some roughness to it ("whiskey," "pans/ Slid," "ear scraped," "beat time on my head"), and the mother disapproved ("Could not unfrown"). Yet the whole experience showed the mutual affection of father and boy: "the waltz was not easy," but the boy was determined to try; "romped on"; the boy clasped his father around the legs ("ear scraped a buckle"); "waltzed me off"; and "clinging."

OPEN HOUSE

In the dominant metaphor of holding an open house, the poet asserts how openly his inner self reveals itself to observers. His "heart keeps open house" and he is "naked to the bone," as he expresses himself in "language strict and pure."

ROOT CELLAR

The strength of the life-urge is illustrated by the action of bulbs, stems, leaf mold, and such in a dark, dank cellar: "Nothing would give up life."

CHRISTINA ROSSETTI

A BIRTHDAY

The title applies not to a chronological birthday but to "the birthday of my life," which is when the speaker's beloved returned to her.

Images of fertility in stanza 1 suggest the overwhelming receptiveness of the woman for the returning man: the bird and the nest on the young branch, the heavily-laden apple tree, and the shell on the sea. Stanza 2 proceeds with a lush though formal description of a raised place (dais) as for a marriage bed.

The whole poem, it might be noted, has a Pre-Raphaelite quality that combines the realistic with the lush and decorative.

GOBLIN MARKET

Goblins tempt Laura to taste their magic fruit. She is about to die because she cannot get a second taste, but her sister Lizzie tricks the goblins and brings back the second taste to her sister.

The goblins call out that they have all kinds of fruit to sell (lines 1-31). Laura and Lizzie fearfully listen to the cry of the goblins (lines 32-80). Laura is tempted, but, she tells them, she has no money. They trade her fruit for a lock of her hair (lines 81-140). When Laura returns home, Lizzie warns her with the story of Jeanie, who had bought the fruit and then died because she could get no more. Laura, however, remains ecstatic. Then they go to sleep (lines 141-198).

At the end of their day's work, Laura lingers near the river bank to catch another glimpse of the goblins, who do not appear (lines 199-241). Laura can no longer hear the goblins cry and she steadily declines (lines 242-298). Lizzie decides to go buy the fruit, to the joy of the goblins, who invite her to join in their feast. Her refusal to stay irritates the goblins, and they attack her. They "squeezed their fruits/ Against her mouth to make her eat." Lizzie steadfastly resists them until they abandon their attempt (lines 299-446). Covered with the juices, Lizzie hurries to her sister. When Laura kisses Lizzie, the taste of the fruit is bitter, and, at last overcome by the taste, Laura collapses (lines 447-523). In the morning, she is fully recovered. In later years, Laura tells her children the story (lines 524-567).

Symbolically, the story is about sin, death, redemption, and rebirth. Laura in her sin (the Biblical sin of sex) becomes sick unto death ("Is it death or is it life?" line 523). She can be reborn only by a redemptive and sacrificial act of love by her sister. To accomplish this, her sister undergoes a temptation similar to Laura's. She resists the temptation, and then returns with the power to restore Laura to life. The theme of forbidden fruit followed by rejection suggests the story of the Garden of Eden.

REMEMBER

The speaker admonishes her lover not to forget her when she is dead. Yet if memory of me should make you sad, she says, it is better that "you should forget and smile."

SONG (WHEN I AM DEAD, MY DEAREST)

The first stanza advises the lover not to grieve when his beloved dies. Perhaps he will even forget her. The second stanza states that the speaker, once dead, will no longer have physical sensation. Perhaps she will remember; perhaps she will forget.

DANTE GABRIEL ROSSETTI

THE BALLAD OF DEAD LADIES

The poet's subject is the death of women, who pass away like "the snows of yester-year."

A wide variety of ladies is mentioned. Those in the first stanza were perhaps real, perhaps legendary, except for Echo, who is mythological. Heloise and Abelard in stanza 2 were famous and ill-fated lovers of the Middle Ages. Then come the names of various ladies famous in the Middle Ages for various reasons, and finally comes the sainted Joan of Arc. All are gone, nor is there any point in asking where they went, any more than there is point in asking "where are the snows of yester-year?"

THE BLESSED DAMOZEL

The damozel in heaven mourns for the lover she has left on earth.

As the damozel leaned over "the gold bar of heaven," she seemed to have come to heaven only in the last day, though in earthly terms she had been there ten years (lines 1-18). To the one she left it had seemed "ten years of years" (lines 19-24). She stood on a rampart of God's house, high in heaven (lines 25-36).

Unlike other, happy souls, the damozel leaned unhappily over the bar. She saw time and she tried to see through it (lines 37-54). She spoke in the night, and the lover below on earth fancied he heard her (lines 55-66). When her lover has joined her, she said, they will bathe together in "the deep wells of light" (lines 67-78). They will see their old prayers granted, and they will lie in the shadow of the mystic tree of life (lines 79-90). She will teach him the songs she knows, but the lover wonders if God will raise his soul to heaven (lines 91-102). They will go where Mary sits with her five hand-maidens, and Mary will approve of their love (lines 103-120). Mary will bring them to Christ, and the damozel will ask Christ that she and her lover may live in love eternally (lines 121-132). Then she stopped, and after a while she wept (lines 133-144).

Stanza 4, stanza 11, stanza 17 and the last stanza tell us that the narrator is the damozel's lover, who is still alive on earth. This perspective suggests that the vision exists only in the lover's imagination. Rossetti's assertion that the poem was suggested by Poe's *The Raven* might support the idea that the incident is an hallucination of the narrator. But it is perhaps more effective to think of the damozel as a vision who actually exists in the heavenly realm.

THE BURDEN OF NINEVEH

The poet muses upon the history and the meaning of the beast unearthed at Nineveh.

As he turns from looking at the Grecian statuary, the poet sees a beast with human face and bull's body—a Minotaur from Nineveh. It brings to mind questions about what kind of religious rites it has witnessed (lines 1-30). Didn't it seem, he wonders, as if life returned to Nineveh when the ancient spell of silence was broken by the excavators (lines 31-40)? The beast now stands, casting its shadow, as it had done in ancient times (lines 71-110).

The poet continues musing, contrasting the present decay and the past glories of Nineveh (lines 111-150). With the moving sun, the shadow disappears and looking at "The god forlorn," he thinks that future times will merge all the past, London and Nineveh alike, into one, so that future ages may confuse the two civilizations (lines 151-190). Finally, the poet sees that, in worship of a burdened and earth-bound existence, Nineveh was like London (lines 191-200).

The House of Life

This sonnet sequence presents Rossetti speaking as a poet on various subjects. Part I (Sonnets 1-59), "Youth and Change," deals with love, and Part II (Sonnets 60-101), "Change and Fate," deals with general questions of reality.

THE SONNET

This sonnet introduces the sequence, *The House of Life.* It defines the sonnet as a poetic form, and it also states the basic themes of the sequence as Rossetti saw them—Life, Love, and Death.

A sonnet commemorates an event, and it should be "reverent" toward this content. Its mood may be light or dark; it will have a "flowering crest" (that is, a beautiful appearance). A sonnet has two sides: one shows the soul (the idea, the occasion, the subject, and so on), and the other shows what is the ultimate force behind it—Life, Love, or Death.

4: LOVESIGHT

The poet wonders when he sees his beloved most: when he sees her in the light or when he sees her "in the dusk hours" alone and his soul sees only her soul. If he should no longer see her, it would be like death.

18: GENIUS IN BEAUTY

The genius of the beloved's beauty equals the harmony of great art, and it bestows as many gifts as Life itself. As one man among many retains the power of writing poetry throughout his life, so this beauty will be secure from the destructive years.

19: SILENT NOON

All about the lovers things are quiet and beautiful. This hour seems to have dropped from heaven. They should clasp it closely, for their "silence was the song of love."

24: PRIDE OF YOUTH

As a child has little grief for the dead because it is now his turn to live and theirs to die, so this New Love arrives without regret for the Old Love. Alas for change and for all the old things that give place to the new. Alas for the loves that "proud Youth lets fall."

28: SOUL-LIGHT

The poet's beloved has an infinite capacity to be loved. After their rapture seems completely full, there still is in her eyes the thrill and fire of Love. As there is a changing wonder in the light of the moon, of the stars, and of dawn, so her eyes and voice move the poet in a varying light with "infinite love."

34: THE DARK GLASS

The poet cannot tell the extent of his love for his beloved, for he cannot measure tomorrow's gift by yesterday's. He asks if these confusing sounds of life and death and other mortal experiences make him blind and deaf. Shall his senses "pierce" love, which is the ultimate creation of eternity? He is only a "murmuring shell" or a small "heart-flame"; yet through his beloved's eyes he may gain the ultimate powers that any mortal may understand.

48: DEATH-IN-LOVE

An image with the wings of Love bore Love's banner, and on the banner was the beloved's face. The poet felt the banner's power in his heart, like the hour of his birth. A veiled woman, following the banner, plucked a feather from the winged figure. The figure had no breath, and she said that she and Love were the same, and that she was Death.

49: WILLOWWOOD–I

The poet sat with Love at a well, and they leaned across the water. Love told his secret through his lute; his eyes and the poet's met in the water. In the sound of the lute the lover heard his beloved's voice. His tears fell, and Love's eyes in the reflection became her eyes. The ripples became "waving hair," and as he stooped to the water, her lips met his.

50: WILLOWWOOD—II

Love's song was full of half-remembered things, as might be the song of a soul waiting between bodily death and a new birth. The poet became aware of mournful forms, each the shade of a past day of his and his beloved. These forms looked on as the lovers clung in their kiss, and the moan of self-pity ran through all. And Love sang.

51: WILLOWWOOD—III

Love addresses all those who are grief-stricken through loss of their loves, and who long for their lost ones. It were better that the soul sleep until death than that the soul wander in the bitter region of Willowwood.

52: WILLOWWOOD—IV

As clinging roses part at evening, so with the end of the song "his beloved's face fell back drowned." Then the poet drank from the water, and as he did so Love drew near him in pity.

53: WITHOUT HER

What is the beloved's mirror without her, and her dress and her accustomed paths and her pillow? So, without her, the poet's heart is "A wayfarer by barren ways."

55: STILLBORN LOVE

The hour of Love is seen as a spirit or child waiting for parents (the lovers) to claim it. It waits in bondage until the "wedded souls" appear, and "the little outcast hour" leaps toward them and claims them as parents.

The House of Life

69: AUTUMN IDLENESS

The sun shines in November over every glade. The grazing deer look as if they had been dappled by the sun. Dawn, moon, and evening have their delights. And here, for the poet, memories renew the past while he wanders over the grass, not knowing what he should do.

71: THE CHOICE–I

The poet advises his beloved to eat and drink, for tomorrow death will come. He pours wine for her, and she will sing. Love is better than work.

72: THE CHOICE–II

Fear death, says the poet, for it will come when man knows it not. Who can tell the future? Of what use are man's actions? Nor can you pretend to take comfort in the happiness of future men when you yourself know only pain. Therefore, "watch, and fear."

73: THE CHOICE–III

Think and act, says the poet. It is not for you that men have struggled. You must exert yourself, for the sea (of life, knowledge, experience) stretches out endlessly.

77: SOUL'S BEAUTY (SIBYLLA PALMIFERA)

The speaker is awe-struck at the sight of Beauty enthroned. She is the principle that draws "bondmen" to her law. She is the Lady Beauty whom you (the viewer or observer) have so long followed trembling.

78: BODY'S BEAUTY (LILITH)

Lilith, Adam's first wife, was deceptive and tempting, and she draws men into her power through her body's beauty: "round his heart one strangling golden hair."

The House of Life

83: BARREN SPRING

Spring once more returns, but brings with it no answering smile, for the poet's life is still entwined with the dead past. And so the spring does not concern him. The poet sees the flowers of spring as destructive agents. He warns his reader to turn from them and not wait till the flower shrivels (and beauty turns to death).

86: LOST DAYS

The poet asks what would his lost days be if he could see them. They are things of value that were misused and wasted (wheat, coins, blood, water). At his death, these lost days will address him ("Each one a murdered self") as lost parts of himself, since his present self is also a lost (or fragmented) being.

101: THE ONE HOPE

When desire and regret both go to death, what shall help him to forget? the poet asks. He wonders if Peace will be "unmet." Or perhaps his soul will find the charm. He prays that when the soul "peers breathless" for the gift, no other magic spell will be there but "Hope's one name," that is, whatever it is that Hope's word is for him.

MURIEL RUKEYSER

BOY WITH HIS HAIR CUT SHORT

The poem describes a boy getting a haircut as he prepares hopelessly to find a job in the impersonal twentieth-century city. Ironically, the neon sign "always reaches its mark," in contrast to the boy, who will not be successful. Also, ironically, the solicitous sister cutting his hair and speaking hope to him denies hope by her "hopeless look."

The House of Life

EFFORT AT SPEECH BETWEEN TWO PEOPLE

A man and a woman make separate efforts at speech. Out of their loneliness and unhappiness, they grope for relationship with one another, but each is most concerned with his own problem. The man speaks in stanzas 1, 3, 5, and 7. He narrates unhappy events of his life at age three, at nine, at fourteen, and yesterday. The woman, speaking in stanzas 2, 4, and 6, tells of an unhappy love affair.

CARL SANDBURG

CHICAGO

The poet celebrates the city of Chicago for its pride, energy, and optimism.

The city is wicked with painted women, crooked with gunmen, brutal with hungry women and children. But the poet can accept such ugliness ("give them back the sneer") because of the other, attractive qualities of the city. His description personifies the city as untamed youth—pride, coarse energy ("slugger"), savagery, and ebullient optimism as it laughs the "stormy, husky, brawling laughter of Youth."

COOL TOMBS

In respect to death ("dust," "cool tombs"), the supreme human experience is love.

The good president Lincoln (stanza 1), with his North-South statecraft (a copperhead was a Southern sympathizer) and his assassination, "forgot" all at death. Likewise the corrupt president Grant (stanza 2), with his crooked money schemes, "lost all thought" in the dust. It is the lover (stanza 3), such as the lovely Pocahontas, whose experience may not be forgotten in the dust ("did she wonder? does she remember?"). Among any group of people (stanza 4), nobody gets "more than the lovers."

FOUR PRELUDES ON PLAYTHINGS OF THE WIND

The vain pride of a blatantly glorious nation is ironically seen against the inevitable fall of civilizations.

Part I personifies time preparing man's tomorrow as a lackadaisical woman doing her hair (reminiscent of the Greek Fates weaving man's destiny). Part II describes the once-glorious city and its boast of being "greatest" set against its subsequent desolation ("broken hinges"). Part III indicates that the rise and fall of nations is a pattern of history. Strong men put up a "city" before, but finally only the rats, lizards, and crows remained. Part IV suggests a finality of desolation. The genealogies of the rats and the shifting of wind and dust suggest a passing of time long enough so that the "greatest nation" is lost in oblivion ("nothing at all").

GRASS

The covering grass suggests the futility of war as it consigns to oblivion ("What place," "Where") the bodies of several battlefields —Austerlitz and Waterloo (Napoleonic Wars), Gettysburg (Civil War), Ypres and Verdun (World War I).

I AM THE PEOPLE, THE MOB

The poet personifies "the People" to express his confidence in the mass, the common man, that it will eventually come into its own.

Important workers of the past have come from the masses—inventors, producers, Napoleons, Lincolns (lines 1-4) and will continue to come even though they are abused (lines 5-7). When the people become wise enough to use the "lessons of yesterday," they will "arrive" (lines 8-9).

ANNE SEXTON

MUSIC SWIMS BACK TO ME

The poet tells how she felt the first night in a mental hospital.

The radio music she remembers is the focal point to emphasize the harsh and impersonal treatment of the numbed patient. She tells her story to an anonymous "Mister," who, as the final question indicates, does not wait to hear.

RINGING THE BELLS

The poet describes the helplessness and frustration of patients undergoing therapy in a mental hospital.

In lines 1-14, the therapist gives a music lesson to the "crazy ladies." In lines 25-29 the patients respond automatically to the useless treatment.

WILLIAM SHAKESPEARE

FEAR NO MORE THE HEAT O' THE SUN

This dirge from *Cymbeline* is sung by two brothers at the grave of their supposedly dead sister Imogen. In stanzas 1-3, they are consoled that she need "Fear no more" the sufferings of life (heat of the sun, tyrant's stroke, slander), for she, as all people must, has "come to dust." In stanza 4, they pray that no evil or disturbance come to her grave.

FULL FATHOM FIVE THY FATHER LIES

In this song from *The Tempest*, the sprite Ariel tells Ferdinand that his supposedly drowned father has undergone a beautiful transformation in the sea. In this "sea-change," his bones have turned to coral, his eyes to pearls—everything has turned to "something rich and strange."

Sonnets

The series of one hundred and fifty-four sonnets by Shakespeare lacks coherent order, but in general sonnets 1-126 are addressed to a handsome, noble, blond young man and sonnets 127-154 deal with the poet's relations with the Dark Lady.

Basic motifs in the sonnets are the urge to perpetuate oneself through offspring, the celebration of friendship, sorrow over separation of friends, broodings upon time and death, rival claims of the poet's male friend and his female friend, and the wooing of the Dark Lady.

12: WHEN I DO COUNT THE CLOCK THAT TELLS THE TIME

The poet advises having children as a defense against the brevity of time.

When the poet sees the short life of the day, the violet, black curls, leaves on the tree (lines 1-8), then he thinks that his beautiful friend also must go "among the wastes of time" (lines 9-12). The only defense against time is to "breed" children (lines 13-14).

15: WHEN I CONSIDER EVERYTHING THAT GROWS

The poet attempts through poetry to preserve his friend's youth.

In lines 1-4, he considers that everything is inconstant, illusionary ("shows"), and subject to the influence of the stars. In lines 5-8, he perceives that men's lives grow and decrease quickly, inhibited by the influence of the stars. In lines 9-14, he sees that time is decaying the youth of his friend, but the poet adds by his poetry what time takes away ("engraft you new").

18: SHALL I COMPARE THEE TO A SUMMER'S DAY?

The beauty of the poet's friend and its permanence is expressed by the extended metaphor of a summer's day. A summer's day is sometimes too cold with "rough winds," or "too hot," or "dimm'd," or "too short." But the poet's friend is lovely, temperate, and eternal, not subject to death. It is the "eternal lines" of the poem which immortalize his friend.

29: WHEN, IN DISGRACE WITH FORTUNE AND MEN'S EYES

The poem tells of the comforts of love in times of bad fortune.

When the poet feels like an outcast of fortune and society (lines

Sonnets

1-4) and when he envies all the good things other people have (lines 5-8), if he thinks of his friend's love, he becomes as happy as a lark and as wealthy as a king (lines 9-14).

30: WHEN TO THE SESSIONS OF SWEET SILENT THOUGHT

The power of friendship can compensate for the losses and griefs of the past.

In lines 1-12, the poet thinks of the past and grieves at the unfulfillments, the waste, the loss of friends and love, and the many woes he has suffered. In lines 13-14, thinking about his friend restores losses and ends sorrows.

33: FULL MANY A GLORIOUS MORNING HAVE I SEEN

The poet uses the image of a cloud hiding the sun to describe a breach in friendship.

Lines 1-8 describe a morning made glorious by the sun until the "basest clouds" hide the sun for the rest of the day. In lines 9-12, the poet compares such a covering of sunlight to separation from his friend. Lines 13-14 assert, nevertheless, that such a breach does not weaken the poet's love.

54: O, HOW MUCH MORE DOTH BEAUTY BEAUTEOUS SEEM

As the perfume of the rose makes it fairer and allows it to survive death, so the poet's verse will preserve the truth of his friend.

Lines 1-4 assert that beauty is increased if it is joined to truth, just as the rose is made fairer by its odor. Lines 5-11 contrast the canker-blooms, or wild roses, which have color but no odor. They are rejected because their "show" is their only virtue. In lines 11-12, roses, unlike wild roses, will survive death by being made into perfume. Lines 13-14 apply the simile to the poet's verse: it will distill and preserve the truth of his friend.

55: NOT MARBLE, NOR THE GILDED MONUMENTS

The poet asserts the durability of love and art.

Through the poet's "powerful rhyme," the memory of his friend

will outlive three things: the marble and monuments of great men
that time besmears (lines 1-4), the statues and masonry that war destroys (lines 5-8), and the oblivion that comes with enmity and death
(lines 9-12). So in "this" poem, the friend will outlast all things until
the judgment day (lines 13-14).

56: SWEET LOVE, RENEW THY FORCE

In asking that love be not dulled, but continually renewing its force,
the poet uses three main similes: appetite, a couple viewing the
ocean, and summer following winter.

In lines 1-8, the poet wants love to renew its force as does appetite, momentarily allayed, but always resharpened. In lines 9-12, he
asks that love be like a newly-engaged couple ("two contracted
new") whose view of the ocean is blessed because of the return of
love. In lines 13-14, he asks that love be "thrice more wished" as is
summer after a winter of care.

60: LIKE AS THE WAVES MAKE TOWARDS THE PEBBLED SHORE

In the face of all-destroying time, the poet hopes through his verse
to keep alive the worth of his friend in times to come ("times in
hope").

Lines 1-4 show the fast movement of life, our minutes hastening
in sequence like waves. Lines 5-8 show the inevitable life cycle—
from nativity to maturity to destruction ("confound"). Lines 9-12
show the corrosive aspects of time. Time transfixes beauty (as a
spear), delves (as a plow), feeds (as a worm), and mows. In lines
13-14, despite this "cruel hand" of time, the poet will try through
his verse to immortalize his friend.

64: WHEN I HAVE SEEN BY TIME'S FELL HAND DEFACED

The poet grieves when he "fears to lose" his love to time and death.
Three main images develop the idea of time producing ruin. The
splendor ("cost") of the past is defaced by time's hand (lines 1-2).
The tower and the enduring brass is razed by the "mortal rage" of

time (lines 3-4). The ocean and the shore struggle with one another (lines 5-8). The ruin seen in these images of "interchange" and "decay" has taught the poet that time will take his love away (lines 9-12). Thus the grief of lines 13-14.

65: SINCE BRASS, NOR STONE, NOR EARTH, NOR BOUND-LESS SEA

The poet laments time's destruction of the beauty of his loved one and hopes to preserve this beauty through poetry.

In lines 1-4, the poet doubts that beauty, delicate as a flower, can endure, since such strong things as brass and stone are overcome by mortality. In lines 5-8, he doubts that beauty, light and sweet as summer, can endure since time decays rocks and steel. In lines 9-12, he asks how he can possibly protect this jewel of beauty from time and concludes in lines 13-14 that the only possible was is through poetry ("black ink").

71: NO LONGER MOURN FOR ME WHEN I AM DEAD

The poet expresses his wish that his loved one should forget him after his death rather than have grief.

The poet tells his friend not to mourn for him after his death (lines 1-4), not to remember him if memory should cause unhappiness (lines 5-8), and not to love him lest a cruel world cause grief through taunting (lines 9-14).

73: THAT TIME OF YEAR THOU MAYST IN ME BEHOLD

Three sets of images develop the idea that love is intensified by awareness of approaching death: winter, night, and a dying fire.

Lines 1-4 compare the poet's life to the end of the year—winter, with the lifelessness of bare boughs after a vital summer. Lines 5-8 compare the poet's ending life to the end of the day—night, which is like death. Lines 9-12 compare his ending life to a self-consuming fire, which must die out. Lines 13-14 state the increase of love which must come with awareness of imminent loss.

87: FAREWELL! THOU ART TOO DEAR FOR MY POSSESSING

The poet laments the loss of friendship.

In lines 1-4, the poet bids farewell to his friend, the bonds between them broken. In lines 5-8, the poet states that he had the friendship not through his own "deserving," but only through the friend's "granting." Lines 9-12 point out that the friendship was apparently founded on the friend's mistaken sense of his own or the poet's worth, and so had to end. In lines 13-14, the poet, therefore, loses his friendship like a beautiful dream of being a king.

97: HOW LIKE A WINTER HATH MY ABSENCE BEEN

The barrenness of winter is used to express the poet's unhappiness at his absence from his friend.

Lines 1-4 compare the absence to winter with its freezings and barrenness. Lines 5-8 point out the paradox that the absence takes place in autumn, the actual season of fruitfulness. Lines 9-14 compare the friend to summer; so that when he is away, there can be no pleasures, no fruit, no happy songs of birds.

98: FROM YOU HAVE I BEEN ABSENT IN THE SPRING

The poet expresses his sorrow at his friend's absence by being unable to be happy in the spring.

Lines 1-4 describe the youthful spirit and joy of spring. Lines 5-10 tell of the poet's inability to find joy in any of the specific delights of spring. In lines 11-14, the reason for the sorrow is that the poet sees in the delights of spring only the "pattern" and "shadow" of his friend. So to him it seems winter still.

106: WHEN IN THE CHRONICLE OF WASTED TIME

In praising the beauty of his friend, the poet says that the ancient praisers of the beauty of ladies and knights were really trying to express just such beauty as the poet's friend has. But neither the ancients who prefigured the friend nor the poet who sees him has the ability to express the friend's great worth.

107: NOT MINE OWN FEARS, NOR THE PROPHETIC SOUL

The poet's love has survived prophesied disasters of the times and through the immortalizing power of poetry will survive death. In lines 1-4, the poet's love is immune to his own fears and to wordly prophecies of disaster. In lines 5-8, his love has survived the bad omens ("eclipses") which astrologists, or "augurs," forecast, but which proved so false that even the forecasters laughed ("mock") at their presage. Lines 9-14 describe the poet's love as surviving death, since the times have become so "balmy" and since his poem provides an immortal monument to love.

116: LET ME NOT TO THE MARRIAGE OF TRUE MINDS

The poet asserts, in lines 1-4, the permanence of love based on the union of minds. Though the loved one may show alteration, love will not change. Lines 5-8 express this permanence in the metaphor of the fixed guiding star of the navigators. Though the worth of the star be not known, its "height" can be used for navigation. Lines 9-12 express the permanence of love through the metaphor of time as the reaper with a sickle. Though time may destroy "rosy lips and cheeks," love will last till the end of time. The end couplet merely emphasizes these beliefs.

129: THE EXPENSE OF SPIRIT IN A WASTE OF SHAME

The power of lust is so strong that though it submits man to "waste" and a "hell," he is unable to desist from it.

Lines 1-4 describe lust as murderously unrestrained in trying to gain its ends. Lines 5-12 describe the unreasonable extremes ("Past reason," "Mad") between lust unfulfilled and lust fulfilled—"enjoyed-despised," "bliss-woe," "joy-dream." Lines 13-14 point out the inability of man to shun this heaven that leads him to this hell.

130: MY MISTRESS' EYES ARE NOTHING LIKE THE SUN

The poet specifically rejects the "false" conventional descriptions of women: "eyes-sun," "lips-coral," "breast-snow," "cheeks-roses," "breath-perfume," "voice-music," "walk-goddess." Yet, while describing his mistress' beauty as much less than these exaggerations, the poet insists on the rarity and genuineness of his love.

144: TWO LOVES I HAVE OF COMFORT AND DESPAIR

The poet describes his conflict between his two loves—a good man and an evil woman.

Lines 1-4 characterize the "better angel" and the "worser spirit," one giving comfort and the other despair. Lines 5-8 tell that the "female evil" is stealing the friend from the poet and is corrupting both friend and poet. In lines 9-12, the poet fears that the two loves are together, and so the angel has turned into a fiend. Lines 13-14 state that the poet will remain uncertain until "my bad angel fire my good one out."

146: POOR SOUL, THE CENTER OF MY SINFUL EARTH

The poem describes the development of the soul at the expense of the body, rather than *vice versa*, as a way of conquering death.

Lines 1-8 question why the soul in the mortal body of "sinful earth" should "suffer dearth" while the body of "outward walls" is given costly attention, since the mansion of the body will fade and worms will eat it. Lines 9-14 suggest feeding the soul by taking "dross" from the body, and so destroying Death by allowing it no food.

WHEN ICICLES HANG BY THE WALL

This song from *Love's Labors Lost* depicts the special joy of winter—the comfort and geniality that man creates for himself to escape the cold. Images of discomfort (icicles hanging, the shepherd blowing on his fingers to warm them, frozen milk, red and raw nose) are offset by images of warmth and genial anticipation (crab apples roasting, the owl singing a "merry note," the maidservant cooling the pot).

Sonnets

KARL SHAPIRO

BUICK

In an erotic love poem to an automobile, the poet shows how much the machine culture has preempted our lives. In a melodious rhythm, the Buick is addressed as a sexual lover—"warm-hearted beauty . . . clocks of excitement . . . all instinct . . . satisfaction of love."

DRUG STORE

The epigraph from *Romeo and Juliet* contrasts the old apothecary's shop, which handled drugs only, to the modern drug store which has added the functions of cafe, tobacconist, and ice-cream parlor. Also, the passionate, love-and-death-romanticism of Shakespeare's lovers contrasts to the lifeless, crude "lusts" and "fellowships" of America's adolescents in their hang-out.

HOLLYWOOD

The extravagances of Hollywood most peculiarly define the soul of America: they show the "crude whim of a beginning people."

The "fabulous metaphors," "Laughter and love . . . industries," "the mystic makes a fortune," "superlatives come true"—such excesses and contradictions show a culture in its early youth, a "possible proud Florence."

NECROPOLIS

Even in the cemetery, the "necropolis," the rich prosper over the poor.

There the wealthy, "owners of rents and labors," have the most elaborate graves—names cut deepest in the stone, Latin, model temples adorning the grave, iron decorations, and shrubbery. In contrast, the poor are buried "thickly herded," with "standard sculpture" and cheap slabs and crosses.

THE DOME OF SUNDAY

The poem is a criticism of the modern city, where the lives of the people are devoid of individuality: "Row-houses and row-lives," "our women are one woman," "their visit to themselves." High up, the poet waits for a "vision" of someone different to "blot out this woman's sheen," but "nothing happens."

THE INTELLECTUAL

The poet attacks the intellectual for his lack of action.

Stanzas 1-7 describe the intellectual for whom "talk is all the value" and whose mind is a "Self-sealing clock." Stanzas 8-10 cry out for the intellectual to break loose, to "Do something!" But he is immune and lacks the will to act. Stanzas 11-13 give the poet's preference for any action—a milkman's, or a barber's. The poet spits, laughs, and fights, while the intellectual swallows his "stale saliva" and still sits.

UNIVERSITY

A modern university in the South is criticized for its senility, growing out of a historically-maintained class system.

In the university, Negros and Jews are outcasts, and newcomers are "outlanders" (stanza 1). "Equals" and "unequals" are distinguished. And sectional snobbery is claimed in considering the North "raw" and the West "unfinished" (stanza 2). The Deans in aloof buildings hold to the past like "dry spinsters over family plate" (stanza 3). A past of degeneracy such as "inbreeding and conformity" produces a "luckless race" (stanza 4). The "true nobleman" has degenerated from shapely thought and broad dream to "senile pleasure" (stanza 5).

PERCY BYSSHE SHELLEY

A LAMENT

The poet laments that grief has replaced joy in his response to nature. He now trembles where once he stood firmly (lines 1 and 2), and his heart, faint from grief, will no longer respond in delight to the seasons (lines 8-10).

ADONAIS

The poem has three general divisions: Stanzas 1-22 deal with the poet's and Nature's desolation at the death of Adonais (Keats), and suggest that the creatures of Keats' imagination also are mourning. Stanzas 23-29 show pity and sorrow being expressed by Urania (goddess of astronomy and also another name for Aphrodite or Venus; probably Shelley conceived of Urania as a universal Mother, the creative principle)—this sorrow is shared by brother poets. Stanzas 30-55 deal with the idea of physical death leading to spiritual life (see especially stanza 52).

The poem opens with the statement of mourning for the dead Adonais. The poet addresses Urania, seen as the mother of Adonais and of other great poets, who had earlier wept for the death of Milton (lines 28 ff). These deaths tell us that great spirits are subject to envy (stanza 5). Now, Urania's youngest son is dead and at peace, though subject to decay.

Now Adonais' inventions ("quick dreams") come to pay homage and to die with him (stanzas 9-13). And all Nature mourns—the morning, the winds, Spring, and so on (stanzas 14-17). With returning spring, when all things are joyous with quickening life, the question arises: Should only the spirit of man die (stanzas 18-20)? Grief is all that remains of Adonais. In sorrow, Urania goes to the corpse of Adonais. She wishes that he had had the strength to destroy his attackers (stanzas 23-28). Now the world is left empty of the "godlike mind."

Along with other "shepherds" (that is, poets) comes "one frail form" (Shelley) to mourn and to identify Adonais' fate with his own rejection (stanza 34), and after him a closer friend (Leigh Hunt). The next two stanzas bitterly attack the anonymous reviewer of Keats' *Endymion*.

Stanza 38 marks the turning point in the poem, from dejection to hope of spiritual life. Though the body returns to the dust, the soul flows "Back to the burning fountain whence it came." At this point, the poet introduces the idea that the immortal spirit returns to its spiritual source, the eternal Absolute. It is actually the mortal men remaining who are dying and decaying (stanzas 38-40). Therefore, let all Nature rejoice, for Adonais is one with Nature, and behind and within Nature is a spirit that gives it form (stanzas 41-43). The influence of great poets is undying. All the spirits of unfulfilled genius welcome Adonais (stanzas 45-46). Do not weep for Adonais, says the poet, but go to the cemetery in Rome. There, among those graves of the long dead and the newly dead, remember that physical death leads to the truth of eternity (stanzas 47-52). The spirit of Adonais calls, and the eternal spirit consumes "the last clouds of cold mortality." In this exalted mood, the poet concludes by asserting that he is now ready to leave this physical existence for spiritual life.

ENGLAND IN 1819

The poet lists the present evils of England: the king, the princes, the aristocracy, a starved people, a Godless religion, and an unjust legislature (Senate). The poet hopes that all these evils may lead to a revolution ("glorious Phantom").

HYMN TO INTELLECTUAL BEAUTY

The poet sees intellectual or spiritual beauty as the power that infuses all things and gives the only permanence and meaning amid the mutability and imperfection of the sensory world.

Stanza 1 tells of the glorifying shadow of the Power that visits the human heart. Stanza 2 describes the imperfections of gloom, hate, and despondency which are left by the Power's absence. Stanza 3 tells of the vain attempts of the past to explain imperfections through Demon, Ghost, or Heaven; for only the light of Intellectual Beauty gives meaning. Stanza 4 says that man would be immortal and omnipotent if Intellectual Beauty prevailed in his heart. Stanzas 5-7 describe the poet's boyhood vision of Intellectual Beauty and his dedication to free the world through Intellectual Beauty.

LINES (WHEN THE LAMP IS SHATTERED)

When the physical object is "shattered" or "broken," the beauty it created disappears (stanza 1). Similarly, when the spirit falls silent, the heart sings nothing but "sad dirges" (stanza 2). Of two lovers, love leaves the stronger heart first; the weaker one is left alone to endure the pain of love that it once had (stanza 3). You (the weaker one) will be rocked by passions and mocked by reason. You will be left exposed and suffering (stanza 4).

LOVE'S PHILOSOPHY

All the creations of nature, from the waters to the flowers, "mix forever/ With a sweet emotion." This example, says the poet to his loved one, should show us that we too should mingle our spirits and kiss.

MUTABILITY (WE ARE AS CLOUDS THAT VEIL THE MID-NIGHT MOON)

We are as impermanent as clouds or as lyres touched to various sounds by the wind. It makes no difference ultimately whether we laugh or weep: "Naught may endure but Mutability."

ODE TO THE WEST WIND

The poet addresses the West Wind as universal "destroyer and preserver" and asks this force to inspire him.

The wind drives the dead leaves before it and carries the seeds to their winter grave, until spring comes. The poet calls upon this spirit to hear him (section 1). Clouds are blown by the wind, forerunners of "the approaching storm." In this time of the dying year, a great storm will break. The poet calls again on the mighty wind to hear him (section 2). In the next section, the poet appeals still once more to this power to hear him. This is the power that woke to activity the Mediterranean from its summer calm, and made giant waves in the Atlantic (section 3).

The poet wishes that he might be a leaf, a cloud, or a wave that knows the power of the wind. Or, he says, perhaps he could be as he was in childhood, when he ran with the wind. Now, he is bowed and chained by the weight of years (section 4). He calls upon the wind to make him its "lyre." He calls upon the wind to be his spirit and so spread his thoughts about the world. There is hope, for Spring must follow Winter (section 5).

OZYMANDIAS

The "colossal wreck" of the statue of the ancient Egyptian ruler, Ozymandias (Ramses II), tells us that only these "lifeless things" survive from that time. This wreck is all that remains of a once cruel and powerful tryant.

PROMETHEUS UNBOUND

Shelley based his drama on the legend of Prometheus, whom Jupiter had ordered to be chained in torment until he revealed the secret that Jupiter needed to know. In Shelley's poem, Prometheus has suffered for long ages and he has learned love. With love and forgiveness for his oppressor, Prometheus is released and the universe returns to love and freedom. The poem in its broadest outlines is an allegory of the triumph of love over evil.

Act I

Prometheus opens with a review of his oppressor, his wrongs, and his pity. He then addresses his mother, Earth, who promises to raise a spirit to recall the curse of Prometheus. The Phantasm of Jupiter appears to repeat the curse, and Prometheus repents of it. Now, Mercury comes with the Furies to torture Prometheus further. In their discussion, Prometheus points out to Mercury that the mind creates evil and also that he, Prometheus, still refuses to submit to omnipotence. The Furies torture Prometheus, tortures which include descriptions of the evil done by men and the evil in men's hearts. A group of good spirits enter. They sing of love and foresee the coming of "Wisdom, Justice, Love, and Peace." The act ends with an allusion to Asia, the spirit of love for Prometheus.

Act II

Scene 1. Panthea comes to Asia to tell her dream of the freeing of Prometheus. The Echoes call to Asia, child of Ocean, to follow them.

Scene 2. As Asia and Panthea travel through a forest, a chorus chants of the dark path they follow and of the "delicate music" that fills the place.

Scene 3. Panthea and Asia now arrive at the entrance to Demogorgon's realm. The entrance is "Like a volcano's meteor-breathing chasm." The peak is surrounded by mists and awesome scenes. They go down to the Cave of Demogorgon as a chorus of Spirits sings a song of descent.

Scene 4. In the Cave of Demogorgon, Asia asks the spirit questions about the creation and about good and evil. Asia is dissatisfied with Demogorgon's answer as to "who reigns," but Demogorgon replies that ultimate knowledge of the real ruler is beyond immediate human perception. There follows a hopeful projection into the future, and the Spirit of the Hour arrives to carry off Asia and Panthea.

Scene 5. Asia undergoes a transformation as the spirit of love begins to flow through the universe. In her last song in this act, Asia forsees man's emergence "to a diviner day."

Act III

Scene 1. In the midst of his pride, Jupiter is taken to the lowest depths by Demogorgon.

Scene 2. Ocean and Apollo say that strife is now replaced by love and peace.

Scene 3. Prometheus describes the cave where he and the others are to live, a place of beautiful harmonies where the arts will have birth. He gives the Spirit of the Hour one last directive, to blow into the mystic shell over the cities of men. The Earth describes the new joy and growth she knows, now that Jove's tyranny has been overthrown.

Scene 4. The Spirit of the Earth tells Asia how she has seen the veil of Evil removed from man. Now beauty has come to the things of the earth. The Spirit of the Hour enters to describe the transformation in men and institutions.

Act IV

Time, carried by the past hours, is buried. A chorus of Hours and a chorus of the Spirits of the human mind hail the joy. Then the spirits separate into groups to pursue their tasks for a "new world of man."

Panthea and Ione hear a new sound. They see a chariot bearing a winged infant and a sphere of complex design in which they see the spirit of the Earth, asleep. They see into the dark recesses of the past.

Earth expresses her joy, and the Moon speaks of life. Love now permeates all things and frees man from "hate, and fear, and pain."

Finally, the voice of Demogorgon makes a last statement: Love is now triumphant, but if in the course of time evil returns, man must endure, forgive, love, and hope in order to regain his freedom.

SONG TO THE MEN OF ENGLAND

This poem is a general call to the proletariat to overthrow their masters and reap the benefits of their labor. The first five stanzas list abuses, the sixth stanza calls for reform, and the seventh and eighth stanzas call ironically for withdrawal to submission and death.

STANZAS: WRITTEN IN DEJECTION, NEAR NAPLES

After describing a beautiful day in stanza 1, when all things seem to have "a voice of one delight," the poet introduces his own isolation (stanza 2) and dejection (stanza 3). His life is now at a point of such low vitality that he could die. But should he die, though some may sorrow for him, they will not remember him with joy.

THE CLOUD

The last stanza tells us that the poet is using the cloud as a symbolic parallel between the natural cycle and the human cycle of life, death, and rebirth. In the preceding stanzas he describes the relation between water, the cloud, and growing things (lines 1-6) and the process by which the cloud moves (stanza 2). He describes the cloud in daylight and at night, in calm and in storm. The last stanza points out the idea of immortality in the cyclic process: "I change, but I cannot die."

THE INDIAN SERENADE

An Indian lover arises "from dreams of thee" to serenade his beloved in the sweet and melodious Indian night. In his suffering for love, he calls upon his beloved to kiss him and embrace him.

TO ——— (MUSIC, WHEN SOFT VOICES DIE)

Music lives in the memory; odors live in the senses they quicken (that is, stimulate or bring to life). When a rose dies, its petals form a bed for it. In such a manner, the speaker concludes, Love (perhaps with the idea that the beloved embodied or in a sense created Love) will slumber on thoughts of you. That is, as the music lingers in the memory, so the thoughts of the beloved in the memory or soul of the speaker will provide a "bed" for Love itself.

TO ___ (ONE WORD IS TOO OFTEN PROFANED)

The speaker says that this word and emotion, love, has been debased in common usage. Nevertheless, he adds, please accept the spiritual need and devotion that I feel, "the desire of the moth for the star."

TO A SKYLARK

The poet's main theme is the spiritual joy he hears in the skylark's song. The bird is "Like an embodied joy" as it flies ever higher from the earth, singing (stanza 2), while its song permeates all the regions of earth and air (lines 16-30). The skylark is like an imperial poet or a maiden filled with love, like a glowworm scattering its beautiful color, or a rose whose scent is spread by the winds (lines 35-55).

Observing that the bird's song surpasses the most joyous sounds that we know, the poet wonders where the song comes from. So pure and joyous is the song that even if we were happier than we are, we could not approach it. The poet concludes that if he had only half the gladness known by the bird he would sing with a "harmonious madness" that would cause all men to listen.

TO NIGHT

The poet asks Night, the weaver of dreams, to come swiftly over sea and land, for he has longed for the day to pass. It is not "Thy brother Death" that he wants nor "The sweet child Sleep" but only "beloved Night."

PHILIP SIDNEY

HAVING THIS DAY MY HORSE, MY HAND, MY LANCE (FROM <u>ASTROPHEL AND STELLA</u>)

The poet gives his beloved Stella the credit for inspiring him to win the tournament. After he won the tournament by guiding so well his horse, his hand, and his lance, various people offer reasons: horsemanship, strength, the skill of experience, chance, appropriate ancestry on "both sides." But all are wrong, says the poet. The true cause is that "her heavenly face" inspired him.

LOVING IN TRUTH, AND FAIN IN VERSE MY LOVE TO SHOW (FROM ASTROPHEL AND STELLA)

The poet rejects the imitative to write his love poetry out of the sincerity of his heart.

In lines 1-5, the poet seeks to please his beloved by writing "fit words to paint" his woe. In lines 6-11, he tries to copy "others' leaves" but finds "Invention" does not come through imitating others. In lines 12-14, the poet's muse counsels naturalness: "look in thy heart, and write."

WITH HOW SAD STEPS, O MOON, THOU CLIMB'ST THE SKIES! (FROM ASTROPHEL AND STELLA)

The poet, rejected by his beloved, projects his unhappiness onto the moon.

In lines 1-8, the poet sees the "sad steps," "wan face," and "languished grace" of the moon as signs that the moon is a lover wounded by the "busy archer" Cupid. In lines 9-14, the poet tells why men and the moon have unhappiness in love. It is because the lovers are constant, but the beautiful women are proud, scornful, and ungrateful.

ROBERT SOUTHWELL

THE BURNING BABE

In an allegory of the Christ Child, the poet, shivering in the snow, has a vision of a burning babe on fire like a furnace fed by Love, Justice, and Mercy. Men's defiled souls will be purified in the furnace and washed in the babe's blood. As the vision fades, the poet recalls that the day is that of Christ's nativity.

STEPHEN SPENDER

I THINK CONTINUALLY OF THOSE WHO WERE TRULY GREAT

The poem praises those who were truly great, that is, those who "fought for life."

Stanza 1 defines the great as those who remember the soul's history, in spirit and desire. Its spirit aspect is expressed in images of sun, fire, and song. Its desire aspect is imaged by blossoms from spring branches. Stanza 2 insists on the value of enjoying the pleasures of these desires ("delight of the blood") with their sources older than mankind ("ageless springs"). Likewise the growth of the spirit must not be smothered by the deadening activities of social living ("traffic," "noise and fog"). Stanza 3 states that nature (snow, sun, grass, cloud, wind) celebrates the names of those who "fought for life" ("sun," "fire's center"), that is, the flowering of the spirit and desires.

NOT PALACES, AN ERA'S CROWN

Constructive change ("light to life") can be brought about only by the fully-realized life in man.

Instead of formal and traditional productions of a culture whose people are "ordered like a single mind," men should "drink energy." Realizing to the fullest the experiences of eye, ear, touch, love, and all senses, they should leave their habitual ways ("gardens" and "singing feasts") to promote the equality and fulfillment of man. The habitual ways are destructive ("killers") and should be destroyed. The method can be militant ("program of the antique Satan"), but the purpose shall be opposite, to bring "light to life."

THE EXPRESS

The poem personifies an express train to enhance its power and motion from a physical on through a metaphysical implication.

The status of the train is enhanced as it moves from the station, along its course, and on to "beyond the crest of the world." It begins in the station with "plain manifesto" and "black statement," then becomes queenlike, passes people, passes death, acquires mystery, begins to sing, moves beyond time into "new eras," moves beyond country and island, moves beyond the world, and finally, cosmic "like a comet," it surpasses earthly nature (bird, bough).

THE LANDSCAPE NEAR AN AERODROME

The poem describes the sordidness of the homes, factories, children, and religion of a city as seen from a descending airliner.

Stanzas 1-2 describe the descent of the airliner. The travelers have been used to the beauty and gentleness of "miles of softness" across "feminine land" and sea. The beauty of the airliner itself is mothlike. In stanzas 3-4, the approach to the industrial city is sordid ("lank black fingers," "squat," "houses moan," "unhomely"). Children at play cry like wild birds and their cries are lost in the city's noise. In stanza 5, by the time the plane lands, the gentle moth beauty of stanza 1 has become a "landscape of hysteria" and religion is uglier than the "charcoaled batteries" of factories and is "blocking the sun."

THE PYLONS

The poet expresses his faith in technology to produce a great new social age.

Stanzas 1-3 describe the country life and landscape violated by the concrete pylons and the power lines they carry. Stanzas 4-5 see the pylons as prophesying the beautiful cities of the future.

ULTIMA RATIO REGUM

The poem is an ironic attack on money as the cause of the war which was responsible for the death of the young soldier.

Instead of war being "the final argument of kings" (in variation from the title), it is here the final argument of money. The money motif is also carried on through "gold," "Stock Exchange," and the irony of "expenditure justified."

The use of irony ("Was so much expenditure justified?") to suggest the boy's unimportance makes his death so tragic and important that the reader is outraged at the cause of death. Further outrage is produced by the callousness of contrasting associations with nature (lead and hillside, bullets and flowers, flags and leaves, hands and branches).

EDMUND SPENSER

AN HYMNE IN HONOUR OF BEAUTIE

The poem develops the Platonic concept that the Idea of Perfection, the "goodly Paterne" by which God created all things, is reflected in beautiful things on earth, particularly the loved woman, in whom the beautiful and the good are identical.

After stanzas 1-4, an invocation to Venus, the Queen of Beauty and the Mother of Love, the poem may be analyzed in five parts: the divine origin of Beauty (stanzas 5-9); the false nature of outer beauty (stanzas 10-14); the true nature of divine Beauty (stanzas 15-23); advice to lovers to seek true Beauty of the soul (stanzas 24-37); and a final tribute to Venus (stanzas 38-41).

The first part (stanzas 5-9) describes the origin of "perfect Beautie." Since God created all things from the divine Pattern, every earthly thing is beautiful to the degree that it partakes of "influence divine" and refines gross matter.

The second part (stanzas 10-14) points out the nature of false beauty. Such is founded on "outward show of things," which are transitory—"white and red" of cosmetics, "blossomes of the field," or "fair pictures."

The third part (stanzas 15-23) describes the nature of true Beauty based on the divine Spirit. Because of the divine origin of the soul, the body will be beautiful to the degree that it reflects the divine Spirit (stanzas 15-20). Though the body may be deformed through various imperfections of matter, accidents, or abuse, the soul remains fair because things "immortal no corruption take" (stanzas 21-23).

The fourth part (stanzas 24-37) gives advice to lovers to seek true Beauty of the soul. They are to shun lust and seek love (stanzas 24-27); they are to seek the soul-mate ordained by heaven for them, as "made out of the same mould" (stanza 30); and they are to love not the outer form, but the soul, "free from fleshes frayle infection" (stanzas 31-37). Lovers, with eyes sharper than those of other men, can see the woman's beauty reflecting her soul—"beams bright," "compassion," "sweet musicke," "thousand Graces," "chaste pleasures."

The final four stanzas (38-41) offer tribute to Venus, to request that her kingdom spread, that the poet's beloved will give him grace, and that the power of Venus' Beauty may relieve his grief.

AN HYMNE IN HONOUR OF LOVE

After the invocation to the God of Love to inspire the poet's hymn of earthly love (stanzas 1-6), the poem may be viewed in two parts: (1) the birth of Love and his influence in the world (stanzas 7-17), and (2) the ennobling effects of the lover's torments (stanzas 18-44).

The first part (stanzas 7-17) begins with the birth of Love (stanzas 7-11). His contradictory nature is apparent: born out of "Penurie and Plenty," he is the oldest and the youngest of the gods. He gets light from his mother, Venus, and moves through the unshaped world. In stanzas 12-13, Love puts order into the world by organizing the four elements out of chaos and by tempering their hostile forces. In stanzas 14-17, Love maintains all things in the world and influences them by the power of love. It is desire for Beauty, the closest to Love's heavenly fire, which makes a man wish to propagate himself.

The second main section (stanzas 18-44) begins with a description of the conventional pains of the lover (stanzas 18-23). Stanzas 24-31 point out the purpose of the lover's pains: to ennoble him, to expel "sordid basenesse," and to make him value his love when he gets it. Stanzas 32-35 describe the bravery of the lover (such as Leander, Aeneas, Achilles, and Orpheus) as he undergoes dangers "her grace to gaine." Stanzas 36-39 describe the jealousy of the lover. Once gaining the beloved's favor, he wishes to be loved "not best, but to be lov'd alone." So, there are the envies and the fears which "make a lover's life à wretches hell." In stanzas 40-42, the consummation of the lover, or his entrance into love's "paradize," is brought about through the "Purgatorie" of his pains. The closing stanzas 33-44 ask the Christian God to give the poet his desire, for which he will sing a heavenly hymn.

AN HYMNE OF HEAVENLY BEAUTIE

The hymn praises heavenly beauty in creation, in God, and in God's Sapience. The invocation (stanzas 1-3) asks God for help to show immortal beauty to men that they may learn to love that "heavenly beautie." Thereafter, the poem may be analyzed in 3 sections: (1) the ascending order of beauty in God's creation (stanzas 4-15); (2) the beauty of God (stanzas 16-26); and (3) the beauty of God's Sapience (stanzas 27-42).

In the first section (stanzas 4-15), the poet praises beauty in creation according to the great chain of being, beginning with the "base world" and mounting through the various degrees to the throne of God, the nearer to God the purer the form. First (stanzas 4-7) are the beautiful forms of earth in ascending beauty through the four elements of earth, water, air, and fire; then on to the sky of stars, especially the Sun and Moon (8-9); the farther stars (10); the first Movers (11); the heaven of happy souls and beyond to the place of Platonic Ideas of pure Intelligences (12); to Powers, Potentates, Princes, States, Dominions (13); and to Cherubim and Seraphim, angels and archangels (14). Finally, in stanza 15, is the "Highest" in its "endless perfectnesse" so far beyond all others in the ascending degrees of beauty that the poet's mortal tongue cannot hope to express it.

The second section (stanzas 16-26) describes God's beauty. In stanza 16, the poet thinks that if the parts of God in creation are so beautiful, how much more glorious are the essential parts of God, such as truth, love, wisdom. Stanza 17 states that God displays himself to all creatures only indirectly, for even the angels cannot endure the sight of God's face. In stanzas 18-19, man, unable to stand such glory, has the Neo-Platonic means of seeing God through "his workes"—that is, all that is beautiful and therefore good. So, in stanzas 20-26, by "heavenly contemplation" we can mount to God's throne, where he sits with the rod of Righteousness on the seat of Truth, which emits glorious light.

The third section (stanzas 27-42) praises the Sapience of God. Stanzas 27-29 show Sapience sitting in God's bosom, as the queen and darling of the Deity, holding a scepter by which she rules heaven and earth. Stanzas 30-34 describe her beauty. It is greater than that of all women and angels (30), greater than that which the painters of Venus could have portrayed and greater than that of Venus herself (31-32), and greater than the poet can describe (33). So, in stanza

34, the poet will let the angels praise her and describe her; he can only be possessed by her. Stanzas 35-40 describe being possessed by God's Beloved. To see her "celestiall face" gives a man all happiness and takes away all earthly wants (35), for she pours upon him heavenly riches (36) and gives him ecstasy which makes him forget all worldly things (37). Henceforth, all worldly things become worthless shadows—fleshly sense, pomp, ambition, riches (38-40). Stanzas 41-42 call upon his hungry soul to cease feeding on worldly shadows but to look up at last to that "Soveraine Light" from which all perfect beauty springs.

AN HYMNE OF HEAVENLY LOVE

The poem praises the heavenly love of Christ as shown in his redemption of fallen man and enjoins all men to love Christ and man and so come to the "Idee of his pure glorie."

In the invocation (stanzas 1-3), the poet repents of his poems to earthly love and asks Christ, the God of Love, to lift him above the earth to sing a heavenly hymn. Thereafter, the poem may be analyzed in four sections: (1) the creation by Love of all beings, leading to man (stanzas 4-17); (2) the fall of man and his redemption through Christ by love (stanzas 18-22); (3) the duty of man to requite Christ's love by loving God and his brethren (stanzas 23-31); and (4) a call to all the world to love Christ and so be filled with his divine Idea and heavenly love (stanzas 32-41).

The first section (stanzas 4-17), begins with the "eternal powre" existing before time and the world and moving in itself by love. Stanzas 5-7 give the origin of the Son and the Holy Spirit. Stanzas 8-14 describe God's "second brood," the Angels. Begotten by love, they served him happily until through pride and ambition the brightest angel led a rebellion that sent millions to Hell. In stanzas 15-17, man is created in the image of God, the "heavenly Patterne," to fill the space left by the fallen angels. Man is made like God, for love likes to see itself in other lovely shapes.

The second section (stanzas 18-22) describes the fall of man and the Redemption. Stanza 18 shows man's fall from grace which brought death to himself and the race. In stanzas 19-22, Christ in his love to redeem man descended to "fleshes fraile attyre," for since guilt came in the flesh, it must be removed in the flesh.

The third section (stanzas 23-31) enjoins us to requite Christ's love by loving God and man. In stanzas 23-27, the poet marvels at the depth of Christ's love in shedding his blood and wonders how we can requite such love. First (stanza 28), we can love God, because he saved us from the "second death" and gave us the food of life, the sacrament. Second (stanzas 29-31), we can love our brethren, who were made in God's image and shall return to him equally redeemed.

The fourth section (stanzas 32-41) calls all to love Christ and so to be filled with his divine Idea. Stanza 32 calls the earth to rise from its dirt and read Christ's mercies. Stanzas 33-35 describe three of these mercies—his nativity, his good life, and the sufferings of his betrayal, trial, and crucifixion. Stanzas 36-41 state that if we so read Christ's mercies, we will love Christ (37), renounce all other loves (38), be so filled with holy fire of Christ (39) that "earthes glories" will seem as dirt (40) and the soul shall be filled with the "Idee of his pure glorie" and "celestiall love" (41).

EPITHALAMION

This epithalamion, or wedding song, is in celebration of the poet's own wedding. The poem may be broken into four parts:

The first part of the poem describes the preparation of the bride (stanzas 1-8). After the muses are invoked (stanzas 1-2), the bridal bower is adorned by nymphs (stanzas 3-4). The bride is awakened and adorned by the three Graces who attended Venus (stanzas 5-6). The groom asks the sun god to let this day be his (stanza 7). The wedding music begins (stanza 8).

The second part of the poem describes the arrival of the bride and the wedding (stanzas 9-13). The bride arrives, wearing white, modest and beautiful (stanza 9). Her beauty of body is described in stanza 10 and her "inward beauty" in stanza 11. The priest performs the wedding, and the Angels sing (stanzas 12-13).

The third part of the poem describes the wedding party (stanzas 14-16). The bride is brought home and the wedding party begins with drinking wine, singing, dancing, and ringing of bells (stanzas 14-15). The day becomes long and weary as the groom waits for the wedding night (stanza 16).

The fourth part of the poem describes the wedding night (stanzas 17-23). The bride goes to bed (stanza 17), and the groom asks the "welcome night" to watch over them (stanza 18) and to keep away evil spirits (stanza 19). He asks Silence to keep watch as the two make love throughout the night (stanza 20). He prays for Cynthia, goddess of the moon and of reproduction, to give them children (stanza 21); for Juno, goddess of marriage, to bless them (stanza 22); and for the high heavens to grant a large posterity (stanza 23). In the final stanza (24) the poet offers the poem as a substitute for "many ornaments," probably wedding gifts.

ONE DAY I WROTE HER NAME UPON THE STRAND (FROM AMORETTI)

The poet expresses his belief in the power of his poetry to immortalize his beloved and their love.

In lines 1-4, the poet writes on the sand his beloved's name, which is washed away by waves and tide. In lines 5-8, she tells him his attempt is vain, since both she and her name must decay. But the poet insists, in lines 9-14, that his verse will make eternal her virtues, her name, and their love.

PROTHALAMION

This prothalamion, or wedding song, is in honor of the double marriage on the same day of two sisters, Elizabeth and Katherine Somerset, to Henry Gilford and William Peter. The two sisters are symbolized as white swans swimming on the Thames.

In stanzas 1-2, the poet, dissatisfied with his lack of professional advancement, wanders along the banks of the Thames, where he sees a flock of nymphs gathering flowers for the bridal day. In stanzas 3-4, two white swans appear, and the nymphs are awed by their beauty—like Leda, or the swans of Venus, or Angels. In stanzas 5-7, the nymphs adorn the swans with flowers and then sing a song wishing them happiness, the smile of the love goddess, Peace, and Plenty. The river affectionately bears the swans along, attended by the other fowls. In stanzas 8-10, they arrive at London, where the poet laments the loss of his former patron (Earl of Leicester) and praises another peer (Essex) for his victory in battle with Spain. The noble Lord descends with the two grooms, who receive the "two faire Brides."

WALLACE STEVENS

A HIGH-TONED OLD CHRISTIAN WOMAN

With the leading premise that poetry is the supreme imaginative act ("fiction"), the poet, speaking to a high-toned old Christian woman, compares the merits of religion and art as ways to the spiritual life. Religion (lines 2-5) begins with the moral law of ascetic self-denial and moves from conscience to church nave to heaven to palms. The artist (lines 6-13) begins with the opposing law of sensuous enjoyment and moves from bawdiness to pagan peristyle to masque to palms. Both laws agree in principle: they arrive at some kind of exalted ordering of experience, symbolized by palms. But sensuous artists (lines 14-20), like flagellants of Christian discipline, may out of their creative act ("whip themselves") reach an experience comparable to the heavenly exaltation of the Christian ("sublime," "among the spheres"). So (lines 21-22), "fictive things" (poetry) are supreme as stated in line 1, for they act ("wink") beyond the disapproval ("wince") of the Christian.

ANECDOTE OF THE JAR

The jar, as a work of art, is used as an example of how the creative imagination imposes order upon an unordered environment.

When the poet placed a jar, with its created form, upon a hill in a wilderness, it imposed its sense of order on the disorder. As the jar "took dominion," the "slovenly wilderness," including hill, bird, and bush, rose up to it and became no longer wild.

ASIDES ON THE OBOE

The "Asides" are imaginative reflections on choosing an ultimate belief. The oboe is one of many musical terms Stevens has used to represent creative imagination and poetry.

Part I offers three choices. (1) The traditional myths being "obsolete," (2) the humanist's idea alone is vital ("philosopher's man," "dew"). But if we imagine this man to be "ever wrong," there is still (3) man idealized ("impossible possible").

In part II, this "central man" for a time gives insight ("transparence") and final meaning ("unless I make thee so").

Then, in part III, death and war show that the idealized-man concept is the "sum of men" only when it includes the "central evil" as well as the "central good."

DISILLUSIONMENT OF TEN O'CLOCK

The "disillusionment" is the dullness of the imagination of most people, as suggested by the commonplace dreams they will have when they go to bed at ten o'clock.

The people's nightgowns are white, not some exotic color combination, and most people will not dream of strange things like "baboons and periwinkles." Only an occasional old sailor has the imagination to dream something as exciting as catching "tigers/ In red weather."

DOMINATION OF BLACK

The poem is an expression of how the imagination can begin with an outer image and move through a series of associated images to produce a related feeling.

The speaker of the poem looks at a fire in a room at night. The imagination sees the fire as like leaves, then moves from a vision of leaves to their resemblance to peacock tails, then to the sound of peacock cries, then to the peacocks' cries as sounds of terror, then to the sound of terror itself ("a cry against"), and so to a feeling of terror ("I felt afraid").

GALLANT CHATEAU

The nothingness of death can be preferable to disagreeable life situations.

In stanza 1 the poet questions whether it is necessarily bad to have found that someone has died ("empty bed"). In stanzas 2-5 he points out several worse situations that one could have found ("tragic . . . bitter . . . cold . . . pitiless verse . . . immense solitude"). The poet concludes in stanza 6 that it is good to find nothingness rather than the endless round of unpleasantness "tuned and tuned and tuned." The "empty bed" can really be the "gracious mansion" indicated by the title.

PETER QUINCE AT THE CLAVIER

The poet uses the dominant metaphor of music-as-feeling to express the theme of the greater permanence of beautiful feeling over the sensory stimulus which evokes it. The title alludes to Shakespeare's *Midsummer Night's Dream*, in which Peter Quince presents a farcical version of a tragic love story. The speaker of the poem, like Peter Quince, interprets a love story. The speaker's love story is about himself and a woman he is thinking of.

In Part I, the speaker, making music on the keys of the clavier, thinks of and desires a woman in "blue-shadowed silk." He compares his feeling to music—an experience of the spirit produced by sensory stimulus. The particular kind of music produced in him by desire is that music, or "strain," produced in the elders by Susanna (of the story of Susanna and the Elders in the *Apocrypha*). The elders are base, thin-blooded, bawdy, and sensual.

Part II describes the "music" of Susanna as she bathes, attended by her Byzantine maids. She, in contrast to the lascivious elders, is langorous, innocent, and beautiful.

Part III suggests the harsh, ugly aftermath of the sensual elders' attempt to violate Susanna.

Part IV deals with the philosophy of the relationship between the lovers of the poem (speaker and "you") as paralleling the elders and Susanna: the feeling (or music) coming from beauty outlives the sense stimulus which evokes it.

Stanzas 1-2 of Part IV describe the relationship between sense, mind, and feeling. Beauty stays but a moment in the mind, since mind is only a "portal" by which the stimulus moves to feeling. But beauty itself ("in the flesh") does not die; it is "immortal," forever remembered. For while the sensory stimulus itself passes ("the body dies"), the beauty of feeling produced lives on in the memory of feeling. Thus maidens, evenings, gardens—the whole Susanna-type situation—die, but the music "plays" on in the immortality of memory.

Stanza 3 of Part IV compares the momentary sensory stimulus of the elders to the permanent "music" of Susanna. They desired her in sense only, not in feeling. The desire stopped with the body, and so "escaping," did not become the feeling that is "music." Their desire ended thus in death's "scraping" while Susanna's music endured.

Since the relationship of the speaker and the woman (of Part I) parallels that of Susanna and the elders ("like the strain" of Part I), the woman's music escaped the speaker. In this ironic aspect, the

Peter Quince of the title applies. The relationship between the speaker and the woman is not a tragic or beautiful love story, but a farce.

STUDY OF TWO PEARS

The two pears offer examples of absolute external reality: the observer can will to conceive of them as "nothing else" but pears. They cannot be seen as viols, nudes, bottles, or flat surfaces with curved outlines. Their own sense data dominates—"yellow forms," "round/ Tapering," "hard dry leaf hangs," "Citrons, oranges and greens."

SUNDAY MORNING

A woman ponders the Christian and other promises of an afterlife and finds that she prefers the sensuous pleasures of this life.

In stanza 1, a woman in the complacencies of her drawing room on a Sunday morning reflects about the "ancient sacrifice" of Christ. Her thoughts pass over the seas to "silent Palestine" to consider the significance of "the blood and sepulchre" of Christ.

In stanzas II-IV, the woman states her preference for the sensuous pleasures of this life to the nonhuman paradise of the next life. The sensuous pleasures such as "Passions of rain," "wet roads," "bough of summer," and "April's green" appeal more than the "inhuman" gods, such as Jove, and the afterlives they promise—"golden underground," "heaven's hill."

In stanzas V-VI, the woman states her preference for death rather than an afterlife; for death, as necessary to change, is "mother of beauty," and changelessness, even in heaven, is dull and ugly.

In stanzas VII-VIII, the woman resolves on the pleasurable things of this world, such as men dancing, deer walking, quail whistling, sweet berries—all the "old chaos of the sun," even though these things perish and life sinks "Downward to darkness" of death.

THE EMPEROR OF ICE-CREAM

The poem describes the meaninglessness of death to modern society.

Stanza 1 describes a wake at which the people treat death with irreverence. The girls show lack of respect by dawdling in everyday dress and the boys by bringing flowers presented not decorously but wrapped in old newspaper. Calling ice cream "concupiscent" and "the only emperor" suggests the dominance of the frivolous, the party mood. The contradiction is sharpened by having the cigar-rolling, muscular man dish up the ice cream. The poet asks that reality ("be") put an end to the seeming that death is frivolous.

Stanza 2 uses harsh details to emphasize the solemn reality of death. Now out of the commonplace (dresser with missing knobs) comes the woman's own self-embroidered sheet, ironically, to "cover her face." The "horny feet" protruding can show "how cold she is, and dumb." The lamp with fixed beam suggests the definiteness of death, and the last line becomes a sardonic mockery of the irreverent mood of the people in stanza 1.

THE GLASS OF WATER

Psychic reality, such as "one's ideas," dominates sensory reality, such as a "glass of water" and "dogs and dung."

Stanza 1 points out a parallel. Just as the outer reality of a glass of water is a "state" between two poles ("melt," "freeze"), so inner reality ("metaphysical") may vary with the perceiving consciousness. Stanza 2 and part of stanza 3 suggest two of the ways one may perceive a glass of water: one may view the water as a pool with the light as a lion which comes down to drink. In "another state" the mind may perceive the glass of water as "parts of poems." In the rest of stanza 3 and in stanza 4, the poet ("fat Jocundus") considers that one's inner reality varies as does the perception of the exterior glass of water. That is, the "centre of our lives" at any one time and place is a "state" dependent upon "one's ideas."

THE IDEA OF ORDER AT KEY WEST

It is the creative imagination that gives order to outer reality and to ourselves. The situation is that of the speaker and a companion standing at the far edge of Florida, listening to a woman singer who, by creatively singing, imposes order on sea, self, and listeners.

Stanzas 1-3 describe the singer as she dominated the sea, singing beyond its "genius" or creative spirit. As she sang above the chaos of the sea with its "empty sleeves," "grinding water," and "gasping wind," she was "maker of the song she sang," and so the listeners heard, not the sea, but her.

Stanzas 4-5 point out how the singing (as an act of creative consciousness) imposed order on disorder. Her song was more than the "voice of the sea" and the "voice of the sky"; it was more than "her voice, and ours." More than a voice, she was "the maker," "the single artificer of the world." So, she turned the disorder into order and meaning for the world ("Whatever self it had") and for herself ("the one she sang").

Stanzas 6-7 describe the order imposed upon the listeners. When the speaker and his companion (Ramon) turned toward the town (stanza 6), order had been imposed ("mastered," "fixing," "zones") not only upon the sea and the night but also upon the listeners. Their urge to order themselves and their origins had become more spiritual ("ghostlier") and "keener."

THE MOTIVE FOR METAPHOR

Man's motive for describing experience metaphorically is to avoid facing the basic reality of himself ("never quite yourself").

The reason for liking autumn (stanza 1) and spring (stanza 2) is that these seasons make but small demands ("half dead," "without meaning"; "half colors of quarter-things"). In such an "obscure world" (stanza 3), one does "not want nor have to be" himself. So, man prefers the resemblance of metaphor to the direct reality of fundamental experiences, described by the series of metaphors in stanzas 3-4 ("noon," "A B C," "X").

THE SENSE OF THE SLEIGHT-OF-HAND MAN

The means of grasping the meaning ("Sense") of nature ("Sleight-of-Hand Man") is not intellectual but emotional and imaginative.

Moments of exaltation ("grand flights," "Sunday baths," "tootings at the weddings of the soul") occur unpredictably ("as they occur"). Nature, too, like a sleight-of-hand man performing magical tricks, shows its moments of beauty unpredictably ("bluish clouds," "leaves," "floods of white," "bluejay," "sun"). This "sense" of nature is not dependent upon "myths" and "gods" nor upon intellectual explanations ("Could you have said . . . ?"). It depends on the capacity to see metaphors ("wheel," "fire-eye," "cornet," "island") and to feel one's life ("mate his life") as one with nature ("the pearly spouse"). Perhaps only the "ignorant man" can avoid intellectualizing enough to achieve such an emotional, imaginative mating with nature.

THIRTEEN WAYS OF LOOKING AT A BLACKBIRD

Truth as perceived is relative to both the object and the perceiver's state of mind. The blackbird is a constant in thirteen different shifts of situation, mood, or concept. There are thirteen or more contexts in which we can look at anything: (1) blackbird as motion; (2) blackbird as choice; (3) blackbird as part of the drama, or "pantomime," of nature; (4) blackbird as part of love or human relation; (5) blackbird as actual and remembered; (6) blackbird as portent; (7) blackbird as available sex, opposed to sexual fantasy; (8) blackbird as songmaker; (9) blackbird as particular appearance, whose movement exposes the underlying general reality; (10) blackbird as harmony; (11) blackbird as death; (12) blackbird as change; and (13) blackbird as timelessness.

JOHN SUCKLING

CONSTANCY (OUT UPON IT, I HAVE LOVED)

The cavalier poet shows his cynical attitude toward women and love. After indicating in stanzas 1-2 the low value he puts upon constancy in love, he does in stanzas 3-4 manage a dubious compliment to the present woman in her rare ability to hold his love for three whole days.

SONG (WHY SO PALE AND WAN, FOND LOVER?)

This is a typical cavalier poem in its cynical, devil-may-care attitude toward women and love.

The poet urges lightness and gaiety in winning women, not being "pale and wan" (stanza 1) or "mute" (stanza 2). And if the woman is not easy to persuade ("of herself"), then the "devil take her!" (stanza 3).

HENRY SURREY

DESCRIPTION OF SPRING WHEREIN EACH THING RENEWS, SAVE ONLY THE LOVER

In the "sweet season" of Spring, all things put on new life except the lover. Hill and vale, nightingale, turtledove, deer, snake, bee— "these pleasant things" show that care is ended. But with the lover "sorrow springs."

LOVE, THAT DOTH REIGN AND LIVE WITHIN MY THOUGHT

This adaptation of Petrarch's *Sonnetto in Vita 91* describes a lover as saddened when the woman rebukes his vigorous expression of love.

Lines 1-4 describe love as a king and warrior who lives in the speaker's thoughts, "built his seat" in the breast, and shows himself as a banner in the face. In lines 5-8, the woman rebukes this "hot desire." In lines 9-14, "coward Love" flees to the heart and the speaker must follow his "lord" there.

ALGERNON CHARLES SWINBURNE

BEFORE THE BEGINNING OF YEARS (FROM ATALANTA IN CALYDON)

This is a statement of man's fate, which is paradoxical and frustrating.

Many elements "came to the making of man," such as grief, pleasure, memory, love, and so on (lines 1-12). The gods took up the ingredients and created "The holy spirit of man" (lines 13-28). They gave man life. They gave him time for work and they gave him time for pleasure. But he has "foreknowledge of death," and his achievements are without fulfillment: "His life is a watch or a vision/ Between a sleep and a sleep" (lines 29-48).

HERTHA

The voice of Hertha, the life-force, describes the process of evolutionary development.

Hertha is the original creative force, existing before all other things, and she permeates all things, subject and object alike (lines 1-30). She tells man to stop looking to God and to find his true origins in the creative force within him, for he is ignorant of the ultimate sources of creation. Such knowledge can come only from the mother herself (lines 31-65). Man should free himself of false ideas of God, for the only God is "To be man with thy might." Man should learn from the divine spirit within himself (lines 66-85). Hertha describes the process whereby man advances in accordance with his increasing knowledge from superstition to truth. These advances occur by gradual changes in the slow process of time (lines 86-135). Growth continues in spite of everything, and in the dim past there evolved the spirit of man. Man should realize himself "with freedom of soul," not bowed to any God (lines 136-185), for the terror of divine wrath gives way to truth. Man lives in freedom in the full development of love and truth (lines 186-200).

HYMN TO PROSERPINE

A Roman regrets the passing of the old pagan religion for Christianity. He addresses Proserpine, the goddess of the underworld.

The speaker says that Proserpine gives sleep and that he is weary of life (lines 1-12). The old gods of wrath are replaced by the new gods of pity, but all that men really need in their bitter life is peace (lines 13-22). The speaker asks if the Galilean (Jesus) will take away all the sensuous joys of living, for this life is the only life we have (lines 23-34). Since the new faith has in the course of things brought an aura of grayness and suffering and death, he defies Christ (lines 35-46). The eternal and destructive power of the sea will survive all the gods, including the Galilean (lines 47-74). The speaker contrasts the mother of Christ, who brought sorrow, with Aphrodite, who brought the joy of life (lines 75-88). Proserpine is the "daughter of earth," and the speaker turns to her as a mother. She shall endure beyond all others, for she gives sleep. And death is stronger than all gods (lines 89-110).

THE GARDEN OF PROSERPINE

The poem asserts that death is a peaceful sleep.

The speaker is watching a peaceful field, and he states that he is weary of life (lines 1-16). Here, in this peaceful place (lines 17-24), there grow only flowers without fruit, except for poppies, the flowers of Proserpine (that is, death), which sleep through the night (lines 25-40). A man's only goal is death, and Proserpine stands ready to gather all living things. She forgets the earth, and all things come to her (lines 41-72). Sorrow and joy are alike unsure, and no loves endure (lines 73-80). We are thankful, says the speaker, that no life goes on forever and that we will finally reach an eternal sleep (lines 81-96).

WHEN THE HOUNDS OF SPRING
(FROM ATALANTA IN CALYDON)

This is a chorus addressed to Artemis, goddess of the moon.

When Spring comes, Artemis (the moon) brings leaves and rain, and the song of the nightingale is less sad (stanza 1). The chorus implores Artemis to come quickly (stanza 2), and they wonder how man can find her (stanza 3). Winter is gone, and the force and fertility of spring permeate everything (stanzas 4-5). The gods pursue the maidens who are their followers (Maenad, Basarid, and Bacchanal) (stanzas 6-7).

ALLEN TATE

ODE TO THE CONFEDERATE DEAD

Tate in his essay "Narcissus as Narcissus" provides an analysis of the poem. He says the poem is about solipsism or Narcissism—preoccupation with self. In eulogizing the Confederate dead, the poet contrasts their social heroism with the modern locked-in ego, symbolized by the blind crab and the jaguar.

The spectator at the Confederate graveyard in his subjective prison, his solipsism, cannot identify with leaves and wind of nature, with the dead, or with the heroism of the entire society. He shows the "cut-off-ness" of the modern intellectual from the world. While the active faith of the Confederate dead showed the ebullient spirit of an entire society, the man at the gate is like the blind crab and the jaguar—they have mobility and energy, but no purposeful world to use them in. Nothing is left to the man at the gate but the "gentle serpent" of time and death, the "ravenous grave."

EDWARD TAYLOR

HUSWIFERY

Using the metaphor of a housewife's making a garment, the poet prays for divine grace to give him godly character.

In stanza 1, the yarn is spun out of God's Word and the poet's affections, soul, and conversation. In stanza 2, the cloth itself is made out of the poet, the Holy Spirit, God's ordinances, and heavenly accoutrements. In stanza 3, the new godly garment is put on the total person—understanding, will, affections, judgment, conscience, memory, words, and actions. He is thus "clothed in holy robes for glory."

MEDITATION ONE (WHAT LOVE IS THIS)

The poet expresses his rapturous devotion to God's love.

In stanzas 1-2 he marvels at God's love, so overwhelming that it could not be contained in his infinity, and so it "Married our manhood," runs over all the world, and overflows hell. In stanza 3 the poet prays to be fired with love for God.

MEDITATION EIGHT (I KENING THROUGH ASTRONOMY DIVINE)

The poem develops the metaphor of Christ as the "bread of life" come to give nourishment to the soul.

Stanzas 1-3 show the poet's soul without the bread of life, because his soul, like a bird of paradise in the cage of his body, had sinned—"peckt the Fruit forbid." In stanzas 4-6, God in his tender mercy made his son into the living bread which he offered to all, and the life-giving bread itself invites: "Eate, Eate me, Soul, and thou shalt never dy."

THE EXPERIENCE

The poet tells of his mystical experience of union with God.

Stanzas 1-3 use the main images of light and flame to express how God "filld my Soul then to the brim" and "did me Enflame." In stanza 4, the poet feels himself superior to the angels in that he is nearer to Godhead by having the Lord's nature. In stanza 5, he asks that he be made a "Golden Harp" to sing praises to God.

THE REFLECTION

The poet, offering adoration to Christ at the Lord's Supper, sees in Christ's redeeming power a "reflection" of paradise before the fall.

In stanzas 1-2, the poet asks why Christ does not "my cup o'erflow." In stanza 3, the poet asks for his sin to be removed, as filth from conduit pipes, so that he can be filled with "Thy sweetness." For, in stanzas 4-5, Christ is able to remove sin. Though "ink-faced sin" once chased paradise away, Christ at the Feast of the Lord's Supper stands "'Tween heaven and earth" and so restores "heaven-lost happiness."

ALFRED, LORD TENNYSON

ASK ME NO MORE

The three stanzas mark three stages in a maiden's gradually yielding to her lover's entreaties.

Stanza 1 implies great reserve ("when have I answered thee?"), and refers to the lover rather distantly and critically as "too fond." Stanza 2 implies that the maiden is beginning to be touched: the lover is now "my friend" and the maiden "will not have thee die!" In stanza 3 the maiden addresses the lover as "dear love" and says that "at a touch I yield."

COME DOWN, O MAID

Metaphorically, the poem invites the maid to abandon a life of thought and abstraction for a more common life of love in less rarified surroundings. Literally, the speaker urges the maid to come down from the mountain heights to the peaceful but productive life of the valley.

In lines 1-17 the shepherd urges the maid to come from the heights, for "Love is of the valley." Love is not found in the forbidding places she is used to. In lines 17-31 the shepherd continues to urge the maid to leave the forbidding heights, and he concludes by describing the sweet sounds of the valley.

In Memoriam

This is an elegy occasioned by the early death of Tennyson's close friend, Arthur Henry Hallam. The shock and grief at his death caused Tennyson to explore the meaning of life in terms of various problems. Some of these problems are universal, such as the loss of loved ones. Some are specifically Victorian, such as the religious doubt raised by scientific discoveries. In its main outline, the poem is an assertion of spiritual faith in the midst of doubt brought on by grief.

PROLOGUE: STRONG SON OF GOD, IMMORTAL LOVE

In a mood of humility, the speaker admits the limitations of his and all men's knowledge. He expresses faith in "immortal Love" and asks forgiveness for "these wild and wandering cries."

Having asserted faith in immortal Love, the speaker defines this force as the creator of Life and Death (lines 1-8). This force is also the creator of man, who must have been created for some purpose. Since this force of immortal Love seems to be an idealized humanity, man is probably destined to form himself according to this model (lines 9-16).

Man's knowledge is incomplete and transitory; his ultimate recourse is faith. As man's knowledge grows, man's reverence should grow with it so that his mind and spirit may become one. The speaker implores help in achieving the ability "to bear thy light " (lines 17-32)

The Prologue concludes with a personal plea for forgiveness for the pride that the speaker sees in himself (lines 33-36), for the grief in the loss of his friend (lines 37-40), and for the poems themselves (lines 41-44).

1: I HOLD IT TRUE WITH HIM WHO SINGS

Although, like the poet Goethe, the speaker believes that men may rise above their former selves, he is doubtful that his grief will result in a future gain. In desperation, he says that his love will cling to the grief. It is better to be obsessed with grief than for Time to destroy the memory of the beloved friend.

2: OLD YEW, WHICH GRASPEST AT THE STONES

The speaker is impelled to identify himself with the yew, the symbol of death, for that "sullen tree" represents unchanging gloom, impervious to the glow and bloom of life. The yew, which is situated in a cemetery, does not seem to produce new birth, as do the flower and the flock. It is impervious to the gale as to the sun. As the speaker gazes on the tree, he seems to become absorbed into it.

3: O SORROW, CRUEL FELLOWSHIP

Sorrow whispers of the blind forces that control the universe and the "phantom, Nature." Sorrow, a cruel companion, tells him that the universe at large is purposeless and "waste"; the sun itself is dying. It appears that Nature is a phantom, her apparent harmony being but an echo of man's own feelings and thoughts. The speaker concludes ambivalently, not knowing whether to accept this blind sorrow as a part of himself or to reject it as a vicious thing before it can enter the mind.

In Memoriam

4: TO SLEEP I GIVE MY POWERS AWAY

In sleep, with his will suspended, the speaker communes with his heart in the chill of grief. But, upon waking, the will asserts itself and says that the speaker shall not be "the fool of loss."

5: I SOMETIMES HOLD IT HALF A SIN

The speaker sometimes feels guilty for putting his grief into words, for words "conceal" the spiritual truth ("Soul") behind them. But, he continues, the act of writing verse numbs his pain. He will wrap himself in these words (to protect himself from the grief), as clothes might protect him from the cold, though the grief described is given only "in outline."

6: ONE WRITES THAT "OTHER FRIENDS REMAIN"

The fact that "loss is common" does not lessen the speaker's grief. Rather, the grief is intensified by the fact that terrible loss occurs daily. Even as a father pledges his son, the son is killed. As a mother prays for her sailor son, he is being buried at sea. Somewhere, a girl is waiting eagerly for a lover who is already dead. The girl will be forever unmarried, and the speaker will be without a friend.

7: DARK HOUSE, BY WHICH ONCE MORE I STAND

The speaker calls upon the house and its doors to behold him—the house where his friend once lived, the doors where the speaker once waited eagerly for the hand he now will grasp no more. "Like a guilty thing," he creeps to the door in the early morning, but the friend is not there. As the city comes to life again, the day breaks with "drizzling rain."

8: A HAPPY LOVER WHO HAS COME

The speaker compares himself to a saddened lover whose beloved has departed. All the brightness and delight in the beloved's home are now gone. So the speaker finds that all the places he formerly went with his friend are now dark without him. But as the saddened lover might find a weather-beaten flower his beloved had raised, so for the speaker his "flower of poesy," though little nourished, still has life. He proposes to plant this flower at his friend's tomb. That is, he will compose these poems in memory of his friend, and in this purpose they will succeed or fail.

9: FAIR SHIP, THAT FROM THE ITALIAN SHORE

The speaker asks that the ship bringing home the body of his friend Arthur may have a fair and fast voyage.

10: I HEAR THE NOISE ABOUT THY KEEL

The ship is bearing home the friend's body. It seems better to the speaker that Arthur be buried in his home soil than be engulfed in the deep.

11: CALM IS THE MORN WITHOUT A SOUND

All is calm and at peace. In the speaker's heart is a "calm despair" and in Arthur's body is a "dead calm."

12: LO, AS A DOVE WHEN UP SHE SPRINGS

In imagination, the speaker's soul leaves his body and flies to the ship and says mournfully, "Is this the end of all my care?"

13: TEARS OF THE WIDOWER, WHEN HE SEES

The speaker compares his grief to that of someone recently widowed. His tears fall like those of the widower, who in a dream sees his beloved wife and then finds her place empty. The speaker's tears weep for a loss forever fresh, for a void and a silence. They weep for his comrade, who is no longer living and breathing. The speaker asks Time to teach him that he does "not suffer in a dream." Now his fancies have time to imagine that the ship brings its regular merchandise and not the burden that it does bear.

14: IF ONE SHOULD BRING ME THIS REPORT

The speaker would not think it strange if he saw his friend coming alive off the ship. He addresses the ship as *thou*.

The speaker makes a series of conditional statements: if he should hear that today the ship had arrived and then he went down to the quay; if standing in his grief he watched the passengers greeting those they knew; if along with these he should see his beloved friend; if the speaker should tell his returning friend of his grief and his friend should comfort him; if he should find his friend still the same—the speaker would not find all this experience strange.

15: TO-NIGHT THE WINDS BEGIN TO RISE

The storm matches the unrest in the speaker's soul. The wind roars and blows the leaves and the rooks. The trees crack and the waves rise. Except for his belief that the ship and its burden are still proceeding smoothly, the speaker could hardly bear the storm. On the other hand, except for the fear that this belief "is not so," the speaker's "wild unrest" would lose itself in the storm.

16: WHAT WORDS ARE THESE HAVE FALLEN FROM ME?

In his confusion, the speaker feels both "calm despair" and "wild unrest." He wonders if, like a dead lake, he knows only the surface reflection of change while remaining unchanged in the depths. Or perhaps the shock has unsettled the speaker so that he has "no knowledge of himself," but confuses old and new, the false and the true, mingling everything without any order.

17: THOU COMEST, MUCH WEPT FOR

The speaker blesses the ship in all its travels for the office that it has done in bringing home the "precious relics" of his friend's body.

18: 'TIS WELL; 'TIS SOMETHING; WE MAY STAND

It is something that Arthur's body is to be buried in his native land, for the bones seem to be blest to lie in the familiar places. The

In Memoriam

speaker calls upon the "pure hands" (the pallbearers) to bear the sleeping head, and he calls upon mourners to hear the burial service. The speaker then asserts that, if it might be, he would breathe into the body his own life, a life that "endures with pain" and slowly develops a stronger mind.

19: THE DANUBE TO THE SEVERN GAVE

Now that Hallam is buried "by the pleasant shore of the Severn," the "deeper anguish" has abated and "I can speak a little."

20: THE LESSER GRIEFS THAT MAY BE SAID

Lesser griefs may be relieved by speech, but this grief is cold and silent. Like servants in a house where the master has died, these lesser griefs may express themselves fully and directly. The servants say that it will be hard to find another place as good as this to work in. The other, deeper griefs seem to freeze at the source. Like the children of the dead man, the vital spark of life itself (the hearth) is chilled and silent at the loss.

21: I SING TO HIM THAT RESTS BELOW

There are some who criticize the speaker for his poems of grief, accusing him of weakness, desire for attention, or irrelevance. But he sings only because he must, as the linnets sing.

22: THE PATH BY WHICH WE TWAIN DID GO

The speaker contrasts the brightness of his friendship with Hallam with the dark Shadow of Death.

For four years the two friends were together, and they went cheerfully, with a sense of fulfillment, from season to season in the annual cycle. But as they entered the fifth autumn in a hopeful mood, the Shadow appeared and wrapped the speaker's friend in the dark mantle (of death). The Shadow bore his friend where the speaker could not follow, and now the speaker thinks that the Shadow waits for him.

In Memoriam

23: NOW, SOMETIMES IN MY SORROW SHUT

Sometimes in his sorrow or as he fitfully writes a poem ("breaking into song"), the speaker wanders alone to "the Shadow" (that is, Death), who holds the secrets of all the religious creeds. He looks back upon the past joy and comments on the change.

Formerly, the leaves and the hills were full of the happy sounds of nature. The speaker and his friend communicated intuitively before the words could verbalize the thought. Everything—present and future—was good. Vitality was in their blood, and the thought and song of Greece were around them.

24: AND WAS THE DAY OF MY DELIGHT

The speaker questions if the past was "As pure and perfect as I say?" Is it that present grief makes former happiness so great? Or does the past have its glory from being so far away?

25: I KNOW THAT THIS WAS LIFE

The speaker says that the burden of his life in the past was eased by Love, which caused his pain to be shared with his friend.

26: STILL ONWARD WINDS THE DREARY WAY

The speaker follows "the dreary way" (of life) in order to prove that his love for Hallam will not die. But if the Power that sees all things should know that the speaker's love will turn to indifference, he would wish death ("the Shadow") to take him before he could outlive his love.

27: I ENVY NOT IN ANY MOODS

The speaker rejects a life "void of noble rage" and a life without freedom and a life without conscience. Nor does he want a life of protected detachment. It is "better to have loved and lost/ Than never to have loved at all."

In Memoriam

28: THE TIME DRAWS NEAR THE BIRTH OF CHRIST

Christmas bells from four hamlets bring the speaker the sounds of "Peace and goodwill." The sounds are a source of grief, since they mark time's passage, as well as a source of comfort, reminding the speaker of how such joyous bells "controll'd me when a boy."

29: WITH SUCH COMPELLING CAUSE TO GRIEVE

The speaker asks how they can have the joys of Christmas in the midst of this grief. Yet they will make a wreath "for Use and Wont," so that Christmas will be observed as before.

30: WITH TREMBLING FINGERS DID WE WEAVE

The shadow of the dead casts sadness on the Christmas festivities, but with Christmas morning comes a note of hope.

In sorrow the family hung the holly. The Shadow hovered over their merrymaking, and they heard the winter winds outside as they sat silently. They sang, in their sorrow, a merry song they had sung the preceding year, and, ceasing, they thought of the sweet sleep that the dead enjoy. Their voices now took on a more assertive note as they sang of the enduring spirit that leaves behind the change and frailty of mortality. The poem ends with a renewed hope as the speaker invokes Christmas morning.

31: WHEN LAZARUS LEFT HIS CHARNEL-CAVE

The speaker recalls that Lazarus rose from the grave and came to Mary's house; but Lazarus did not reveal what death was.

32: HER EYES ARE HOMES OF SILENT PRAYER

The speaker imagines that Mary, the sister of Lazarus, in the midst of her grief for the death of her brother, turns her eyes upon Jesus. All her confusion ("subtle thought" and "curious fears") is driven away by her gladness in the true Life she sees.

In Memoriam

The last stanza draws the moral that the truly blest are those whose lives are their prayers (like Mary's action in the presence of Jesus) and whose earthly loves are encompassed within a higher (that is, divine) love.

33: O THOU THAT AFTER TOIL AND STORM

The speaker admonishes those who have come to their faith the hard way (through difficult intellectual effort) not to distrust the simple faith of one who follows the simple forms. The simple faith may be the better one.

One who seems to have attained "the purer air" of a hard-won faith and whose faith, free of traditional forms (and creeds), is universal, should be tolerant of the simpler person. Nor should this person of independent faith try to insinuate doubts into the simpler person's mind. Through the form of its practice this simple faith is pure, and this person of simple faith does good more quickly than does the person of more complex mind, for "the flesh and blood" of the simpler person have been formed wholly in accordance with the divine truth. So, warns the speaker, the person who holds his faith by his reason should take care that he not fail in the sinful world for lack of those of simple faith.

34: MY OWN DIM LIFE SHOULD TEACH ME THIS

The speaker says that the uncertainty and obscurity of his own life and its aims should lead him to a belief in immortality. Without the prospect of eternal life, there is no ultimate goal, and so any choice that he might make in this world would be without meaning. Without such purpose, it would be better to die at once.

35: YET IF SOME VOICE THAT MAN COULD TRUST

If death is all, then, the speaker says, he might struggle to keep Love alive for as long as possible. But the thought of inevitable Death will destroy Love. The speaker admits that if Death were really seen as Death, then Love would not have been or would have existed at only a lower level.

36: THO' TRUTHS IN MANHOOD DARKLY JOIN

The deepest truths of man were embodied in Christ, the speaker thinks, who through his life made these truths available to all. Although truths may be present in man at the deep levels of his being, we should bless Christ, who made the truths current and readily accessible. Truth in the form of a tale may be understood by the humble. The divine Word, stronger than the imaginative thought of poetry, created the sublime creed through human action. No matter what their occupation or condition of life, all men may understand this divine example of the deepest truths.

37: URANIA SPEAKS WITH DARKEN'D BROW

Urania (the muse of astronomy and of the harmony of the spheres) delivers a reproach for the speaker's humble and uncertain expression of faith. Melpomene (the muse of elegy) explains that the song comforts the bereaved, who thus gives voice to his brooding on the beloved dead.

38: WITH WEARY STEPS I LOITER ON

The speaker says that in his weary and limited life, he gets some solace from the thought that the spirit of Hallam may get a degree of pleasure from these poems.

39: OLD WARDER OF THESE BURIED BONES

The old yew partakes of life, but Sorrow "fixed upon the dead" is permanent, just as even the flowers of the yew eventually wither and pass "into gloom again."

40: COULD WE FORGET THE WIDOW'D HOUR

The speaker compares the absence of Hallam to that of a bride that leaves the home of her parents for a new home. Whereas the woman can revisit the old house, the dead can never return.

In Memoriam

41: THE SPIRIT ERE OUR FATAL LOSS

The speaker finds an impossible separation between himself and the departed spirit of his friend.

While Hallam was still alive, his spirit was always rising to new heights. Now that Hallam is dead, he is experiencing a kind of change that the speaker cannot participate in. And the speaker wishes that he could leap over the "grades" or degrees that separate him from Hallam's spirit. Although, the speaker continues, he does not fear death, he sometimes does fear that he will not be with his friend again. Although he (the speaker) has aspired in his secular existence to follow Hallam's spiritual achievements, he fears that he will always be behind his friend (who now grows in his completely spiritual state).

42: I VEX MY HEART WITH FANCIES DIM

At first discouraged by the thought of how much the spirit of the other outstripped his own, the speaker then takes comfort in the idea that in his "spirit's inner depths" he can learn from the other a truth of larger experience.

43: IF SLEEP AND DEATH BE TRULY ONE

If death is only a trance until the ultimate spiritual birth, then the dead one's love at his spiritual birth will be the same as it was when he was alive.

44: HOW FARES IT WITH THE HAPPY DEAD?

If the dead may have a slight remembrance ("touch") of past life, the speaker hopes that the memory of him will come to his departed friend's spirit.

45: THE BABY NEW TO EARTH AND SKY

As the baby grows, the speaker thinks, he learns to distinguish between the "I" and the not-I. Perhaps this self-identification is the purpose of mortal life, since it may prepare us for the after-life.

46: WE RANGING DOWN THIS LOWER TRACK

When we are alive, the speaker thinks, the past lies in shadows. With the spiritual revelation after death, the full "tract of time" will be revealed and the full extent of Love will be seen.

47: THAT EACH, WHO SEEMS A SEPARATE WHOLE

The idea that the individual identity will merge into "the general Soul" is too vague a faith, the speaker thinks. Eternal form shall still divide the eternal soul from all else, "and I shall know him when we meet." At least, they will know each other before the final spiritual parting.

48: IF THESE BRIEF LAYS, OF SORROW BORN

These short poems, inspired by Sorrow, are not intended to resolve "grave doubts" nor do they plumb the depths, the speaker says. Sorrow's purpose is not to analyze and prove but to make doubt subordinate to Love. And so she (Sorrow) makes poetry ("plays with words"). But she does not try for the deepest insights nor the broad subject. Rather, she makes short (lyric) poems that are touched with sadness.

49: FROM ART, FROM NATURE, FROM THE SCHOOLS

Beneath the relatively superficial influences from art, nature, and the schools, the speaker's sorrow lies deep and overwhelms "The bases of my life."

50: BE NEAR ME WHEN MY LIGHT IS LOW

The speaker asks that the spirit of Hallam be near him when "the heart is sick" and life seems to be without meaning.

In Memoriam

51: DO WE INDEED DESIRE THE DEAD

The speaker asks if we really want the dead near us to see into our innermost beings. Such doubt wrongs the dead, though, for the dead watch us with a broader understanding and sympathy.

52: I CANNOT LOVE THEE AS I OUGHT

The speaker fears that his love is not worthy of its object. The Spirit of true love replies that it will always be with him and at death the true wealth (of love) will be "gathered in."

53: HOW MANY A FATHER HAVE I SEEN

Despite the temptation to see that good somehow grows out of evil, the speaker says, we should hold firm to the good. For philosophy may lead us to Hell by its sophistries.

54: O, YET WE TRUST THAT SOMEHOW GOOD

Nevertheless, the speaker says, we "trust" that the ultimate purpose of life is good, and that "not a worm is cloven in vain." The speaker admits that in his ignorance he is "An infant crying in the night."

55: THE WISH, THAT OF THE LIVING WHOLE

When the speaker compares his belief in God's purpose with Nature's savage ways, he doubts there is an after-life. Then he can only "stretch lame hands of faith."

56: SO CAREFUL OF THE TYPE?

Does Nature's indifferent destruction of species apply also to man, and is man's faith in love, truth, and justice only an illusion?

Nature seems to cry that, in the cycle of life and death, spirit means only breath. Shall man, the speaker asks, who had such a high purpose, who sang psalms and built temples, who believed in love despite the destruction of Nature, who battled for the right—shall man be nothing? Such an idea is nightmarish discord, like a gruesome conflict between prehistoric monsters. The speaker wishes for the voice of Hallam to soothe him. The answer lies "Behind the veil" (of life).

57: PEACE; COME AWAY: THE SONG OF WOE

The speaker suggests to a companion (probably his sister Emily, who was engaged to Hallam) that the song lamenting the dead should cease. He says that they do the dead man wrong with such wild singing. Your cheeks are pale, the speaker continues to his companion, but he himself has parted with half his life. His friend is richly and memorably buried, but he himself is an insignificant failure. Ever in his ears he will hear the bell tolling the departure of the sweetest of all human souls, and he took an eternal farewell.

58: IN THOSE SAD WORDS I TOOK FAREWELL

The speaker's words of farewell fell like the echoes of drops of water falling in sepulchres, and the sound (of the words) reminded the hearers of their mortality. The high muse, Urania, reproached him for disturbing others and advised him that, with patience, he would find a better way to take his leave.

59: O SORROW, WILT THOU LIVE WITH ME

The speaker conceives of Sorrow as a wife. He asks Sorrow to rule and to be sometimes lovely and gentle, if she will have him "wise and good." Although his grief will not lessen, he will take pleasure in it, as with one beloved. And he will so present his Sorrow mixed with Hope that, although he will know her identity, some could hardly recognize her. (That is, in the speaker's appearance and actions there will be little obvious trace of sorrow.)

60: HE PAST, A SOUL OF NOBLER TONE

The speaker compares his soul in its love for Hallam to a girl who loves a man above her in station. The girl's daily life is miserable and at night she weeps.

In Memoriam

61: IF, IN THY SECOND STATE SUBLIME

Although he is much less than the spirits with whom the spirit of Hallam may be conversing, the speaker says that his love is as great as that of any spirit could be.

62: THO' IF AN EYE THAT'S DOWNWARD CAST

Perhaps the speaker's love is now to be forgotten by the spirit of Hallam in his new existence. The spirit will turn from a lesser to a more worthy love.

63: YET PITY FOR A HORSE O'ER-DRIVEN

As the speaker has sympathy for a horse or any dog, so Hallam's gentle spirit may watch him when he weeps. Love extended to a lower creature is not a chain or weight that drags down the spirit.

64: DOST THOU LOOK BACK ON WHAT HATH BEEN

The speaker asks if Hallam looks back on his earthly life as a gifted and successful man might look back on his humble past. The speaker compares Hallam to a man of superior abilities who rises from humble origin by a combination of good fortune and determination. At the height of his success, he pauses in his activity and contemplates nostalgically the stream and the hill where he once played at politics with his earliest friend, a friend who now, in his still hard labor, pauses to wonder if his successful friend remembers him.

65: SWEET SOUL, DO WITH ME AS THOU WILT

In his troubled musings, the thought comes to the speaker that, since Hallam had such an effect on him, his friendship may likewise have had an ennobling effect on Hallam.

66: YOU THOUGHT MY HEART TOO FAR DISEASED

People may wonder that the speaker can be gay. He explains that his loss has made him kindly with his fellows. He is like a blind man who gets along well with others but still feels inwardly his loss.

In Memoriam

67: WHEN ON MY BED THE MOONLIGHT FALLS

As the moonlight falls on his bed, the speaker knows that Hallam's tombstone appears bright. As morning approaches he knows that "Thy tablet glimmers in the dawn."

68: WHEN IN THE DOWN I SINK MY HEAD

The speaker dreams of his friend as still alive, but he is troubled nevertheless. When he awakes, he discovers that in his dream he has transferred his own youthful troubles to his friend.

69: I DREAM'D THERE WOULD BE SPRING NO MORE

The speaker dreamed that Nature had lost her power of rebirth. Going into a wood, he put a crown of thorns on his head. He was scoffed at by the townspeople, but it seemed to him that an angel, speaking softly to him, touched his crown so that it turned into a leaf. Although the angel's voice did not convey grief, "The words were hard to understand."

70: I CANNOT SEE THE FEATURES RIGHT

When he tries to picture his friend's face, the speaker sees only gigantic, murky scenes. Then, suddenly, the face appears.

71: SLEEP, KINSMAN THOU TO DEATH AND TRANCE

The speaker asks Sleep, which brings him pleasant memories of a visit to France, to increase his pleasure by eliminating his sense of wrong. He recalls in his dream the talks he had with Hallam and the scenes where they were.

72: RISEST THOU THUS, DIM DAWN, AGAIN

The speaker reproaches the day (the anniversary of Hallam's death) for bringing in the sad hours with a storm. The day continues in gloom and storm, as though marked "with some hideous crime."

In Memoriam

73: SO MANY WORLDS, SO MUCH TO DO

The speaker thinks that Hallam's death left many good deeds undone. He also considers that worldly fame dies and that all of the soul's energy is now directed into spiritual force.

74: AS SOMETIMES IN A DEAD MAN'S FACE

As he looks upon the face of his dead friend, the speaker sees Hallam's kinship to the great and the wise. There is also something greater than this that the speaker sees that he leaves unsaid.

75: I LEAVE THY PRAISES UNEXPRESS'D

The speaker does not express praise of Hallam but leaves his friend's greatness to be inferred from the depth of his own grief. Neither the most expert writer nor the most richly-toned singer can describe Hallam as he really was. Nor does the speaker want to raise only a passing bit of praise for Hallam with his poems. Since Hallam died young he will not receive praise for what might have been, for the world recognizes only what has actually been done. But in his spiritual existence Hallam does much and is acclaimed.

76: TAKE WINGS OF FANCY, AND ASCEND

The loftiest fancy and the highest foresight of the speaker's songs are vain. They shall be gone "Ere half the lifetime of an oak."

77: WHAT HOPE IS HERE FOR MODERN RHYME

Modern rhyme seems inferior to the songs and lives of the past, and these songs of the speaker may pass into oblivion. Nevertheless, they serve to express love.

78: AGAIN AT CHRISTMAS DID WE WEAVE

The second Christmas finds them calm, and in their festivities there is "no mark of pain." The deep-lying grief is still with them, but the tears no longer flow.

In Memoriam

79: MORE THAN MY BROTHERS ARE TO ME

The speaker apologizes to his brother Charles for saying that Hallam was more to him "than my brothers" (see section 9). The speaker explains that whereas he and his brother "are one in kind" from having the same rearing, Hallam in his unlikeness better supplied the wants in the speaker's personality.

80: IF ANY VAGUE DESIRE SHOULD RISE

If the speaker sometimes has a wish that he had died before Hallam, he thinks of how Hallam would have borne the loss, turning the sorrow into growth. The thought of how Hallam would have reacted helps to sustain the speaker.

81: COULD I HAVE SAID WHILE HE WAS HERE

The speaker asks himself if, while Hallam still lived, he might have said that his love was fully matured. More years would have made him love his friend more. But Death says that sudden death brought sudden maturity.

82: I WAGE NOT ANY FEUD WITH DEATH

The speaker does not blame Death for taking Hallam because in the "eternal process" the spirit goes on "From state to state." The speaker is angry only because he and his friend can no longer "hear each other speak."

83: DIP DOWN UPON THE NORTHERN SHORE

The speaker calls upon the new year to come and bring the flowers. Then Spring will release the "frozen bud" of the speaker's sorrow and fill "a fresher throat" with song.

84: WHEN I CONTEMPLATE ALL ALONE

The speaker thinks regretfully that Hallam would have married his sister and that Hallam's sons would have been his nephews. Hallam would have had a long, productive life. Then, he and Hallam might have died at the same time and entered Heaven "as a single soul."

85: THIS TRUTH CAME BORNE WITH BIER AND PALL

The speaker replies to a friend's questions about the quality of his life and whether the sorrow has affected his religious faith. (The friend is Tennyson's future brother-in-law, Edmund Lushington.) When Hallam at his death went to heaven, he (the speaker) became depressed. Yet he also felt the spiritual support of his dead friend. With consciousness of spiritual strength, he seeks again the companionship of others, though his and Hallam's friendship is beyond the touch of time, except as associations in nature recall his love. Remembering his full commitment to Hallam, he reaches out to a new friend.

86: SWEET AFTER SHOWERS, AMBROSIAL AIR

The speaker asks the evening breeze to fill him so that his fancy can fly far away to where "A hundred spirits whisper 'Peace.'"

87: I PAST BESIDE THE REVEREND WALLS

The speaker revisits Cambridge and recalls the old days there. The poem opens with a description of sound as the speaker wanders through the town: the tumult in the halls, the "storm" and "thunder-music" of the organs, the shouts and noise associated with the racing shells. Last, the speaker came to the rooms where Hallam had lived. Inside were the noises of boyish gaiety. It was here that the speaker and his companions once had debates on various subjects. Among them were speakers of varying skills, but Hallam shone above them all with a divine light from within, and about his eyes he seemed to resemble Michael Angelo.

88: WILD BIRD, WHOSE WARBLE, LIQUID SWEET

The speaker asks the bird (the nightingale) for the secret of the power that reconciles or joins conflicting elements, such as grief and joy. Whereas the bird in its music expresses a "secret joy" in its grief, the speaker finds that his command of his own music is uncertain—after a moment, the note of glory passes.

89: WITCH-ELMS THAT COUNTERCHANGE THE FLOOR

The speaker recalls Hallam's delight in simple pastimes, which dispelled the cares of his work. Hallam enjoyed the shadows cast on the lawn by the elms and the sycamore. Shaking from himself the influences of the city, he entered into the simple pastimes of the country. He enjoyed the cool air and the sound of the scythe and the gusts of wind. Sometimes the group would gather around Hallam on the lawn while he read Dante and Petrarch to them. At times someone would sing to them. Sometimes they would go on a picnic to the woods, where they would discuss various things. But if the speaker chanced to praise town life, Hallam would strongly object, saying that the town destroyed individuality. The poem concludes with a description of the peaceful sights and sounds of the country.

90: HE TASTED LOVE WITH HALF HIS MIND

Some cynical person commented that people do not really wish the beloved dead to return. There would be too much change and confusion. The speaker says that he, however, can find no reason for not wanting Hallam back.

91: WHEN ROSY PLUMELETS TUFT THE LARCH

The speaker asks that Hallam appear to him. If in the spring, Hallam should come in the guise known on earth; if in the summer, he should be in the full splendor of spiritual light.

92: IF ANY VISION SHOULD REVEAL

If the speaker should have a vision of Hallam, he would count it a delusion, no matter how plausible it might seem.

In Memoriam

93: I SHALL NOT SEE THEE

Although the spirit of the dead will not return in physical form, the speaker pleads that the spirit of Hallam descend to him.

94: HOW PURE AT HEART AND SOUND IN HEAD

The speaker says that there must be calm and purity within the breast that would hold communion with the dead. The imagination, the memory, and the conscience must all be at peace, for where the heart is troubled and doubt is present, the spirits cannot enter, for they hear only discord.

95: BY NIGHT WE LINGER'D ON THE LAWN

This poem begins at night and ends at morning. The speaker recounts a mystical experience that occurred during the time. The poem has two climaxes. The first recounts the mystical experience itself (lines 21-43), culminating in the intense vision (lines 35-43). The second climax occurs in the last stanza, where the dawn becomes the symbol of eternal truth, spiritual reality, and faith.

The poem has three phases. First, the family group was gathered on the lawn. It was a calm evening, and they enjoyed a quiet and genial companionship (lines 1-16).

Second, the others gradually withdrew, leaving the speaker alone. As he sat reading Hallam's letters, he fell into a trance. A voice spoke to him silently, expressing faith, and suddenly the dead man touched him. Then, their two united spirits rose to the "heights of thought" and partook of the ultimate knowledge of Being itself (lines 17-43).

Third, the speaker's trance ended and doubt entered. It is difficult to state in words or even to remember clearly what the experience was. Dusk now revealed the scene around. A breeze moved the trees and the flowers, and then, having seemed to herald the dawn, died away. Then East and West in the motionless air joined in the single emerging light of day (lines 43-64).

96: YOU SAY, BUT WITH NO TOUCH OF SCORN

In reply to a woman who has said that doubt comes from the Devil, the speaker replies that Hallam had doubts, struggled with them, and came through to "a stronger faith." For "there lives more faith in honest doubt . . . than in half the creeds." Truth dwells in the darker side also, as over Mt. Sinai, when God gave the Commandments to Moses.

97: MY LOVE HAS TALK'D WITH ROCKS AND TREES

The speaker compares the relationship of his spirit to Hallam's as that between man and wife. As a wife holds a humble position in relation to the husband's superior powers, so his spirit can only humbly love Hallam's.

98: YOU LEAVE US: YOU WILL SEE THE RHINE

The speaker addresses his brother, who is about to leave for Vienna. The speaker says that, for him, Vienna will always have deep associations of death. It will always seem to him that births and weddings are haunted by evil, that here friends are oftener parted, that more fathers lose their sons, that men suffer from more wants, and that sadness overshadows the royal glory. Yet the speaker admits that he has heard Hallam say that nowhere are carriages more stately in their movement through the parks, that nowhere is there more content and gaiety in the crowds with their dances and their firework displays.

99: RISEST THOU THUS, DIM DAWN, AGAIN

The speaker addresses the dawn of the second anniversary of Hallam's death. It is loud with the sounds of birds and animals. This dawn seems to tremble upon the stream that runs by the meadows and woodlands closely associated with Hallam. The dawn also brings a song that takes no notice of the coming sorrow. Also, the dawn brings to many people memories of weddings and births and to many more it brings memories of death. Wherever these mourners may be, they mourn with him, although they do not know him.

100: I CLIMB THE HILL: FROM END TO END

In the surrounding area, the speaker finds that everything carries with it some memory of his friend. As he prepares to leave this place, it seems as though his friend once more dies.

101: UNWATCH'D, THE GARDEN BOUGH SHALL SWAY

The speaker continues to prepare to move from his home. He thinks that the trees, the flowers, and the brook will thus be left alone until gradually a new inhabitant makes this country familiar to himself.

102: WE LEAVE THE WELL-BELOVED PLACE

As the speaker and his family prepare to leave their home, two spirits address the speaker: the spirit of his boyhood love for the place and the spirit that enhances this love through memory of Hallam. These spirits seem to struggle for ascendancy, but finally fuse into "one pure image of regret."

103: ON THAT LAST NIGHT BEFORE WE WENT

In a dream-vision the speaker finds himself in a hall with maidens (the Muses, the Arts) singing. He is summoned to the sea (of eternity). As he proceeds upon the river that leads to the sea, the maidens grow in power and he grows in size (that is, his spiritual power and his power as an artist grow). He sees a ship, and on this ship he finds Hallam, who is also larger than life-size. They embrace. Although the speaker in his joy has forgotten the maidens (his talents and power as an artist), Hallam tells them to come along.

The allegory involves the themes of spiritual growth, artistic growth, and the relationship of art to the spirit. In the hall (of settled life) the speaker is happy in his art and in the worshipful memory of Hallam (the statue) toward which the songs are directed. When the speaker enters upon the river, which comes from the "hidden summits" (mysterious origin), that will take him to the sea (of eternity), his growth suggests an increase in spirit, and the growth of the maidens suggests an increase in artistic powers as they sing of ever-greater themes. It seems that in life a lingering self-centeredness or weakness yet caused the speaker's spirit to dissociate itself from the aesthetic powers. But the insight of a greater spirit (Hallam's) welcomes these artistic powers. Art, too, partakes of eternity.

The poem also climaxes the speaker's contemplation of his moving from the place which held so many memories of his departed friend. With this fact in mind, the reader may see this poem as an allegory which describes (1) the speaker's singing of his dead friend in the place which was their home (that is, the hall); (2) the need to make a change, which would result in spiritual and artistic growth (the river journey); (3) the result of this growth, that the spiritual and artistic powers would eventually be joined (the final scene of acceptance).

104: THE TIME DRAWS NEAR THE BIRTH OF CHRIST

The third Christmas finds the speaker in a new place, where the bells sound "Like strangers' voices."

105: TO-NIGHT UNGATHER'D LET US LEAVE

Christmas Eve falls strangely in this new home. They do not keep the old forms of Christmas celebration. There is no motion except the cosmic movement that will lead to eternal good.

106: RING OUT, WILD BELLS, TO THE WILD SKY

This is a call at Christmastime to ring out the old world of falsehood, grief, and strife and to "Ring in the Christ that is to be."

107: IT IS THE DAY WHEN HE WAS BORN

It is the day of Hallam's birth, a cold, dark, bitter winter's day. But inside they will "keep the day" with warmth and cheer.

108: I WILL NOT SHUT ME FROM MY KIND

The speaker determines that, rather than confine himself to isolated grief, he will go among his kind, though he will have to take the fruit of sorrow which life inevitably brings.

109: HEART-AFFLUENCE IN DISCURSIVE TALK

The speaker recalls Hallam's fine qualities: he was full of rich talk on household matters, and he had a clear, critical insight into highly intellectual regions, such as the arts and philosophy; he had a high and forceful intellect that overcame men's doubts; his logic was "impassioned" and quick; his moral nature was pure but not ascetic; he loved freedom but rejected unbridled license; in his manhood was such grace that a child could find comfort there. If, the speaker concludes, he has looked on these virtues and not been ennobled by them, his should be the shame.

110: THY CONVERSE DREW US WITH DELIGHT

The speaker describes Hallam's effect upon others. His talk attracted the young and the older, and it gave heart to the weak-spirited. It chastened the proud and the deceitful. His talk had an improving effect on the stern, the flippant, and the fool. Although the speaker says that he does not have Hallam's ability to influence others, his love impels him to imitate Hallam's tact and skill.

111: THE CHURL IN SPIRIT UP OR DOWN

No matter how high his position, the low-spirited person will at times let his true vileness show through. But Hallam was a true gentleman: his social graces matched his inner spirit.

112: HIGH WISDOM HOLDS MY WISDOM LESS

The speaker holds others, great and small, of little worth in comparison with Hallam, who produced order and control in his thoughts.

113: 'TIS HELD THAT SORROW MAKES US WISE

Although it is said that sorrow will bring us wisdom, the speaker implies that probably more wisdom was lost at Hallam's death than was gained in the grief that resulted from it. Had Hallam lived, he would have been a powerful political force for righteousness in the face of violent disturbances.

In Memoriam

114: WHO LOVES NOT KNOWLEDGE? WHO SHALL RAIL

The speaker says that knowledge, separated from love and faith, is wild and lusts for power. Knowledge must be made subordinate to Wisdom, reverence, and charity, as it was in Hallam.

115: NOW FADES THE LAST LONG STREAK OF SNOW

As spring returns to the land, spring also wakens in the speaker's breast. The snow fades and flowers appear. Everything is brighter. The birds are active. Spring comes to the speaker's breast, and his sorrow is transformed into "an April violet."

116: IS IT, THEN, REGRET FOR BURIED TIME

Spring causes the voice of new life to rise within the speaker. Although he does not forget his dead friend, he now looks more to the future.

117: O DAYS AND HOURS, YOUR WORK IS THIS

The longer he remains separated from Hallam, the speaker says, the sweeter will be the eventual reunion.

118: CONTEMPLATE ALL THIS WORK OF TIME

The speaker thinks that from evolutionary development a higher race is gradually emerging. Man is the herald of this higher race, and man should help promote it by struggling for spiritual growth.

Time is still young in his labors, says the speaker. We should not think of "human love and truth" in the same way we think of the ordinary natural elements ("dying Nature's earth and lime"). Rather, we should trust that the dead now are spirits with expanding goals. It is said that the earth, which began as a fiery mass, developed by chance into its various forms, culminating in man. Man prospered and became the forerunner of a still "higher race," and now shows too that he can grow within himself. Man shows that life is not inert but is composed of gloom and shaped by fears and sorrows and "the shocks of doom." The speaker then calls upon man to purge the sensual and the beastly in himself and to strive upward.

119: DOORS, WHERE MY HEART WAS USED TO BEAT

Once again the speaker visits the house where Hallam had lived in London. This time, the atmosphere is cheerful and the speaker's thoughts are pleasant.

120: I TRUST I HAVE NOT WASTED BREATH

The speaker cannot accept the assumption that man is only a complex mechanism. If science should prove that man is only clay with no soul, then neither science nor life would have meaning for him. He concludes that although this new man might adapt himself to the materialistic point of view, the speaker himself would not live with such an attitude, because he was *born* (that is, intended) to a higher destiny.

121: SAD HESPER O'ER THE BURIED SUN

Venus, as both evening star (Hesper) and morning star (Phosphor), symbolizes to the speaker the unity that exists behind the changing surface of things.

Hesper, ready to sink with the sun, watches over the earth as it gets dimmer, with the glory of the day fading. Men's labor comes to an end and sleep follows. In the morning Phosphor appears, "fresher for the night," and as the world's work begins, the sun rises. The speaker sees his past and his present, like the morning and the evening star, as two aspects of one phenomenon.

122: O, WAST THOU WITH ME, DEAREST, THEN

Addressing Hallam's spirit, the speaker asks if his friend was with him earlier when he was striving for spiritual insight. He asks that Hallam's spirit be with him now so that he may achieve a greater fulfillment. He will escape from "thoughts of life and death." With his Fancy unencumbered, there will be a rainbow in every dewdrop, the "wizard lightnings" will glow intensely, and his thoughts will flower beautifully.

In Memoriam

123: THERE ROLLS THE DEEP WHERE GREW THE TREE

Though the external world changes with time, the speaker holds to the inner truth of his dream (of spiritual reality).

124: THAT WHICH WE DARE INVOKE TO BLESS

The speaker says that his faith did not come from the external world nor from the intellect, but from a feeling within, a feeling similar to that which a child has when, in doubt and fear, he "knows his father near." The speaker concludes that his present self ("what I am") saw again reality ("what is"), a reality that "no man understands." From the darkness came (to enlighten and uphold him) the power that reaches through nature to mold man.

125: WHATEVER I HAVE SAID OR SUNG

Despite some bitterness in the speaker's songs, Hope remained vital. In his songs full of care as in his songs full of sweetness and strength, Love was with him, and Love continues with him.

126: LOVE IS AND WAS MY LORD AND KING

Love, the speaker's "lord and king," brings him hourly "tidings of my friend." Love guards him while on earth, and he is reassured "that all is well."

127: AND ALL IS WELL, THO' FAITH AND FORM

The speaker retains his faith that, despite the most violent disorders, the spirit will triumph. Although formal creeds have been separated from faith, those who hear "A deeper voice" have a strong faith in the midst of earthly struggle. The voice proclaims that "social truth" and "justice" shall prevail despite the most violent upheavals. The spirit of Hallam looks upon the worldly tumult with the knowledge that "all is well."

128: THE LOVE THAT ROSE ON STRONGER WINGS

The speaker trusts in the ultimate purpose of things, despite the setbacks and reversals that mark human history. Development in time has a deeper meaning than merely to gloss and rearrange past events and old ideas. The love that became stronger in the face of Death is like the love that sees the course of human events. Without doubt, there will be movements contrary to the mainstream of human progress, yet the speaker is confident that there is a real force for good operating. He would have contempt for the whole process if time ("Wild Hours") had no purpose but meaningless change, useless destruction, to deceive the mob, to disrupt established beliefs, to modify the meaning of a word, to change or move (rather than destroy) some "arbitrary" power, and (at a trivial level) to make a student keep at his desk until he is cramped or to cover some old tower with grass. But the speaker sees within his limited perspective some purpose in the struggle.

129: DEAR FRIEND, FAR OFF, MY LOST DESIRE

When the speaker feels most intensely the difference between lower and higher, physical and material, he "dreams" (envisions) all the world mingled in Hallam's spirit, "a dream of good."

130: THY VOICE IS ON THE ROLLING AIR

The speaker perceives the spiritual presence of Hallam pervading nature. The speaker's love is now greater than before because now it encompasses both the past and the expanding present, "God and Nature."

131: O LIVING WILL THAT SHALT ENDURE

The speaker says that our will should purify us and enable us to lift our voices to the eternal power, with faith that will ultimately be resolved in spiritual union.

In Memoriam

EPILOGUE: O TRUE AND TRIED, SO WELL AND LONG

The speaker is happy at the coming marriage of his sister, though the memory of Hallam, who was to have married another of his sisters, prevents him from writing a marriage ode.

In the years since Hallam's death the speaker feels that he has grown to such an extent in spirit that the earlier poems now seem inferior in the light of the greater love that has developed within him.

The bride and the groom are both truly worthy, and their marriage is cause for happiness. The speaker's spirits are now "genial," though his thoughts return to the dead Hallam.

After the couple leaves, the festivities continue. The moon rises and spreads its light and shadows over everything. The speaker continues with a projection or prophecy of a higher type of man, of which Hallam was a forerunner. The speaker ends with an assertion that the universe is moving to "one far-off divine event" envisaged as God's purpose (or perhaps as the fulfillment of God).

LOCKSLEY HALL

The poem consists of a series of thoughts in the mind of a young man who has been jilted. He is bitter. He is also impulsive, one thought giving way to another in rapid succession, so that he ranges over a number of topics. He seems to be an intense and intelligent person, given to emotional outbursts and prone to self-pity. He likes to think in broad terms (lines 11-16), but his thoughts soon turn to his lost Amy. His thoughts about love are both strident and idealistic (lines 21-38), and he cannot escape a bitter resentment as he thinks that the man she married will drag her down (lines 45-56). He attacks the materialism and social traditions that separated them (lines 59-62). Later, thinking of present greed and selfishness, he desires to free his spirit in action, a thought that leads to visions of progress and war and then peace (lines 97-130). He swings back to despair at the slow rate of progress (lines 131-144). Impulsively, he scorns his weak resentment and thinks that an escape into primitive life is good (lines 145-172). But he catches himself and, with an optimistic turn, admits the superiority of civilized life (lines 173-188). The poem ends in a mixture of gloom and self-assertion.

LOCKSLEY HALL, SIXTY YEARS AFTER

The speaker is generally pessimistic in his view of society and man's future prospects. This attitude is partly attributable to his age (eighty) and partly to a disillusionment with the Victorian idea of progress ("Forward"), which reflected an optimistic interpretation of the theory of evolution. The speaker begins with a specific comparison. His grandson's Judith is shallower than his own lost love, Amy, had been (lines 17-24). After giving an idealized picture of his wife, Edith, and the boy's father (lines 47-66), he raises the question of whether man has really progressed from primitive savagery (lines 73-102). He fears the democratic tendency of the times (lines 109-138). He attacks the degenerate literature of the day (lines 139-150) and questions the hope for a brighter future (lines 151-174). The last hundred lines intersperse objections to new attitudes and comment on unsavory urban conditions with pleas for a larger knowledge of God. The poem concludes (lines 255-292) with a plea for Love, Light, and Right, thus rounding off the conservative tone that dominates the poem.

MAUD

Tennyson himself described this poem as "the history of a morbid poetic soul" who is redeemed through love. Through the speaker, Tennyson unites love, death, and war in a single morbid vision. Death and madness pervade the poem. Even the accounts of love are interspersed with mad suspicions and impulses.

Part I recounts the speaker's development from morbid despair to the joy of love. From the beginning he equates peace with social evils (Section I), an idea that is paralleled later by Maud's song of war which brings Death and Honor (Section V). Although he saw her first as "Dead perfection" (Section II), he finally realizes the inspiration and joy of love (Sections XVII, XVIII, XXI, XXII). Throughout, the antagonism with Maud's brother is a major problem (for instance, Section XIX).

Part II shows that this antagonism precipitates the tragedy. The speaker kills the brother and flees the country (Sections I and II), and in the midst of his despair he learns of Maud's death (Section III). Brooding on his loss, he withdraws still more into himself (Section IV), until he actually goes mad and is put in a madhouse (Section V).

Part III develops the theme that war is socially and morally useful because it gives men a higher purpose than money and comfort.
Then, "I am one with my kind,/ I embrace the purpose of God, and
the doom assigned."

NOW SLEEPS THE CRIMSON PETAL (FROM THE PRINCESS)

The speaker presents a series of parallels between things in nature
and the relationship between himself and his beloved:
The firefly wakens and now, he says, you should waken to me
(line 4). Like a ghost, suggested by a peacock, "she glimmers on to
me" (line 6). As the Earth lies open to the stars, "thy heart lies open
to me" (lines 7-8), and so on with increasing intimacy at each step
in thought (line 10) with finally a complete enfolding of the beloved
(lines 13-14).

TEARS, IDLE TEARS (FROM THE PRINCESS)

The refrain, "the days that are no more," states the cause of the
"idle tears."
After the occasion ("looking on the happy autumn fields") and
the thought "of the days that are no more" in the first stanza, the
speaker (a maiden) proceeds to a series of parallels to describe the
quality and the nature of the season. These past days are "fresh,"
"sad" (stanza 2), "sad and strange" (stanza 3), and "dear," "sweet,"
"deep," and "wild with all regret" (stanza 4).

THE HIGHER PANTHEISM

The poem states that the physical universe is the vision or dream of
God. We cannot perceive spiritual reality through the senses. If we
could penetrate beyond the senses, that vision would be God.

THE LADY OF SHALOTT

Tennyson said that the theme of this poem is that "The new-born
love for something, for someone in the whole world from which she
has been so long excluded, takes her out of the region of shadows into that of realities."

Part I establishes the fact of the isolation of the Lady of Shalott. Part II describes the Lady as she weaves the sights reflected in the mirror and concludes with her thought that she is "half sick of shadows."

In Part III, the Lady sees Launcelot in her mirror, and she is drawn to him, though there is a curse on her if she turns from her mirror to look directly upon the world.

Part IV is the account of the dying Lady's drifting down the river to Camelot, where her dead body arrives to interrupt "the sound of royal cheer."

THE LOTOS-EATERS

Those who eat the lotos lose all desire to work or labor for a goal. When Ulysses' men eat the lotos, they lose the desire to return home.

The introduction (lines 1-45) sets the scene. As Ulysses and his followers come to the land of the Lotos-Eaters, they see a place where the air and the streams move lazily. The Lotos-Eaters come and offer them the lotos, which causes the voyagers to lose themselves in dreams.

In the choric song, stanzas 1-3 raise the question of why the men should not have rest when soft music invites rest (stanza 1) and leaves, apples, and flowers fade after they pass maturity. Stanza 4 is a protest against any idea of struggle. Then, in stanzas 5 and 6, under the influence of the drug, they dream of their past lives and reject any thought of returning home. The remaining lines describe the sweetness of this land (stanza 7), and state the determination to exist above the strife, avoiding all conflict (stanza 8).

THE SPLENDOR FALLS ON CASTLE WALLS (FROM THE PRINCESS)

Like the bugle that sends its echoes afar, love sends its "echoes . . . from soul to soul."

Stanzas 1 and 2 describe the beauty of the scene and the sound of the bugle and its echoes. The last stanza draws the parallel between the bugle with its answering echoes and love with its spreading influences.

THE TWO VOICES

The poem consists of two internal dialogues. The first dialogue (lines 1-402) is a dialogue between the speaker and the first voice, which is the voice of death and despair. Following this first and longest part of the poem is a transitional description of a Sabbath morning; it goes from line 403 to line 426. The second voice now appears at line 427 for a brief dialogue, to line 441. This second voice is the voice of life and hope. Lines 442-462 are a concluding affirmation of life.

The beginning of each section of the dialogue is clearly marked by such phrases as "To which the voice did urge reply" (line 7). The voice's statement is followed by the speaker's response.

The voice is the voice of despair, saying in various ways that life is not worth living. At first, the "I" is depressed but he struggles to assert that life is worthwhile for various reasons. Because of his mind, man is the supreme creation of Nature (lines 16-21), and each man is a distinct individual (lines 34-36). The "I" is also fearful. He worries that people will say that he is afraid (lines 100-102), and he says that he finds it hard now to struggle for truth (lines 118-158). Yet a spiritual insight emerges (lines 202-225; 265-315; 334-384), leading to the conviction that it is life that we really want (lines 388-399).

It is now the Sabbath morning. The "I" sees the people going to church, among whom he notices a family walking in "unity so sweet." The first voice disappears.

Now the second voice (Life, Hope, Love) begins its dialogue with the "I," speaking of a hope which may not be put in words (lines 227-441). In conclusion (lines 442-462), the "I" is now pervaded by the spirit of love and the joyful vitality of Nature.

ULYSSES

The theme of the poem is the ideal of eternal aspiration in the face of "time and fate."

In the first part (lines 1-32), Ulysses expresses his dissatisfaction with his current "idle" existence and then defines the purpose of life, which is "to follow knowledge like a sinking star." In the second part (lines 33-43), Ulysses acknowledges the worth of the person of opposite temperament (Telemachus), the prudent rather than the adventurous ("He works his work, I mine"). In the third section (lines 44-70), Ulysses, despite old age, declining strength, and impending death asserts his vigorous determination "to strive, to seek, to find, and not to yield."

YOU ASK ME WHY, THOUGH ILL AT EASE

The poet states why he believes in England's political system despite certain doubts.

Although the poet has doubts (stanza 1), England is the land of freedom (stanza 2) where, because of "settled government," freedom is of gradual growth (stanza 3). Factions and conflict seldom develop so that improvement is slow and sure (stanza 4). However, should group pressures ever force the individual to be quiet (stanza 5), then, though Britain were ever so powerful and rich (stanza 6), the poet would seek another land.

DYLAN THOMAS

A REFUSAL TO MOURN THE DEATH, BY FIRE, OF A CHILD IN LONDON

The poet states his refusal to mourn the death of the child because of the majesty of her death and because she has become one with the cycles of nature.

In lines 1-13, the speaker says he will not mourn until the world ends, in "darkness," "silence," and the "still hour." Then all things ("mankind," "bird," "beast," "flower," "sea") will end and the poet will return to spiritual union with the cycles of nature ("water bead," "corn"). In lines 14-18, the speaker further says he will not by elegies and moralizings violate the majesty of the child's death, as representative of universal mankind. Lines 19-24 give a reason why the girl need not be mourned: she has joined all the past dead ("first dead") and has united with the eternal origins of things ("long friends," "grains," "veins of her mother"). Death cannot touch her now ("there is no other").

AND DEATH SHALL HAVE NO DOMINION

The title and refrain line give the theme—the final triumph of man over death. The Biblical title (Romans 6:9) and the imagery suggest the calling forth of the dead at the Second Coming of Christ ("shall rise again") and the consequent end of death. Here the dominion over death is achieved by man's being made one with nature ("shall be one/ With . . . moon").

DO NOT GO GENTLE INTO THAT GOOD NIGHT

In telling his aged father nearing death to resist dying, the poet uses four kinds of aged men as illustrations. Wise men, good men, wild men, and grave men all resist dying as they near death and find the respective achievements of their lives unsatisfactory. The paradoxes in the poem ("dark is right," "blinding sight," "curse, bless") increase tension and help produce the sense of "rage."

ESPECIALLY WHEN THE OCTOBER WIND

The heart of the poet is "drained" when he observes the omens of winter in October wind, sun, and birds (stanza 1), in women and children among the trees (stanza 2), and in the clock and meadow grass (stanza 3). In each instance, he offers to express ("make") the ominous signs in vocal terms—letters, vowels, syllables, tongue, speeches, notes, and so on.

FERN HILL

In a nostalgic mood, the adult poet recalls the innocence, carefreeness, and wonder of childhood, which time inevitably had to take away.

Stanzas 1-4 describe the poet's childhood. Time allowed him a world of happiness, of wonder, of innocence ("Time let me play," "green and golden," "blessed," "lamb white days"). It was like the beginning of the world with "Adam and maiden . . . in the first, spinning place." Stanzas 5-6 point out that the child was unaware ("Nothing I cared") that time allows but a very brief span for the childhood wonder ("so few . . . morning songs") before the farm is made "childless" by the child's growing up.

The last two lines emphasize the basic contradiction of the poem: even while he lived in the wonder and vitality ("green") of his childhood, time was taking it from him ("dying"). Even while he sang in the carefreeness of childhood, he was in bondage to time as the sea is in bondage to the shore.

IN MEMORY OF ANN JONES ("AFTER THE FUNERAL, MULE PRAISES, BRAYS")

An elegy in tribute to Ann Jones (Thomas' aunt), the poem itself serves as a monument of praise ("monumental/ Argument of the hewn voice") to the humble woman whose love was so great it might bring life out of death ("fox twitch," "fern lay seeds").

The poem has three parts. Lines 1-9 describe the burial, whose activities cannot express the grief of the boy. Lines 10-20 describe the lifeless tone of the feast ("stuffed fox and a stale fern") and the lone boy's preparation to offer a memorial. Lines 21-40 describe the character of Ann Jones and the poet's praise of it in the main meta phor of a piece of sculpture.

IN MY CRAFT OR SULLEN ART

The vocation of the poet is practiced for the lovers. He does not write for his own ambition, bread, or public acclaim ("strut and trade"). Neither does he write for the proud or the dead, but for the lovers with all their griefs, even though the lovers do not heed him.

LIGHT BREAKS WHERE NO SUN SHINES

Senses, intuition, and emotions are superior to intellect and "logics" as life-giving forces.

Using the extended metaphor of man-as-universe ("poles of skull and toe"), the poet shows man bringing life ("light," "dawn," "smile," "spring") to a forbidding universe ("where no sun shines," "where no flesh," "Where no seed stirs," "waste allotments"). The life-giving force is not intellectual ("logics"), but sensory ("grows through the eye," "blood jumps"), intuitive ("thoughts smell"), and emotional ("waters of the heart").

POEM IN OCTOBER

On his thirtieth birthday, the poet remembers and still feels the freshness and immediacy of the child's vision of nature, and he hopes that in a year he will have the same "heart's truth."

Stanzas 1-2 relate the poet's going in "rainy autumn" from the town to the country where he spent his youth. In stanzas 3-4 the feeling of autumn changes to summer as he climbs a hill into the sun and looks down on the rainy town. In stanzas 5-6 the poet's thoughts turn ("weather turned round") to a metaphoric summer of life—his childhood relation to nature which he still feels ("mystery/ Sang alive/ Still"). The poet then senses (stanza 7) that this "summer noon" will pass, for the town that he must return to "lay leaved with October blood," not summer. So the poet makes his closing wish that his child's joy may be with him a year hence.

POEM ON HIS BIRTHDAY

At midlife (Biblically, at thirty-five), the poet balances his awareness of impending death with his exultant love of life.

In stanzas 1-5, the poet sees his own life as moving towards death ("ambush of his wounds," "sings towards anguish," "slaves to his . . . end"). Likewise, nature around him works at death and destruction ("dying trails," "claw tracks of hawks," sunken ships, otters pasturing on small fishes, seals killing). Even the herons (usually sacerdotal in Thomas' poetry) "walk in their shrouds."

In stanzas 6-7, the poet is caught between belief and unbelief (God is fabulous, but dear; Heaven "never was" but is "always true"). The poet considers a God who turns death to joy in a possible heaven (or "brambled void") where he could be with the spirits of the bay (eagles, whales, geese).

In stanzas 8-9, the poet prays, still doubting ("Faithlessly"). He wants to mourn his approaching death ("voyage to ruin") and to count his blessings.

In stanzas 10-13, the poet counts his blessings of flesh ("elements"), of five senses, of his being a "spirit in love," and this last blessing of life's becoming more precious to him the closer he moves to death. This love of life leads to a "triumphant faith," a sense of holiness in nature ("angels ride/ The mansouled fiery islands"), and an exultant acceptance of death ("no more alone/ As I sail out to die").

THE FORCE THAT THROUGH THE GREEN FUSE DRIVES THE FLOWER

The individual has a common fate with all other things and with the processes of the universe (nature, life, death). All are moved by the same force, which leads ultimately to death.

The poem is built on three sets of paradoxes: (1) the same force works in both man and nature ("flower—age"; "water—red blood"); (2) this same force is both creator and destroyer (drives and destroys; leeches "to the fountain head"); (3) the poet's stated inability to communicate ("dumb to tell") with other doomed things, such as the crooked rose, the hanging man, and the lovers, is contradicted by both his compassion for them and also his awareness of their common fate.

THE HAND THAT SIGNED THE PAPER

The poet condemns the misused political power that betrays a people through a treaty. The sovereign, by signing the paper, betrayed the people to division, sickness, and poverty—"halved a country," "bred a fever," "famine came." Such a sovereign cannot sympathize with the people, "does not pat the brow," and has "no tears to flow."

TWENTY-FOUR YEARS

The poet's twenty-fourth birthday reminds him of the connection between birth and death.

As soon as the poet emerged from the "natural doorway" of his mother's womb he was starting on a journey to death ("Dressed to die"). The "sensual strut" and "red veins" of his life of flesh will end at the "elementary town" of death when his "money" (life's blood) is spent.

WHEN ALL MY FIVE AND COUNTRY SENSES SEE

The poem develops the idea that the heart is sensual and is served by the five senses. Although the poet's five senses are not quite the standard five, he does describe five senses as serving the heart through serving love.

Line 1 leads into the idea that when the five senses function correctly ("see"), they do not so much work with the world around them ("forget green thumbs") as they serve the heart as "witnesses" to mark the course of love. In lines 2-5, fingers and eye mark how "Love in the frost is pared." In lines 6-7, the ears "watch love." In lines 8-9, the tongue cries of the wounds of love. In line 10, the nostrils see love as divine, that is, as Moses' burning bush. In most of these uses of the senses, their functions are interchanged (as "nostrils see").

Lines 11-14 point out that even if the senses cease functioning by sleeping ("five eyes break"), love is served by the heart, which is also sensual.

FRANCIS THOMPSON

THE HOUND OF HEAVEN

The poem describes God's pursuit of a man's soul in terms of a hound pursuing its prey.

The speaker fled from God in time and in his mind, in sorrow and in joy, but always the "strong Feet" followed (lines 1-15). He did not have the wit to evade, but Love knew how to pursue (lines 16-24). He searched everywhere for a place to hide. God's servants would not hide him, and swiftness itself was to no avail (lines 25-51).

Children were plucked from the speaker by their guardian angels. He turned to Nature, but although he grew close to her in the rain and the sky, in the morning and the evening, he found that Nature could offer him no comfort (lines 52-110). Now, the speaker found himself stripped and defenseless (lines 111-117). His whole life was pulled down in ruins, his past and even his dreams. The speaker asked if he must be completely crushed in order to be overpowered by the divine love. Now he hears a trumpet from eternity and sees him who sends the summons (lines 118-154). A Voice admonishes the speaker for trying to gain love apart from God. But love comes only from God, and without this gift the speaker is unworthy of love. This shadow that the speaker has fled is really God, Who reaches out to him in love (lines 155-182).

HENRY VAUGHAN

THE RETREAT

The poet tells of his longing for the divinity of childhood and the heavenly state of his soul before earthly existence.

In lines 1-20, the poet tells of his happiness in childhood. Then, this earthly existence ("second race") had not taken him far from his celestial origins (lines 1-6). He could see God's "bright face" (lines 7-10), could see shadows of eternity in nature (lines 11-14), and was moved by "everlastingness" rather than the sins of sense (lines 15-20).

In lines 21-32, the poet uses the main image of a traveler across the plain of life to tell of his longing to retreat at the "dust" of death to the heavenly state from which his soul came.

THE WORLD

The poet has a vision of Eternity and a view of earth-bound men, and wonders why more men do not soar to Eternity's light.

After his vision of Eternity's "ring of pure and endless light" (lines 1-3), the poet sees Time as a shadow in which the world and men move (lines 4-7). Then follows a view of various imperfect men on earth: the doting lover (remainder of stanza 1); the statesman like a fog or mole (stanza 2); the miser hugging his pelf, the sensuous epicure, and other weaker sorts (stanza 3). In stanza 4, the poet sees some "soar up into the ring" of light and wonders at the "madness" of others for preferring dark earth to God's abode. God whispers in the last two lines that heaven is for Christ and the Church.

THEY ARE ALL GONE INTO THE WORLD OF LIGHT (DEPARTED FRIENDS)

The poet longs for heaven and knowledge of what is beyond death.

In stanzas 1-4 the poet envies his friends "gone into the world of light." The light of their walking in the "air of glory" makes his days seem dull and kindles his love to seek heaven. In stanzas 5-8, the poet laments that we cannot see the mysteries beyond death, just as we cannot tell where the bird has flown nor see the star confined in a tomb. In stanzas 9-10, the poet calls upon God to either let him see heaven clearly or else take him to heaven.

EDMUND WALLER

ON A GIRDLE

The poet praises his beloved's beauty through the image of her belt or sash which enclosed "all that's good and all that's fair."

By encircling her waist, the girdle draws the envy of monarchs (stanza 1). It was a world or enclosure which contained all the poet could want (stanza 2). If he could have the woman it bound, he would want nothing else (stanza 3).

SONG (GO, LOVELY ROSE)

In a *carpe diem* ("seize the day") manner, the poet compares his beloved to a rose in urging her to let her beauty be admired.

Though the beloved is fairer than the rose (stanza 1), just as the rose must be seen to be admired (stanza 2), so must the woman (stanza 3). The death of the rose will show her what a brief time beauty has to be admired (stanza 4).

JOHN WEBSTER

CALL FOR THE ROBIN REDBREAST AND THE WREN (CORNELIA'S DIRGE)

In this dirge from the play *The White Devil*, a mother laments over the body of her son, who has just been murdered by his brother. She calls for robin and wren to cover his grave (lines 1-4), for ant, mouse, and mole to warm him (lines 5-8), but does not wish the wolf to desecrate the body (lines 9-10).

WALT WHITMAN

A NOISELESS PATIENT SPIDER

The aspiring soul is compared to a spider sending out its filaments.
Stanza 1 describes the spider silently and patiently sending its filaments to reach some point in the "vacant vast." Likewise, in stanza 2, the soul in its "measureless oceans" flings its "gossamer thread" to "catch somewhere."

CROSSING BROOKLYN FERRY

A sense of human community is carried by the images associated with the river and the city. From the people and the sights he records, the poet is aware of a mysterious unity between himself and the people of the present and the future (section 2-4). The poet asks the question, "What is it then between us?" (section 5) and suggests in answer the integrity and unifying power of bodily experience (section 5), his own emotional and moral identity (section 6), and the spiritual awareness (section 7) of his fellows. Section 8 declares that the spiritual unity is established ("We understand then do we not?") and leads into the summarizing and concluding section, which restates the theme of spiritual unity in man and the objects of his experience.

GIVE ME THE SPLENDID SILENT SUN

The two parts of the poem show the speaker's conflicting love for both nature and the city. In part I, the speaker desires the "splendid silent sun" with all the accompanying aspects of nature "aside from the noise of the world a rural domestic life." In part II, the speaker rejects the "sun" and "quiet places" in nature to desire the bustling city life, "Manhattan faces and eyes."

OUT OF THE CRADLE ENDLESSLY ROCKING

The poet recalls a childhood experience that spoke to him of death and awoke him to his poetic purpose. The strong life-images in the poem—the cradle, the birds at their nest, the child listening and learning—take on a deeper significance as the death theme is introduced (the disappearance of the female bird) and the sound of the sea, both of which have entered into the poet's songs (lines 174-183). After the introduction (lines 1-22), which suggests the close relationship between the poet and the bird, lines 23-143 recount the story of the bird as the boy had observed it. The mating birds begin in joy and the promise of life (lines 24-40). Suddenly the female disappears and her mate calls to her in his sorrow (lines 41-129). The remainder of the poem deals with the effects of the experience on the poet as he absorbed understanding from the bird singing in sorrow and "the savage old mother," the sea, whispering "that strong and delicious word," death.

PASSAGE TO INDIA

This is a song of progress, of material progress and then of spiritual progress. It first deals with man's scientific and material accomplishments and concludes with a challenge to spiritual development (sections 7-9). The occasion for the poem is the thought that the world is now more closely joined by the Suez canal, the transcontinental railroad in the U. S., and the trans-Atlantic cable (lines 5-7). The poet praises voyagers such as Columbus who have brought distant and unknown lands closer together so that we know their culture and their magnificence (for instance, in sections 2-5). Such voyagers are a preparation for the greatest voyager of all, the poet, who will

make the voyage of spiritual discovery to God as "the whole earth
. . . shall be completely joyous" (lines 102-116). The search for
spiritual knowledge is a greater adventure, a journey "to primal
thought" (line 166), to the "moral, spiritual fountain" (line 199),
and to the mastery of "strangling problems" (line 232).

SONG OF MYSELF

The poet celebrates the mystical unity of mankind, which he sees in
all aspects of human life and activity (as, for instance, in section 15).
The creative force is universal, past and present, good and evil, personal and impersonal, as in section 22, where the poet uses the sea
as a symbol of this concept. The poet believes in the physical body
as the sign of life: "Divine am I inside and out" (section 24); we
could learn from the animals to accept our bodies (section 32). The
poet gives extensive and descriptive lists which in their cumulative
effect make his point that he identifies himself with all things and
all people, seeing the unity behind the tremendous variety of life (as,
for instance, in section 33). The poet's perception is a somewhat
pantheistic idea of God, whom he sees manifested in life. The poet
sings the divinity of the soul of man and of God in man (section 48).

THERE WAS A CHILD WENT FORTH

The poem develops the idea that a person's environment becomes
part of the person. After stating this theme in lines 1-4, the poem
gives a catalogue of varied objects and experiences which "became
part of that child."

TO A LOCOMOTIVE IN WINTER

The poet sees the motion, power, and freedom of the locomotive as
emblems of modern life.
   In lines 1-17, the poet describes the motion and power of the
locomotive. In lines 18-25, the poet calls the locomotive an emblem
of the modern, the "pulse of a continent," and asks this emblem to
infuse his verse, not only with motion and power, but also with its
"lawless music" of freedom.

WHEN I HEARD THE LEARN'D ASTRONOMER

The poet expresses his attitude that one's experiences with nature should be immediate, personal, and vital.

When the poet heard the statistical, pedantic lecture about the stars (lines 1-4), he became "tired and sick" (line 5), and wandered off alone to look up in "perfect silence at the stars" (lines 6-8).

WHEN LILACS LAST IN THE DOORYARD BLOOM'D

This elegy on Lincoln is generally organized through the recurring symbols of the lilac (love), the thrush and its song (the poet's grief), and the evening star (Lincoln), all introduced in sections 1-4. They are "twined with the chant of my soul" (line 205). The coffin journeys through a mourning nation (sections 5-6), and the poet brings his offering of lilac to death (section 7). As he thinks of the woe surrounding Lincoln (section 8), the song of the thrush inspires his own chant (sections 9-14). The poet sings of the beauty of America and its images of life. He is reconciled with the release of death (section 14), and he sees that even those who died in battle "were fully at rest" (section 15). In the last section the poet joins hands with his comrades in grief and brings together the dominant symbols in constant memory of "the sweetest, wisest soul of all my days and lands."

JOHN GREENLEAF WHITTIER

ICHABOD

Whittier said this poem was the result of his surprise and grief at Daniel Webster's support of the Missouri Compromise and the Fugitive Slave Bill. The title, from I Samuel 4:21, suggests that the "glory is departed" from America in the figure of Webster.

Stanzas 1-4 describe Webster as a man who might have "lighted up and led his age," but now is fallen and lost to the Tempter. Stanzas 5-9 call for lamentation for the dishonored "fallen angel."

LAUS DEO

The title, "Praise God," indicates Whittier's rejoicing at hearing the bells ringing when the slaves were freed by constitutional law. Stanzas 1-2 proclaim that "It is done," the slaves freed. Stanzas 3-7 ask for worship of God for bringing about "this wonder of our days." Stanzas 8-10 call for world-wide rejoicing for the "fresher life" that may now begin.

MASSACHUSETTS TO VIRGINIA

The poem reproaches Virginia for its slavery after a slave, George Latimer, was seized without warrant in Massachusetts and returned to his master in Virginia.

Stanzas 1-5 describe Massachusetts as engaged in peaceful "commerce" and "honest labor" amid difficulties, but the people do not live, as Virginians do, in fear, slavery, and war. Stanzas 6-9 remind the Old Dominion that the two states were sisters in the Revolutionary War's fight for freedom, though now Virginia is asking Massachusetts to destroy freedom by returning "your wretched slaves." In stanzas 10-11, Massachusetts says she will do anything for Virginia except carry for her the "dark loathsome burden" of slavery. In stanzas 12-14, she washes her hands of the "sin and shame and curse" of Virginia's brutal treatment of men, women, and children. Stanzas 15-24 describe the "man-thief" from Virginia seizing the slave in Massachusetts with its traditions of freedom. In consequence, the "free sons and daughters" rise up to say there will be no slave-hunt, pirate, fetters, or "slave upon our land."

RICHARD WILBUR

A BAROQUE WALL-FOUNTAIN IN THE VILLA SCIARRA

A pagan wall-fountain at a Roman villa is contrasted to the jet fountains of St. Peter's Cathedral to show two ways of life: the life of pleasure and sensuality and the life of Christian effort and aspiration.

Stanzas 1-7 describe the pagan fountain with faun and fauness and the water's "effortless descent," suggesting that the "pleasure, flash, and waterfall" are too simple for us. Stanzas 8-10 suggest we are better expressed by St. Peter's jets, its water "struggling aloft." Such upward struggle can best give us a "fine/ Illumined version" of ourselves. Stanzas 11-13 pose the pagan fauns against the Christian water-saints, arguing that the fauns offer "rest in fulness of desire," just as the saints offer a pattern of virtue ("areté"). Stanzas 14-15 provide a resolution through St. Francis: lying in freezing snow and praising God, he experienced both pleasure and struggle simultaneously. Both fountains, then, are a "shade of bliss"—a "dreamt land" man reaches for either by struggle or by pleasure.

A WORLD WITHOUT OBJECTS IS A SENSIBLE EMPTINESS

In refutation of Thomas Traherne, from whom the title came, the poet says the world without objects is not a sensible emptiness: one cannot find spiritual reality by denying the physical.

Stanzas 1-2 describe asceticism, the "camels of the spirit," which seeks a world without sensory impressions. Stanzas 3-4 tell these "connoiseurs of thirst" that "pure mirage" of spiritual existence is cursed without being "shaped and borne" by sense. Even the "painted saints" were sensory. Stanzas 5-7 call for a turn from the "sleights" and the emptiness. The spirit's oasis is in "light incarnate," shown through trees, creeks, bracken, supernova, and steam of beasts.

JUGGLER

The fascination of the juggler for us is his ability to conquer gravity.

An ordinary bouncing ball, subject to gravity, gradually bounces less and less. But a juggler draws our applause by winning "over the world's weight," first by juggling balls and then by juggling a broom, a plate, and a table.

LOVE CALLS US TO THE THINGS OF THIS WORLD

Attitudes toward laundry hung on a line in early morning show a person's capacity to accept both imagined transcendence and real ugliness.

In stanzas 1-4, the just-waking person, "for a moment bodiless," sees the laundry outside his window as angels and wishes that "there be nothing on earth" but such. In stanzas 5-6, the soul accepts the "waking body," and the laundry suggests an uglier reality—thieves, lovers "to be undone," and nuns keeping their "difficult balance."

STILL, CITIZEN SPARROW

The poem praises the life of venture and commitment as seen in the vulture and Noah in contrast to the routine, timid life as seen in the sparrow.

The sparrow is like an ordinary citizen in the "rotten office," afraid to venture ("childheart"), and willing to die without learning much. But the "unnatural" vulture reaches "heaven's height," and in venturing against death "keeps nature new." Noah, also, rejecting the status quo ("bedlam hours") and working at his venture, became a hero.

THE BEAUTIFUL CHANGES

Here the poet asserts the power of a beautiful person to transmit beauty to the environment.

As the Queen Anne's Lace flowers look like lilies in water, as the chameleon seems to change the forest's color, and as the mantis makes the "leaf leafier," so the "you" of the poem changes all things "back to wonder."

THE DEATH OF A TOAD

The death of a toad by a power mower seems to reproach our mechanized civilization which wastes and spoils life.

The precious worth of the toad's life is suggested by such images as "sanctuaried," "heart-shaped," "a final glade," "rare original heartsblood." Such images as a "lost Amphibia's emperies" and "antique eyes" suggest that this death is not just a single death due to our technology ("the castrate lawn"), but is a tragedy involving the larger natural kingdom.

WILLIAM CARLOS WILLIAMS

LOVE SONG

In a gentle *carpe diem* ("seize the day") poem, the poet urges human love ("come with me") and love of nature ("elm," "burst of fragrance") because of the brevity and insignificance of one's life.

THE RED WHEELBARROW

By use of a sharp image composed of a red wheelbarrow, rain, and chickens, the poet asserts the significance ("so much depends") of sharp perception of a wheelbarrow.

THE YACHTS

The yachts, in preparing to race and in racing over the waves, symbolize the struggle between two social classes—the upper and the lower, the powerful and the weak, the served and the servant.

Stanzas 1-6 describe the beautiful yachts, the contrasting lumbering craft and ant-like crew which attend the yachts, and the protected "arena of open water" in which the yachts contend. Stanzas 7-11 describe the race. The sea waves are personified as human bodies, "beaten, desolate," as the "skillful yachts pass over."

TRACT

The "tract" opposes funerals of pomp and ceremony which detract from the real dignity of the man while living.

With the device of telling his townspeople how to perform a funeral, the poet gives advice in four areas: hearse, flowers, driver, and bereaved. In stanzas 1-3, the hearse is to be "rough plain," not fancy or adorned. In stanza 4, some "common memento" of the dead is preferred to wreaths and hot-house flowers. In stanza 5, the driver is to remove his silk hat and walk inconspicuously beside the hearse. In stanza 6, the bereaved are to walk behind, showing some sense of inconvenience as if they had grief. By such simplicity and show of inconvenience, the townspeople "are ready" to conduct a funeral properly.

WILLIAM WORDSWORTH

A SLUMBER DID MY SPIRIT SEAL

Stanza 1 states that while the girl was alive, she seemed to the speaker to be beyond the reach of time. Now she is dead, as lifeless as the "rocks, and stones, and trees" (stanza 2).

COMPOSED UPON WESTMINSTER BRIDGE, SEPTEMBER 3, 1802

The poet recounts his awed reaction to the sight of London clad in the "beauty of the morning," with the sun shining splendidly and "that mighty heart" lying quiet.

ELEGIAC STANZAS

In the first six stanzas, the poet describes his impression of Peele Castle at the time he lived near it. All was bright and calm according to this earlier view. Yet, he says, his impression of "steadfast peace" was a "fond illusion." Now, the poet has a different view of the scene, so that he agrees with the painter Beaumont's conception of violent storms. In the intervening years, he has learned to welcome such sights, for with them come "fortitude, and patient cheer." The "deep distress" was the death of his brother, John. This sorrow occasioned the mood expressed in the word "elegiac" in the title.

I TRAVELLED AMONG UNKNOWN MEN

Travelling in foreign lands taught the poet how much he loved England. For here was the "joy of my desire," and here too is where the cherished Lucy lived.

I WANDERED LONELY AS A CLOUD

The poet describes the effect of a crowd of daffodils upon himself. At first lonely, the poet suddenly sees the crowd of daffodils. They are dancing and tossing their heads in a most joyous manner. The poet becomes gay at the sight. Later the scene comes into his mind, and his heart "dances with the daffodils."

IT IS A BEAUTEOUS EVENING, CALM AND FREE

As he contemplates the "beauteous evening" and listens to the sound of the sea, the poet concludes that the child with him, who is apparently "untouched by solemn thought," has the presence of God "when we know it not."

LINES COMPOSED A FEW MILES ABOVE TINTERN ABBEY

The poem states the poet's idea of the manner in which the divine force works in man. The divine force creates a unity between Nature and man, and the memory of the experience provides inspiration at a later date. The poem has two main sections: Verse-paragraphs 1-3 describe the scene from the standpoint of the past and discuss the effect that the memory of the scene had upon the poet in the intervening five years; with paragraph 4, the poem comes to the present scene and to thoughts of the even greater sustaining value it will have in the future.

The poet first recalls that he saw this same scene five years before. He hears the same waters, he sees the same cliffs, and he observes all the various suggestions of human habitation (lines 1-22). In the intervening years, these sights have brought him feelings that sustained him and brought him "that blessed mood," in which "We see into the life of things" (lines 23-49). The poet's spirit has often returned to this scene (lines 50-57).

The poet realizes that now the scene will serve as sustenance for future years, though, being older, he does not have the same unreflecting joy in the experience that he had when he was younger. But the maturity has brought with it a profound sense of the force that "rolls through all things" (lines 58-111).

Now the poet turns to reflect upon his sister and Nature's effect on her, for he knows that Nature has the power to comfort her in the future. She will remember him and his service to Nature, and she will also remember that the scene was dearer to him, both for the images of Nature and for her sake (lines 112-159).

LONDON, 1802

The poet calls upon the spirit of Milton, who with his bright soul and great poetic gift had assumed the "lowliest duties." Now England needs Milton, for she needs "manners, virtue, freedom, power."

MICHAEL

Michael's story is one of endurance. Because he had signed a surety for his brother's son, Michael was forced to pay a large sum when his relative failed to pay his debt. Michael decided that, rather than give up a part of his farm, he would send his son Luke to the city to work to pay off the debt. But the son fell into bad company, and Michael and his wife died severely disappointed.

Michael acquired the power of endurance through his long, close association with nature. He realized the importance of the land for himself and his wife. That is why he would not sell it to pay off the debt. And after the tragic news of their son's deterioration, the land helped old Michael to endure, for he "as before,/ Performed all kinds of labor for his sheep,/ And for the land" (lines 459-460).

MY HEART LEAPS UP WHEN I BEHOLD

These lines define a good and meaningful life as a vivid emotional reaction to a natural object, here specifically a rainbow. This spontaneous reaction is what makes life worth living—whether in childhood, maturity, or old age. The poet emphasizes the importance of childhood experiences in forming the adult's reactions: "The child is father of the man." That is, what the child enjoys will be what the adult enjoys (for instance, the rainbow).

ODE: INTIMATIONS OF IMMORTALITY FROM RECOLLECTIONS OF EARLY CHILDHOOD

The ode has three general sections. Stanzas 1-4 are concerned with the loss of the speaker's former joy in nature. Stanzas 5-8 describe the child's spiritual development in and through nature. Stanzas 9-11 discuss the relationship of the adult to nature.

In specific relationship to the title, stanzas 1-4, having pointed out the fact of the loss, prepare the way for the retrospect of stanzas 5-8, which begin by describing the "intimations of immortality" which the child is born with and carries with him for a number of years. In stanzas 9-11 the poet praises those "obstinate questionings" of the senses, questionings which give hints of "that immortal sea which brought us hither." Now, these "shadowy recollections" "Are yet the fountain light of all our day."

The poet begins by contrasting the "celestial light" that once seemed to clothe everything with his present loss of this glory (stanza 1). Although the rainbow, the rose, and the other things of nature are still beautiful, a glory has passed from the earth. In the midst of all the surrounding joy, the poet says in stanza 3, only he is sorrowful, and he determines that his grief shall not do wrong to the season. Still, though he joyfully hears the sounds of nature's creatures, the poet asks "Whither is fled the visionary gleam?" (stanza 4).

Stanza 5 describes the Three Ages of Man. The infant is the most nearly spiritual, "trailing clouds of glory" from the place of the soul's origin. Then, further removed, the Youth still has "the vision splendid" about him. Finally, the man sees the vision "fade into the light of common day." Earth, the poet continues in stanza 6, tries to make man forget the glories he has left behind. In stanza 7 the poet describes the child at play, assiduously imitating the life he sees about him. Then, in stanza 8, the poet praises the child as a "seer blest" who can "read the eternal deep." And the poet wonders why this "best philosopher" is eager to take on the world's weight and put by his immortality.

Yet in maturity is cause for joy, something different from "Delight and liberty" of childhood. Now we have "high instincts" and "shadowy recollections" that let "Our souls have sight of that immortal sea/ Which brought us hither" (stanza 9). Although we cannot now feel "the radiance which was once so bright," we find "strength in what remains behind," "the primal sympathy" and "the faith that looks through death" (stanza 10).

The poet concludes in stanza 11 on a note of consolation. He now realizes that his feelings are different from those of childhood. Now, "Thanks to the human heart," he has a deeper, a broader, and more humane relationship with nature than formerly.

ODE TO DUTY

The poet states his belief that right action comes from Duty rather than from "the genial sense of youth." Though, the poet says, there should be no reproach for those who rely upon their own impulses, he is aware that he now needs the "firm support" of Duty. In the last three stanzas the poet develops the idea that Duty speaks as the lawgiver for the universe. Humbly, the poet asks strength and direction from this Power: "in the light of truth Thy Bondman let me live!"

RESOLUTION AND INDEPENDENCE

The poet introduces his story with a description of a bright and joyous scene in lines 1-21. Suddenly, the poet's thoughts turn darker. He is depressed (lines 22-49). The rest of the poem is concerned with his observation of the old leech-gatherer and with what the poet learns from him. Although the old man is feeble, his speech is stately (lines 92-98) as he tells of making his livelihood by gathering leeches. Lines 106-112 mark the high point of the poem as the imagery brings out the (spiritual) unity which the leech-gatherer exemplified to the poet, for whom the old man took on the semblance of a dream or a mysterious stranger. The poet ends on a note of admiration for the leech-gatherer's firmness.

SHE DWELT AMONG THE UNTRODDEN WAYS

This lament for Lucy describes the beauty of the maid in her isolated surroundings. Its conclusion states the speaker's intense grief.

SHE WAS A PHANTOM OF DELIGHT

The poet describes his developing appreciation of his ideal woman. At first, "She was a phantom of delight," and an airy spirit. Then (stanza 2), "upon nearer view," the poet sees her as a woman also. Finally, he sees the total woman, mortal but strong and intelligent and still retaining "something of angelic light."

STRANGE FITS OF PASSION HAVE I KNOWN

This poem recounts an incident that culminated in a premonition of death.

One evening the lover rode toward Lucy's cottage. He kept his eye on the moon, and, as he and his horse climbed the familiar hill, the moon came nearer and nearer to Lucy's cottage. Suddenly, the moon dropped behind the roof, and the fearful thought came into the lover's head that Lucy may have died.

THE PRELUDE

The Prelude is the most extended poetic statement by Wordsworth of his philosophical and poetic theories. It also contains numerous allusions to Wordsworth's own early life and to what he learned from these experiences.

Book I
Book I concerns mainly episodes of the poet's schooldays. The poet describes the effect Nature had on him as a boy. By beauty and fear (lines 342-343) Nature through her various forms communicated the eternal spirit to the growing child.

Book II
Book II continues the theme of Book I, with a more abstract and philosophical cast. The poet describes the process of developing the creative imagination (lines 232 ff.), which enables the child to learn from Nature "through the growing faculties of sense" that a creative spirit pervades all. Through this interaction with Nature the poet has "felt the sentiment of Being" (line 401) which has profoundly influenced his life and has been his support in evil times.

Book III
After saying that he accomplished little in the way of formal education, the poet says that at times he withdrew from the college to refresh his spirits in the fields. He "looked for universal things" (line 106). The natural scenes "spake perpetual logic to my soul" (line 164).

Book IV
Book IV covers a vacation from July to October, 1788. The poet writes of three experiences: his walk around the lake, his dedication, and his encounter with a desolate soldier. In his walk the poet felt

that his soul was "in the presence of his God" (line 151). After leaving a party he walked home as the morning sun rose, and her "vows/ Were . . . made for me" (lines 334-335). When the poet meets the miserable soldier he at first feels pity, but then comes to respect the man's patient trust in God.

Book V

Book V, "Books," is mostly concerned with children's reading and children's education. After opening with praise of man, the poet proceeds in a somewhat disorganized manner to discuss books, nature, and their influence on man. Toward the end the poet develops particularly the theme of educating children through close contact with nature as well as through reading great books.

Book VI

Book VI, entitled "Cambridge and the Alps," covers the poet's second and third years at Cambridge, the vacation period between them, and the vacation period in France and Switzerland after them. The earlier parts are pervaded by a sense of the eternal. The poet also writes in praise of the abstractions of mathematics, which are a relief from the images that throng a poet's brain. He has much to say in praise of idleness. But the most significant part is the vacation in Europe, especially when he reaches the Alps. The famous Simplon Pass episode, which begins around line 523, is one of the finest passages in Wordsworth's poetry of mystical vision, where the poet describes "The types and symbols of eternity" (line 639).

Book VII

Book VII, "Residence in London," telescopes several London visits into an account of the poet's first stay in 1791. His reactions to the city are ambivalent. On the negative side, the poet's boyish dreams of London are disappointed. In its totality, London impresses him with its confusion, its moral and physical ugliness, and a sense of alienation. Yet there are positive aspects to the city. The poet greatly enjoyed the theater: "Yet was the theatre my dear delight" (line 407). He had a variety of stimulating experiences, such as hearing the aged Burke. And at times he even felt a sense of unity in the city and, as he describes the father holding the sick child, he was impressed with a sense of "love unutterable." Even here, the poet concludes, he felt that "the soul of beauty and enduring life/ Vouchsafed his inspiration."

Book VIII

Book VIII, entitled "Retrospect—Love of Nature Leading to Love of Man," is actually concerned with the dignity and glory of man rather than with the theme of love. This book opens with an extensive description of a fair, where "gaiety and cheerfulness prevail." Then the poet discusses the fact that, through her pleasant aspects and especially through her stormy, violent periods, Nature transfers her genius to the shepherds who are close to her all their lives. Because he saw these shepherds as a boy, the poet "was early introduced/ To an unconscious love and reverence/ of human nature." He was filled with a sense of man's glory and dignity, given by such shapes of men "Instinct with vital functions." Man's glory is distinctive among all creatures because man is "instinct with godhead."

The poet's experiences in London support his observations of man's dignity. In the great city he "conversed with majesty and power" and he saw "affectingly set forth . . . the unity of man,/ One spirit over ignorance and vice."

Book IX

Book IX, "Residence in France," deals with the poet's sojourn in France. He entered into the spirit of the French Revolution: "my heart was all/ Given to the people." Observing the economic and social evils of the country, he recalls his own childhood, when he absorbed Republican ideas into his spirit. Pervasive throughout Book IX is the idea of the dignity of the common man. Then Book IX concludes with an allusion to the story of Vandracour and Julia, which tells how Vandracour was ruined by adverse social and political conditions.

Book X

Book X, "Residence in France (Continued)," continues the poet's thoughts on the French Revolution and its aftermath. He muses on the violence that had come to France and trusts that peace has now come. The impulse to freedom is unconquerable because the "sovereign voice . . . within the soul" rejects tyranny. After the poet returned to England he experienced a deep shock to his "moral nature" when England declared war on France. He was torn by conflicting loyalties—to his home country and to the spirit of liberty that France symbolized.

Then came the Terror in France and with it an even more terrible confusion to the poet. He was beset by evil dreams at the thought of the atrocities occurring daily in France in the name of liberty. Yet he came to realize that not liberty was to blame but the centuries-long accumulation of abuses—"a terrific reservoir of guilt/ And ignorance filled up from age to age/ That could no longer hold its loathsome charge,/ But burst and spread in deluge through the land" (lines 477-480).

The book closes on a more hopeful note at the news of Robespierre's death.

Book XI

Book XI, "Residence in France (Concluded)," describes the poet's progress from intellectual optimism to disillusionment and then to recovery and rededication with new spirit. He tells how in his youth, when "to be young was very Heaven," he found that Reason held the answers to all questions. But the poet's faith in rationalism was shaken when the French Revolution turned to oppression. Despairing, he tested all his beliefs at the bar of Godwinian rationalism and finally he "yielded up moral questions in despair." The poet was rescued from this despondency by his sister, by "Nature's self," and "By all varieties of human love."

Book XII

Book XII, "Imagination and Taste, How Impaired and Restored," does not proceed as clearly as the title implies. By Imagination Wordsworth meant the spiritual and creative faculty and by Taste he meant the rational, analytical faculty. As the rational, analytical faculty grows stronger, the power of the imagination decreases.

The poet's disillusionment has impaired his ability to perceive the unity in things—in man and in Nature. His appreciation of Nature has grown superficial, "aesthetic," concerned with surface forms rather than inner spiritual truths. Despite periods when the rationalistic taste dominates and when our minds are led to the superficial aspects of things, the poet finds that the early influences of Nature will eventually triumph and once more free the imagination.

The means by which Nature operates is by "spots of time." There are moments in our lives "That with distinct pre-eminence retain/ A renovating virtue . . . whence . . . our minds/ Are nourished and invisibly repaired." These moments come unexpectedly, as with the sight of a ruined gibbet, or of a girl leaning into the wind, or of a bleak day.

Book XIII

Book XIII, "Imagination and Taste, How Impaired and Restored (Concluded)," is concerned with Nature's healing and instructive power. Because of this power, the poet returns to Man as "an object of delight,/ Of pure imagination, and of love" after the disillusionment following the Reign of Terror in France. As he thinks of men in public places, the poet wonders why all men cannot attain the highest and fullest personal development. He examines his experience to find the answer.

Only a few, the poet concludes, have the privilege of knowing Nature as it really is, for example, while walking peacefully in the fields and in the woods. It is in these rural ways that one learns the true depth and goodness of man, not in the busy and artificial life of the cities.

The poet dedicates himself to writing of these simple country people in whom humanity is highest: "my theme/ No other than the very heart of man,/ As found among the best of those who live." The poet concludes this book with the optimistic idea that the world is "ruled by those fixed laws/ Whence spiritual dignity originates."

Book XIV

Book XIV, "Conclusion," opens with an impressive description. The poet is climbing a mountain with a companion and a guide. Suddenly, there bursts upon him the sight of the moon, the sea, and the sky. The poet hears "the roar of waters," the sea, the torrents, and streams, as though they were one voice "Heard over earth and sea . . . and . . . felt by the starry heavens."

This vision seemed to the poet "the type/ Of a majestic intellect." He makes the observation that the highest minds have a "glorious faculty" akin to Nature's: "They build up greatest things/ From least suggestions." With the full impact of this vision upon him, the poet states that freedom is repose in the full harmony of the universe.

The individual knows love as an individual. More broadly, this individual love is included in the broader power of spiritual love and is also dependent upon the Imagination. Imagination, which the poet defines as "Reason in her most exalted mood," he notes has been the theme of the poems, as also has been intellectual love, the "feeling intellect" (or intuition).

The poet acknowledges the influence of his sister, Dorothy, who helped him to turn from a too-exclusive interest in the sterner aspects of Nature, an interest that even tended to dwell upon that side of Nature that produced terror.

The poet then addresses himself to Coleridge at some length, in effect discussing this poem with him. He summarizes the purpose, which was to trace the development of man through contact with Nature. The poet ends on the hope that future generations will read and profit from the writings of both himself and Coleridge as "Prophets of Nature."

THE SOLITARY REAPER

A "solitary Highland Lass" is "Reaping and singing by herself." Her melancholy song thrills the listener, and, not understanding the language, he wonders if she sings of "far-off things" or of humbler "matter of to-day." As he leaves, he hears the "music in my heart."

THE WORLD IS TOO MUCH WITH US

All of nature is closed to us because "We have given our hearts away" in order to get and spend. The poet concludes that he would rather be a pagan so that he could "Have glimpses that would make me less forlorn."

THREE YEARS SHE GREW IN SUN AND SHOWER

Nature speaks of her plans for educating and forming the girl (Lucy). The girl will feel within her "an overseeing power/ To kindle or restrain." She will be "sportive as the fawn," and she will also have "the silence and the calm/ Of mute insensate things." Natural objects shall pass by sympathy into her being, so that she will be formed by "vital feelings of delight."

Abruptly, the last stanza states that, having been formed by Nature, Lucy is dead (taken at last by Nature and become a part of it), and the speaker is left with the quiet of the scene and the memory of Lucy.

THOMAS WYATT

MY LUTE, AWAKE! PERFORM THE LAST (THE LOVER COMPLAINETH THE UNKINDNESS OF HIS LOVE)

The poet complains through his lute that the woman is rejecting his love.

In stanzas 1-3, the poet says he sings his last song to his lover because she has cruelly repulsed his "suit and his affection." Stanzas 4-7 describe the vengeance that shall fall upon her. She too shall one day "wish and want" in vain. When she lies "withered and old" on cold winter nights, then, too late, she will know her beauty is gone. The final stanza echoes the first in saying that this is the last song the poet will sing to the unkind woman.

THE LOVER COMPARETH HIS STATE TO A SHIP IN PERILOUS STORM TOSSED ON THE SEA

The poet develops the metaphor of a storm-tossed ship to describe his despair at being neglected ("forgetfulness") by his lover. His lord and enemy, Love, steers cruelly between rocks. Oars, wind, rain, clouds become thoughts of death, sighs, tears, and disdain. The star of reason that could guide the poet to port has been drowned.

THEY FLEE FROM ME, THAT SOMETIME DID ME SEEK

The poem laments the fickleness of a woman.

Stanza 1 shows the woman as once true and loving, "gentle, tame, and meek," but now "seeking with a continual change." Stanza 2 recalls one special scene of intimate love when she "sweetly did me kiss." Stanza 3 insists that the incident "was no dream." But she that was like a tame and meek animal has now become "wild." In her fickleness ("newfangleness") she has forsaken the poet, and he ironically wonders if she deserves the same unkind and unnatural ("kindely") treatment as she gave him.

WHOSO LIST TO HUNT, I KNOW WHERE IS AN HIND

Vain pursuit of a woman is described through the main metaphor of a deer and hunter.

Lines 1-8 give the man's reasons for giving up the chase. He is wearied through vain efforts, lags behind, is unable to get her out of his mind, and realizes that he cannot catch her any more than he can catch the wind in a net. Lines 9-14 warn others that pursuit is vain. She wears the sign "touch me not," because she is Caesar's (traditionally believed to refer to Henry VIII's claim to Anne Boleyn).

ELINOR WYLIE

LET NO CHARITABLE HOPE

The poet asserts her will-to-live philosophy in spite of the meager lot life has given her by virtue of her own nature, her being human, and her being woman.

The poet's character (stanza 1) is meager, not having the strong, graceful features of eagle and antelope. Her lot in life (stanza 2) is meager. She is "alone," and "hard beset." Life itself passes (stanza 3, line 1-2), offering no serious genuineness ("masks outrageous") or abundance ("austere"). Yet (in the last two lines), the poet has met this meager lot with neither "fear" nor bitterness.

PURITAN SONNET

The poet, observing a scene of natural "richness," expresses her Puritan's hatred of such sensuous luxuriance and her love for the opposite: an ascetic austerity.

In landscapes (lines 1-10), she loves the unadorned ("austere, immaculate . . . bare . . . cold . . . thin . . . sparse . . . meager"), The poet's love of the four seasons (lines 11-14) suggests a withdrawal from life itself. Three of the seasons she loves for their brevity, and winter she loves for its likeness to death.

SANCTUARY

The poet, like a bricklayer building a brick room, withdraws like a recluse in her inner "cell" of "dreams, and quiet, and cool" (lines

1-10). The diction suggests tragedy in such withdrawal ("thud," "blood," "bone," "shivering," "Dead nor living"). Lines 12-14 confirm that the poet is indeed "fool" to build such a "Sanctuary."

THE EAGLE AND THE MOLE

The poet offers two ways to avoid following the mass mores: the way of the eagle or that of the mole.

The eagle (stanzas 1-2) symbolizes "stoic," isolated, triumphant life "above the storms" and the "polluted" crowds. The mole (stanzas 3-6) symbolizes the life of negation and withdrawal ("underground," "bones"). Though the mole's way is not as desirable as that of the eagle, it offers a better way than the "lathered" and "steaming" crowd.

WILLIAM BUTLER YEATS

A COAT

The poet describes his poetry and themes ("my song") as dressed in a coat "embroidered" with mythological allusions (lines 1-4). But when "fools" (imitators) stole the myth and metaphor of his earlier works, the poet was glad to yield (lines 5-7). He believes it is better to write the message plain ("naked"), not coated with myth (lines 8-10).

A DEEP-SWORN VOW

The poem concerns the lasting impression made by a deep attachment which has been broken off. Though the poet has made other friends and apparently forgotten the other person since the vow was broken, the impression is imprinted in the deeper self. The person's face always appears when ordinary conscious existence is set aside— in times of danger, of sleep, and of intoxication.

A DIALOGUE OF SELF AND SOUL

The soul and the self debate some of the basic questions of man's existence: the sensuous as opposed to the spiritual, the conscious (day) as opposed to the unconscious (night), and the intellect as opposed to intuition.

In part I, the soul argues for the spiritual ("stair," "ascent," "star") to deliver man from the "crime of death and birth," for man, being "deaf and dumb and blind," is unable to see the value and meaning in life. The self argues for the active and sensuous life, countering that war and love ("blade" and "dress") are the "emblems of the day."

In part II, the self's final long argument is that though life is miserable, it is good to live it. Growing up is distressing (stanza 1), enemies malign (stanza 2), life is a "blind man's ditch," and love is unrequited (stanza 3); yet the self insists that all experience is good, that we are "blest by everything" (stanza 4).

A PRAYER FOR MY DAUGHTER

The poet prays that his newborn daughter may recover the "radical innocence" that will preserve her from the horrors of future years. He sees that her hopes lie in the symbols of the Horn of Plenty (civilized ceremony) and the laurel tree (good customs).

In stanzas 1-2, the poet walks and prays for his daughter in the horrible years to come that he has foreseen. In stanzas 3-4, he prays that she be granted beauty, but not the excessive beauty that brought trouble to Venus and to Helen of Troy. In stanza 5, he prays that she be given courtesy as the chief quality. In stanza 6, he asks that she have a joyful disposition. In stanzas 7-9, he wishes her free of hatred, especially intellectual hatred such as that which troubled "the loveliest woman ever born" (probably Maud Gonne). He prays that her soul will recover the "radical innocence" that makes her self-sustaining so that her "soul's sweet will is Heaven's will." In stanza 10, he prays that her bridegroom provide her the means to the "rich horn" and the "laurel tree" (civilized ceremony and good customs).

AMONG SCHOOL CHILDREN

The poet ponders the relationship between the idealized child and the adult it can actually become, concluding that if all human faculties could be brought into harmony, the real and the ideal would become the same thing.

Stanza 1 sets the scene of a sixty-year-old "public man" questioning what the school children are learning.

Stanzas 2-4 pose the ideal Ledaean woman against the actuality of any present school child's growing up to be Ledaean. The speaker recalls (stanza 2) the graceful figure of one with whom he had a sympathetic union (probably Maud Gonne); the union is likened to the two parts of man trying to find each other (as in Plato's *Symposium*.) The speaker wonders (stanza 3) if the Ledaean woman when a child was like those in the schoolroom, for even children of high birth ("of the swan") can be like those of low birth ("paddler's"). The Ledaean woman, unlike in her youth (stanza 4) is now "hollow"—like the portraits of the fifteenth-century Italian painters ("Quattrocento"). The speaker also once had "pretty plumage."

Stanzas 5-8 deal with the ideal and the actual of what a child can become. An idealizing mother (stanza 5) would not think her son a compensation for the pangs of birth if she could see him sixty years later. Plato, Aristotle, and Pythagoras (stanza 6) propounded idealistic views in contrast to the solid reality of birth and death, described in a scarecrow metaphor as "old clothes upon old sticks to scare a bird." The mother too (stanza 7) has an ideal of what her child can become, worshipping her inner image of him just as a nun worships an image of marble or bronze. The apparent disparity between ideal and actual can be resolved (stanza 8) if all parts of the human being relate harmoniously as in a cosmic dance or a chestnut tree. Then neither the body, soul, beauty, or wisdom would be developed at the expense of the other human faculties.

AN IRISH AIRMAN FORESEES HIS DEATH

An airman's life without values has led to a balance point at which past and future are meaningless as compared to this moment which joins life and death.

In lines 1-10 the airman sees his fate in the clouds as based on none of the traditional personal or social values, such as hate, love, patriotism, law, duty, public pressure, or fame. His only motive for acting (lines 11-12) is impulse which brings him to a balance point (lines 13-16). Past and future are a "waste of breath" and life and death are synonymous.

BYZANTIUM

The poet uses Byzantium as a symbol of aesthetic experience by which man may be purged of the flesh, "the fury and the mire of human veins."

Stanza 1 sets the scene for purging to take place. At night the "unpurged images" (mortal men) of day recede. That is, the fleshly life symbolized by drunken soldiery gives way to the transcendence of night, which disdains all man's complexities and bodily passions.

Stanza 2 considers death or the next life as a means of purgation of the flesh. The poet perceives a mummy-like figure from the dead. As a "superhuman" guide related to both life and death, this figure may "unwind" the "winding path" of one's personal history, thus undoing the mortal life with its complexities of flesh.

Stanzas 3-5 provide examples of aesthetic experience which may purge the spirit of the flesh.

In stanza 3, the art object is a golden bird made by the smithies. It is seen as a "miracle" of art which is able to scorn the flesh, the "complexities of mire or blood." For the art in the object makes it "changeless" and eternal, unlike an ordinary bird or human flesh.

Stanza 4 describes another art object—mosaics of flame designed in marble in the pavement. These flames by means of their aesthetic force cause men of flesh ("blood-begotten spirits") to leave their flesh ("complexities of fury"). For the flames, as art, are not physical flames ("cannot singe a sleeve") but "An agony of flame" which can lead to a spiritual stasis or trance.

Stanza 5 gives a recapitulation of the aesthetic experiences of the bird and the flames: The unpurged human "images," or spirits caught in the flesh ("dolphin's mire and blood"), come to seek purging through art. They come, spirit after spirit, to seek in art (birds of the smithies, marble flames in the pavement) the means to stem the "flood" and the "furies" of flesh.

The spirit tries to throw off the flesh. Mortal man that begets children ("Fresh images beget") is caught in the sea of flesh, but he is torn and tormented by his spiritual urges (dolphin, gong) to escape from flesh.

CRAZY JANE TALKS WITH THE BISHOP

From the simple and outcast (Crazy Jane), rather than from the respectable traditional authority (Bishop), comes the paradoxical wisdom that antinomies (fair—foul, love—excrement, whole—rent) are united.

EASTER 1916

The poet praises the heroic dead of the Irish Republican forces that, fighting for Irish independence from Britain, rebelled on Easter Sunday, 1916. The poet knew individual rebels living ordinary lives at work, at home, at clubs, or in "meaningless" conversations along the streets. He saw these commonplace lives transformed by the fight for freedom from "casual comedy" to "terrible beauty."

FOR ANNE GREGORY

The poet tells a woman that a young man can love her for her yellow hair, not for herself alone (stanza 1). When she replies that she will dye her hair so that a young man will love her for herself (stanza 2), the poet replies that only God could love her for herself (stanza 3).

LEDA AND THE SWAN

The rape of Leda by the swan symbolizes the joining of knowledge and power with the body. The poem raises the question as to whether such a union is fully possible.

In Greek mythology, the mating of Zeus (the swan) and the mortal Leda produced Helen of Troy, a birth that led to the fall of Troy and the murder of Agamemnon.

Lines 1-8 describe the union of Zeus and Leda. Lines 9-11 prophesy the Trojan-Greek era out of the union ("shudder in the loins engenders"). Lines 11-14 raise this question: when Leda entered with her body into the creative union, she put on the god's power, but did she put on the knowledge to foresee the terrible history of the Trojan War and its consequences?

NO SECOND TROY

The poet contrasts a noble, beautiful woman with the pettiness of the times in which she lived.

The people are ignorant and lack courage, while she has nobleness and a beauty "not natural in an age like this" (lines 1-10). She must spend her efforts on this petty time because there is not a second grand Troy worthy of her nobility (lines 11-12).

SAILING TO BYZANTIUM

An old man seeks to move from the dying world of flesh and nature to the world of mind and spirit, where things are permanent and beautiful, as symbolized by Byzantium. Byzantium (Constantinople) was noted for its holiness, rarefied intellectual life, and exquisite and unnatural art.

In stanza 1, the aged are out of place in a world of flesh. "Sensual music" is for the young, who neglect the timeless and spiritual ("unaging intellect"). The music metaphor is carried on into stanzas 2 and 3. Stanza 2 says that the aged, whose flesh is only a "tattered coat," must emphasize spirit—must teach the soul to "clap hands and sing." The soul's method of learning ("singing school") is to study monuments of the soul's magnificence, that is, creations of man's spirit, such as the culture of the "holy city of Byzantium." In stanza 3, the speaker calls on the "singing-masters" (such as, perhaps, the figures of the holy sages on the walls of the noted Byzantine church of Saint Sophia). They are to teach him how to escape from the physical body, the "dying animal," and move to the spiritual ("artifice of eternity"). In stanza 4, the speaker is glad to be free of nature and "bodily" form and to have a spiritual form, such as that made by Grecian goldsmiths. Their works are products of imagination, not external nature, and are thus spiritual and timeless.

THE CAP AND BELLS

The jester's love for the queen was not accepted until he gave his total self—represented by his cap and bells.

When the jester gave his soul (stanzas 1-3), the queen closed the window. When he gave his heart (stanzas 4-5), she fanned it away. Then he sent his cap and bells (stanzas 6-7), though it meant his death, and she accepted them. She then accepted (stanzas 8-9) both his heart and his soul.

THE FIDDLER OF DOONEY

The fiddler of Dooney expresses the theme that "the good are always the merry."

In stanzas 1-2, the fiddler contrasts his merry life with that of his brother and his cousin, priests who spend their time somberly at prayer. In stanzas 3-5, the fiddler asserts that it is he, because of his merriment, who will go first into heaven and continue his merrymaking there.

THE LAKE ISLE OF INNISFREE

The adult poet wants to return to the idyllic country of his childhood. (Innisfree is an island in Lough Gill, County Sligo, Ireland, where Yeats lived when a boy.)

Stanzas 1-2 describe the lonely, peaceful, idyllic life in Innisfree. Stanza 3 describes the poet in his alien present with its "pavements gray," always feeling deeply at his "heart's core" the call to the Innisfree of his childhood.

THE LOVER TELLS OF THE ROSE IN HIS HEART

The poet-lover is reluctant to let the unpleasantness of life affect his dreams.

Stanza 1 tells of the common daily affairs that are disturbing the ideal image of the loved one—things broken, a child's cry, a cart's creak. In stanza 2 the poet says that his romantic sensitivity is so upset ("too great to be told") by "unshapely things" that he desires to remake the world into a setting for his dreams of love.

THE MAGI

The poet has a vision of the wise men returning to the birthplace of Christ at some time after the Crucifixion, because they are "unsatisfied" by the "turbulence" of Calvary. Apparently having hoped for a different outcome, they found the "mystery" of the Nativity "uncontrollable."

THE ROSE OF THE WORLD

The rose symbolizes supreme, eternal beauty, specifically in the love of the ideal woman ("these red lips").

Stanza 1 describes the beauty of the past as not transitory, though the Trojan heroes and the Irish heroes ("Usna's") died for love of beautiful women (Helen and Deirdre). In stanza 2, beauty now ("this lonely face") lives on amid men's souls, though we and the world are passing away. Stanza 3 suggests that beauty was before time and existed with God before the archangels. The world was made for beauty to wander in.

THE SECOND COMING

The present civilization, its two thousand years drawing to a conclusion, is about to be supplanted by a "rough" new age.

Portents of dissolution are seen in stanza 1 in the destruction and corruption so like the signs to precede the Second Coming of Christ—anarchy, bloodshed, unbelief, loss of civilized behavior ("ceremony"). As the falcon in spiraling flight ("gyre") goes farther and farther away from the falconer (the center of control), so the center of civilization is lost and "things fall apart."

Stanza 2 gives the poet's momentary vision of the age soon to be born—a sphinx-like beast appearing out of the spirit of the world ("*Spiritus Mundi*"). It slouches toward "Bethlehem" (any place where a new era may be revealed) to be born and to end the two-thousand-year Christian era begun by the Nativity ("rocking cradle").

THE SONG OF WANDERING AENGUS

This song of the Celtic love god, Aengus, is based on an Irish legend of a man who caught a fish that turned into a princess who had been under a spell.

In stanza 1, the speaker catches the trout. In stanza 2, it changes into a "glimmering girl" who entrances the man and disappears. Stanza 3 describes the effect of love's spell—the girl has become the dream object of the man's life-long pursuit.

THE STOLEN CHILD

A band of fairies calls a human child away from a world full of weeping to a carefree life in nature. In stanzas 1-3, the fairies entice the child to leave the world of trouble, and, in stanza 4, he goes with them.

THE WILD SWANS AT COOLE

The unchanging "passion and conquest" of the swans contrast with the poet's own change.

As the poet in autumn counts the fifty-nine swans at Coole Park (stanza 1), he recalls that nineteen years have passed since he first counted them (stanza 2). He is sad that "All's changed" in his own life (stanza 3). By contrast, the swans, unwearied still, with hearts "not grown old," still seek "passion and conquest" (stanza 4). In stanza 5, however, the poet foresees that the swans as symbols of continuing vitality someday will "have flown away."

WHEN YOU ARE OLD

The poet suggests to the woman he loves that when she is old she will fully appreciate that he was the one of her many admirers who loved her for her "pilgrim soul" and her sorrows.

In stanza 1, the poet bids the woman he loves to read when she is old his poems about her ("this book") and so remember the beauty she once had. Stanza 2 points out that though many loved her for her "glad grace" and beauty, the poet loved her for her pilgrim soul. According to stanza 3, remembering these things, she may be sad that his love for her "fled." That is, he with his love for her had to remain lonely and apart.

WHO GOES WITH FERGUS?

Fergus, an Irish legendary hero, voluntarily gave up his throne to learn by dreaming and meditation the wisdom of the poet and philosopher.

In the poem itself, those who join Fergus in his search turn from brooding on hopes, fears, and "love's bitter mystery." Instead, they search for wisdom ("pierce the deep wood's woven shade") and gain control ("rules").

INDEX OF INDIVIDUAL POEMS FROM SEQUENCES AND OTHER LARGER WORKS

Note: Since this book is arranged alphabetically by authors' names and, under each author, by poem titles and first lines, the following index lists only those poems which occur in poem sequences and other larger works. When the individual poem is readily identified by title, the entry is made by title. Otherwise the poem is identified by the first line. Individual poems from the following works are indexed: E. B. Browning, *Sonnets From the Portuguese*; Hart Crane, *The Bridge* and *Voyages*; John Donne, *Holy Sonnets*; T. S. Eliot, *Four Quartets*; Ezra Pound, *Hugh Selwyn Mauberly*; Dante Gabriel Rossetti, *The House of Life*; William Shakespeare, *Sonnets*; and Alfred, Lord Tennyson, *In Memoriam*.